Garfield
thinks big

BY: JIM DAVIS

Ballantine Books • New York

Copyright © 1997 by PAWS, Incorporated.

All rights reserved under International and Pan-American Copyright
Conventions. Published in the United States by Ballantine Books, a
division of Random House, Inc., New York, and simultaneously in
Canada by Random House of Canada Limited, Toronto.

http://www.randomhouse.com

Library of Congress Catalog Card Number: 97-94053

ISBN: 0-345-41671-6

Manufactured in the United States of America

First Edition: October 1997

10 9 8 7 6 5 4 3 2

THINGS WE NEED MORE OF...

marathon naps
all-night smorgasbords
bacon
wrestling on TV
jelly donuts
back scratchers
scary movies
dog muzzles
fuzzy slippers
Elvis impersonators
cheese
roller coasters
teddy bears
weekends
pizza

THINGS WE CAN DO WITHOUT...

dogs
aerobics
brussel sprouts
decaf coffee
polka
spiders
bagpipes
fruitcakes
houseguests
lawyers
disco
tattoos
diets
Mondays
dog breath

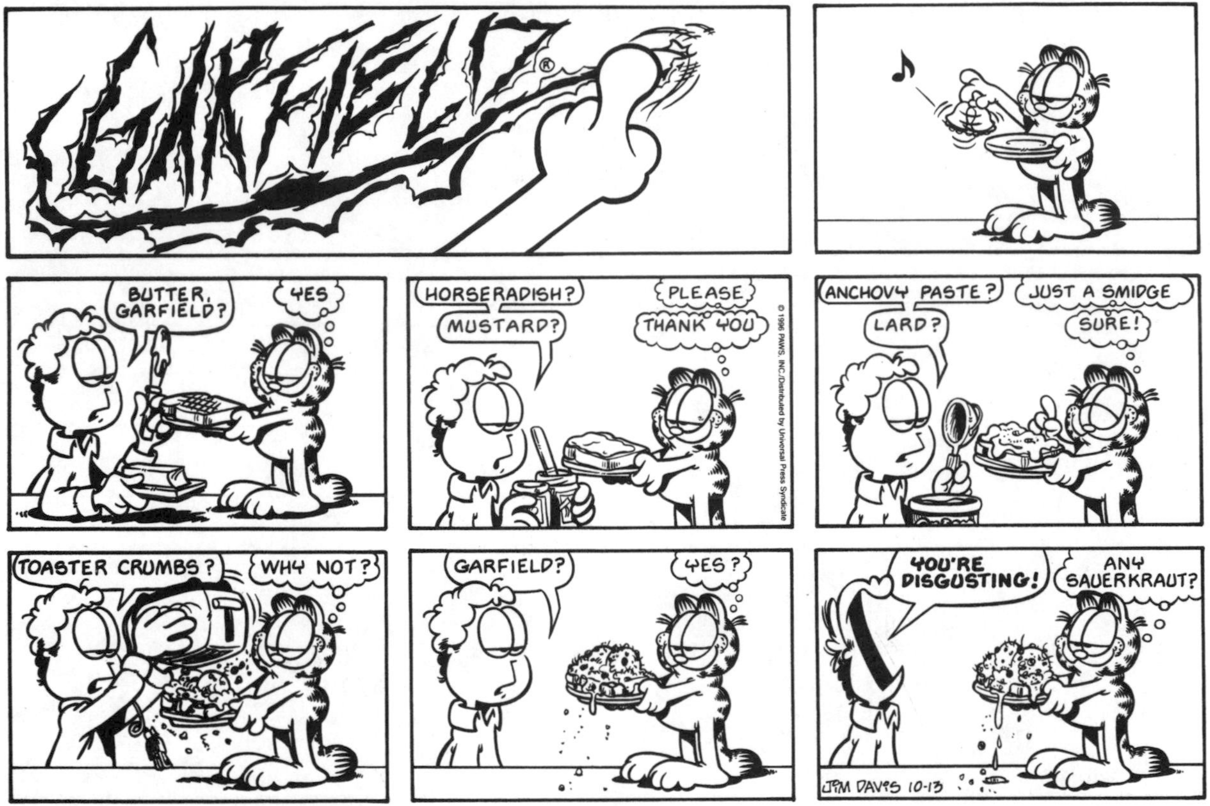
GARFIELD®
BUTTER, GARFIELD?
YES
HORSERADISH?
PLEASE
MUSTARD?
THANK YOU
© 1996 PAWS, INC./Distributed by Universal Press Syndicate
ANCHOVY PASTE?
JUST A SMIDGE
LARD?
SURE!
TOASTER CRUMBS?
WHY NOT?
GARFIELD?
YES?
YOU'RE DISGUSTING!
ANY SAUERKRAUT?
JPM DAVIS 10-13

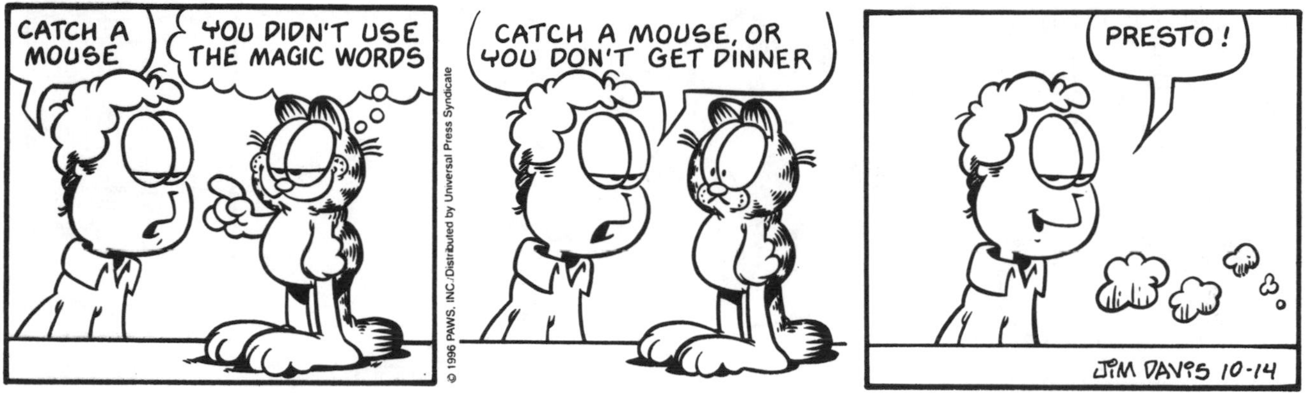
CATCH A MOUSE
YOU DIDN'T USE THE MAGIC WORDS
© 1996 PAWS. INC./Distributed by Universal Press Syndicate
CATCH A MOUSE, OR YOU DON'T GET DINNER
PRESTO!
JIM DAVIS 10-14

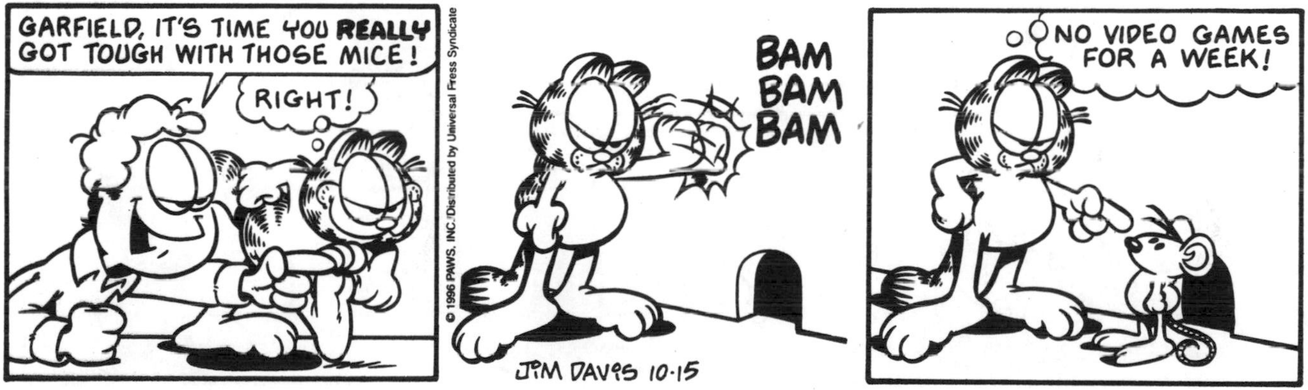
GARFIELD, IT'S TIME YOU **REALLY** GOT TOUGH WITH THOSE MICE!
RIGHT!
© 1996 PAWS. INC./Distributed by Universal Press Syndicate
BAM BAM BAM
JIM DAVIS 10-15
NO VIDEO GAMES FOR A WEEK!

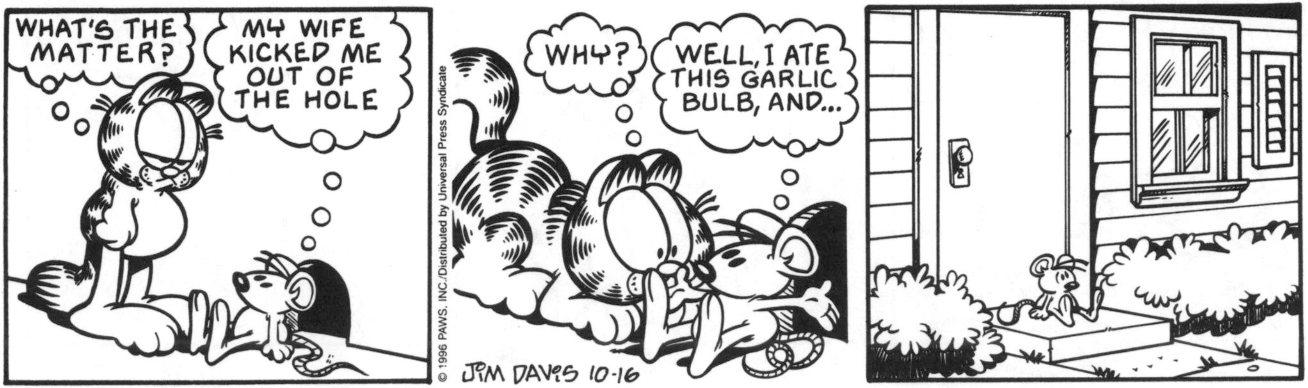
WHAT'S THE MATTER?
MY WIFE KICKED ME OUT OF THE HOLE
WHY?
WELL, I ATE THIS GARLIC BULB, AND...
JIM DAVIS 10-16
© 1996 PAWS, INC./Distributed by Universal Press Syndicate

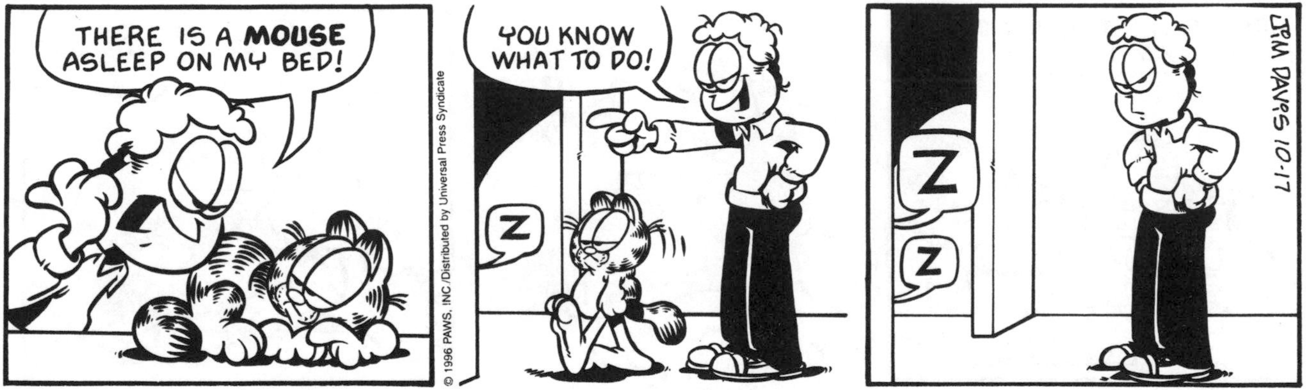
THERE IS A **MOUSE** ASLEEP ON MY BED!
YOU KNOW WHAT TO DO!
Z
Z
Z
JIM DAVIS 10-17
© 1996 PAWS, INC./Distributed by Universal Press Syndicate

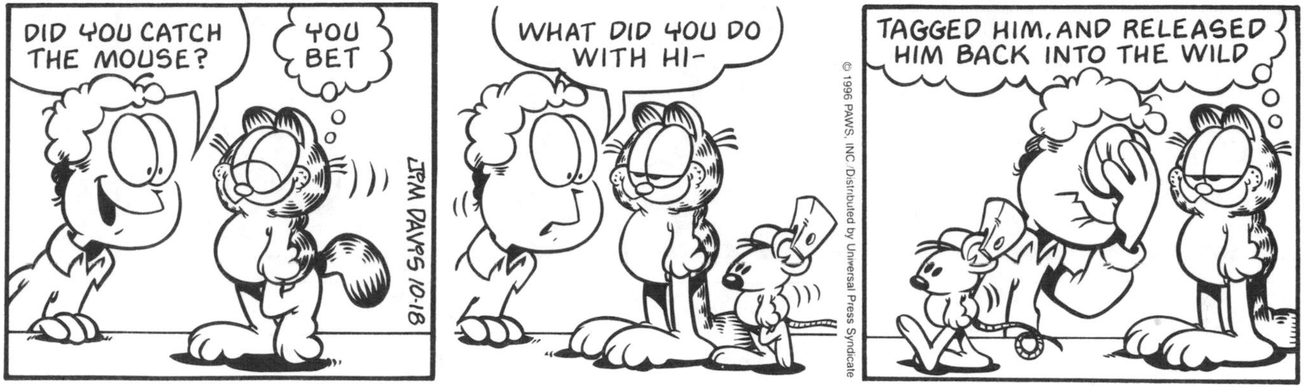
DID YOU CATCH THE MOUSE?
YOU BET
WHAT DID YOU DO WITH HI-
TAGGED HIM, AND RELEASED HIM BACK INTO THE WILD
© 1996 PAWS, INC./Distributed by Universal Press Syndicate

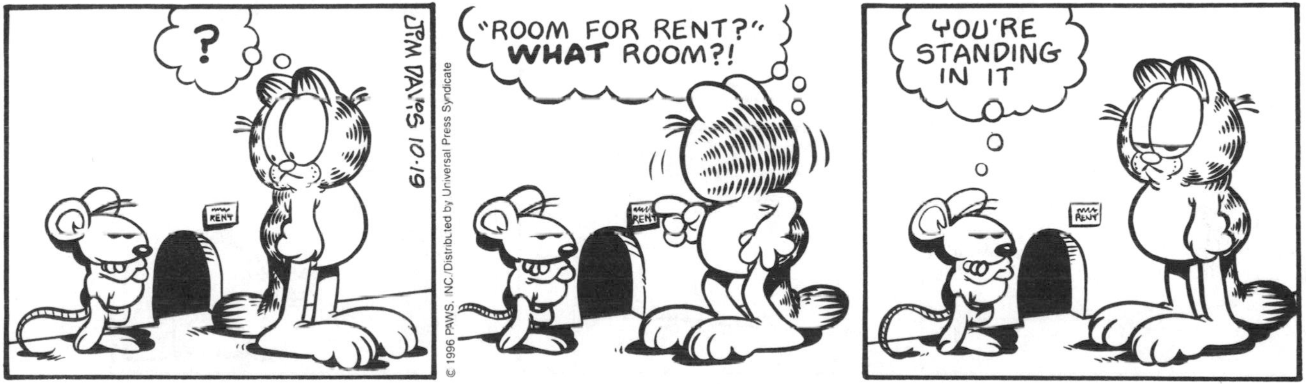
?
RENT
"ROOM FOR RENT?" **WHAT** ROOM?!
YOU'RE STANDING IN IT
© 1996 PAWS, INC./Distributed by Universal Press Syndicate

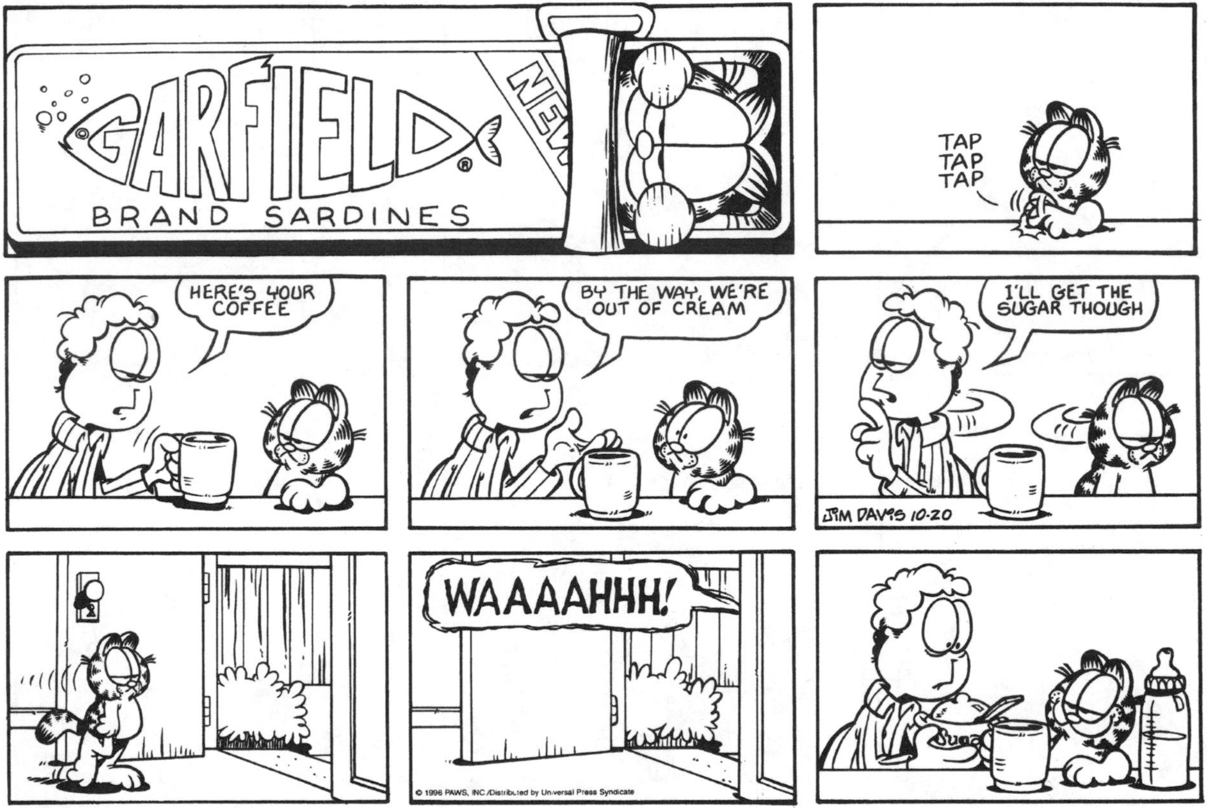
GARFIELD®
BRAND SARDINES
NEW
TAP
TAP
TAP
HERE'S YOUR COFFEE
BY THE WAY, WE'RE OUT OF CREAM
I'LL GET THE SUGAR THOUGH
JIM DAVIS 10-20
WAAAAHHH!
© 1996 PAWS, INC./Distributed by Universal Press Syndicate

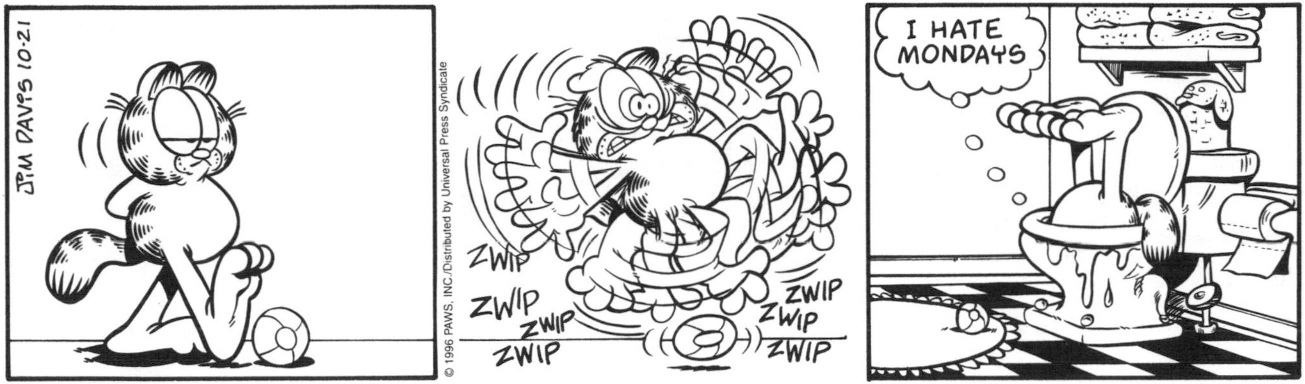
JIM DAVIS 10-21
© 1996 PAWS, INC./Distributed by Universal Press Syndicate
ZWIP
ZWIP
ZWIP
ZWIP
ZWIP
ZWIP
ZWIP
I HATE MONDAYS

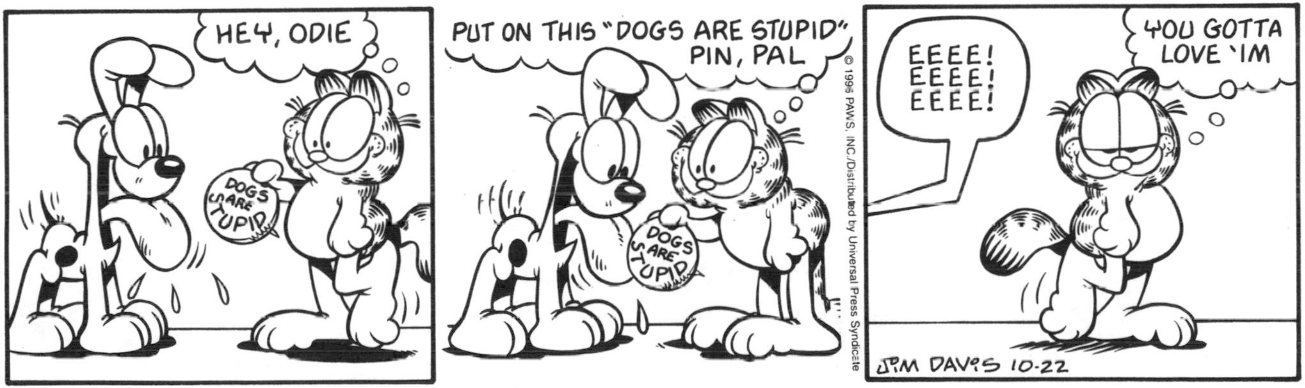
HEY, ODIE
DOGS ARE STUPID
PUT ON THIS "DOGS ARE STUPID" PIN, PAL
DOGS ARE STUPID
© 1996 PAWS, INC./Distributed by Universal Press Syndicate
EEEE! EEEE! EEEE!
YOU GOTTA LOVE 'IM
JIM DAVIS 10-22

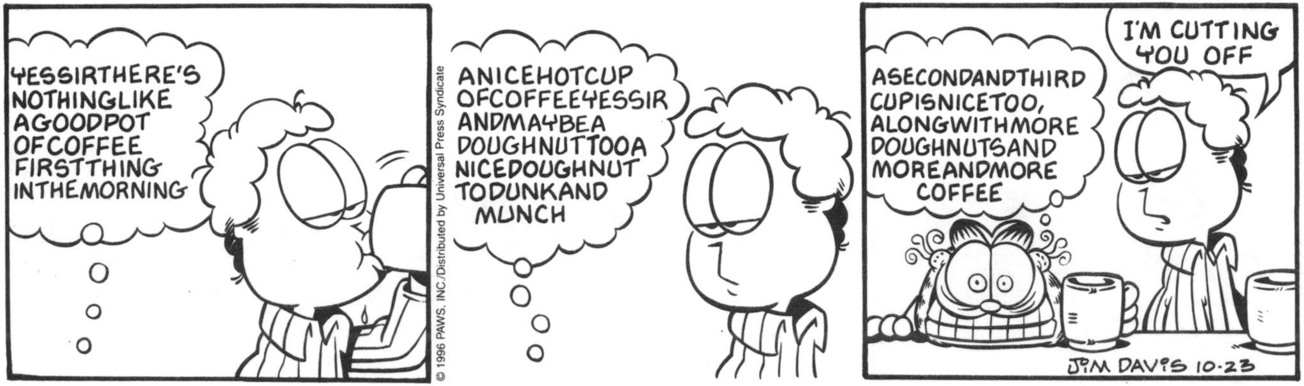
YESSIRTHERE'S NOTHINGLIKE AGOODPOT OFCOFFEE FIRSTTHING INTHEMORNING
ANICEHOTCUP OFCOFFEEYESSIR ANDMAYBEA DOUGHNUTTOOA NICEDOUGHNUT TODUNKAND MUNCH
ASECONDANDTHIRD CUPISNICETOO, ALONGWITHMORE DOUGHNUTSAND MOREANDMORE COFFEE
I'M CUTTING YOU OFF
JIM DAVIS 10-23
© 1996 PAWS, INC./Distributed by Universal Press Syndicate

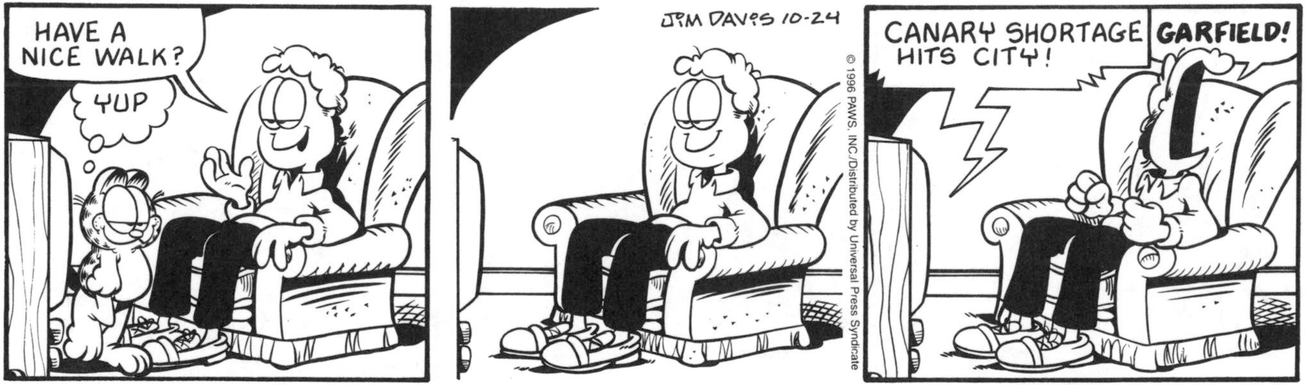
HAVE A NICE WALK?
YUP
JIM DAVIS 10-24
CANARY SHORTAGE HITS CITY!
GARFIELD!
© 1996 PAWS, INC./Distributed by Universal Press Syndicate

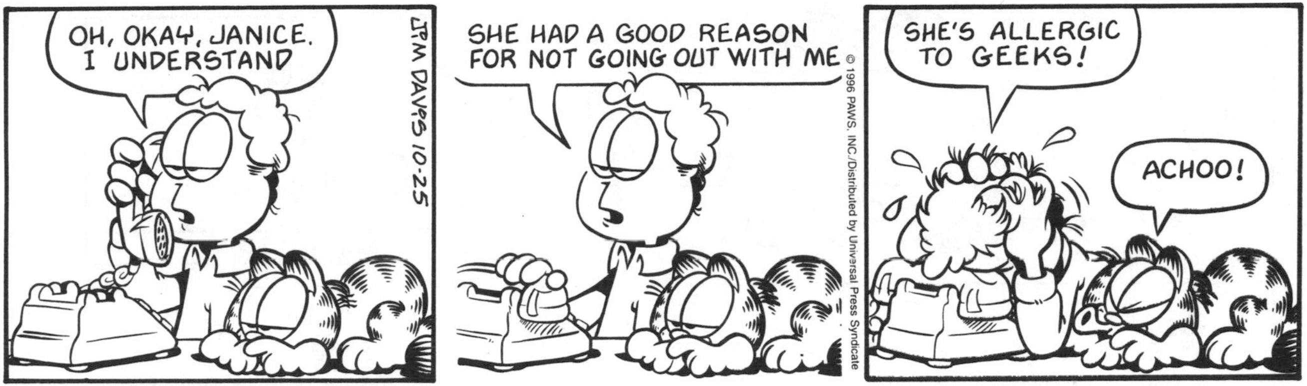
OH, OKAY, JANICE. I UNDERSTAND
JIM DAVIS 10-25
SHE HAD A GOOD REASON FOR NOT GOING OUT WITH ME
© 1996 PAWS, INC./Distributed by Universal Press Syndicate
SHE'S ALLERGIC TO GEEKS!
ACHOO!

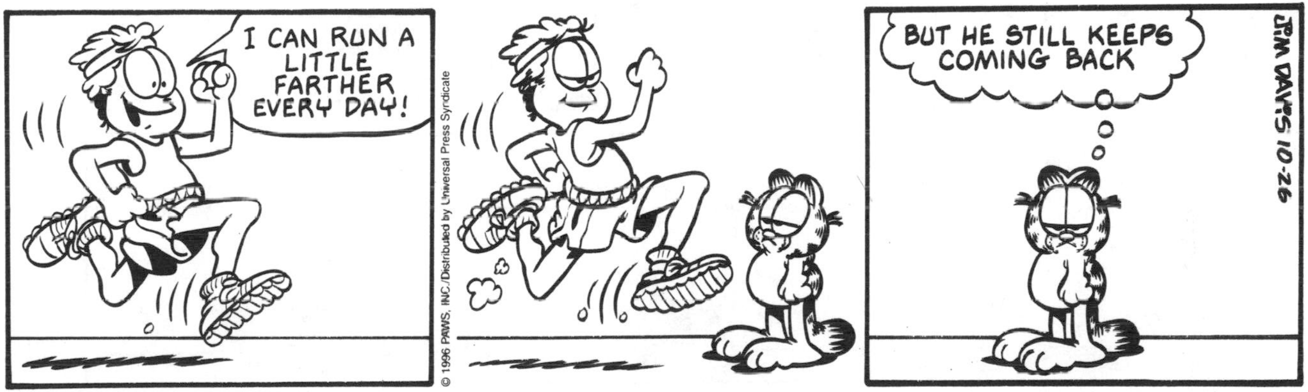
I CAN RUN A LITTLE FARTHER EVERY DAY!
© 1996 PAWS, INC./Distributed by Universal Press Syndicate
BUT HE STILL KEEPS COMING BACK
JIM DAVIS 10-26

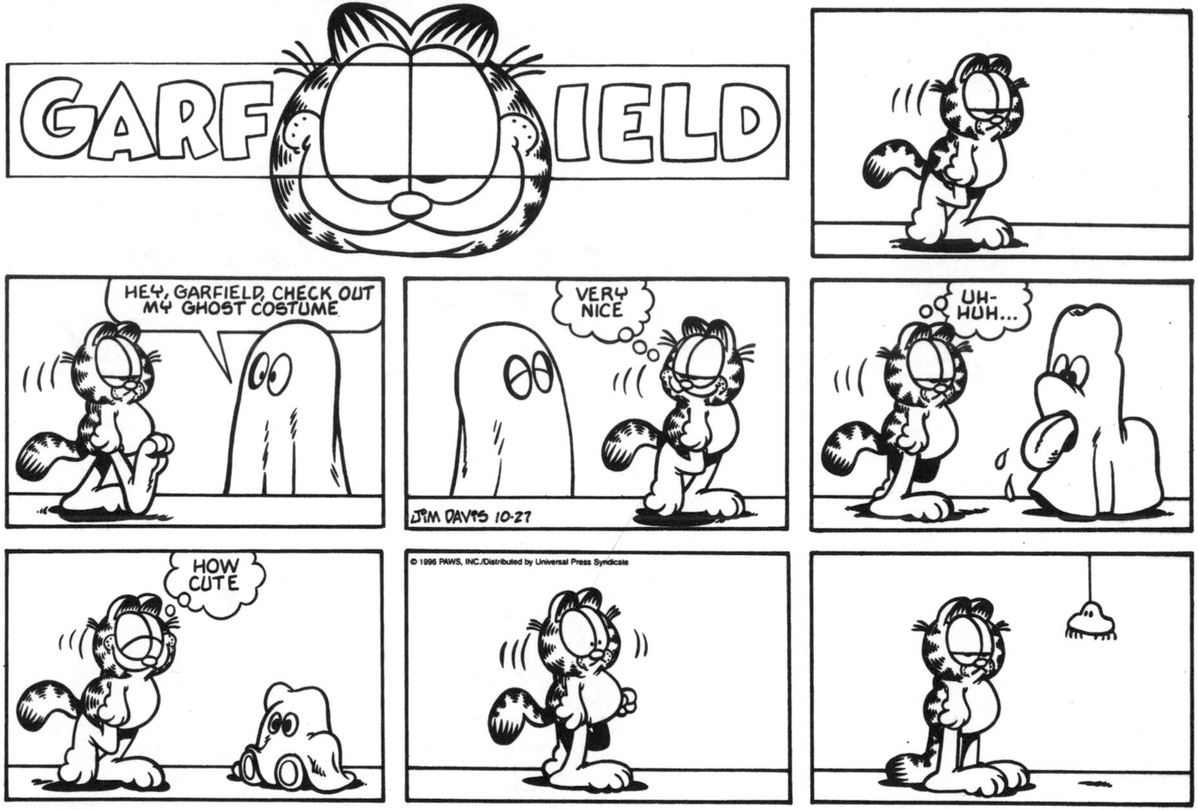
GARFIELD
HEY, GARFIELD, CHECK OUT MY GHOST COSTUME
VERY NICE
JIM DAVIS 10-27
UH-HUH...
HOW CUTE
© 1996 PAWS, INC./Distributed by Universal Press Syndicate

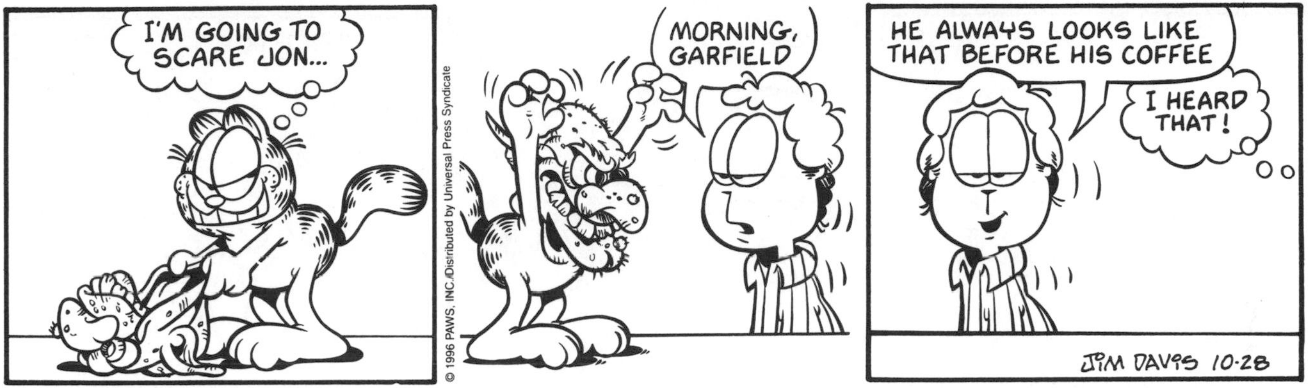

I'M GOING TO SCARE JON...
MORNING, GARFIELD
HE ALWAYS LOOKS LIKE THAT BEFORE HIS COFFEE
I HEARD THAT!
JIM DAVIS 10-28
© 1996 PAWS, INC./Distributed by Universal Press Syndicate

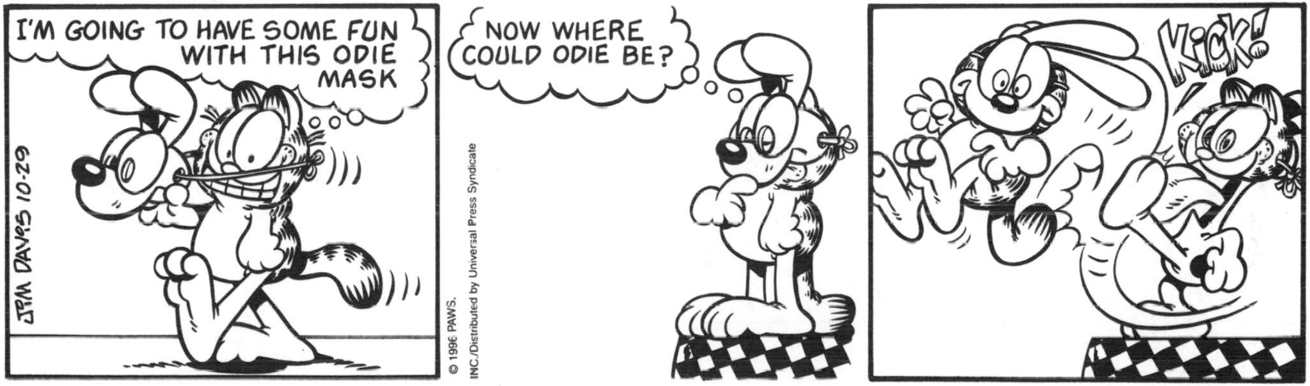

I'M GOING TO HAVE SOME FUN WITH THIS ODIE MASK
JIM DAVIS 10-29
© 1996 PAWS. INC./Distributed by Universal Press Syndicate
NOW WHERE COULD ODIE BE?
KICK!

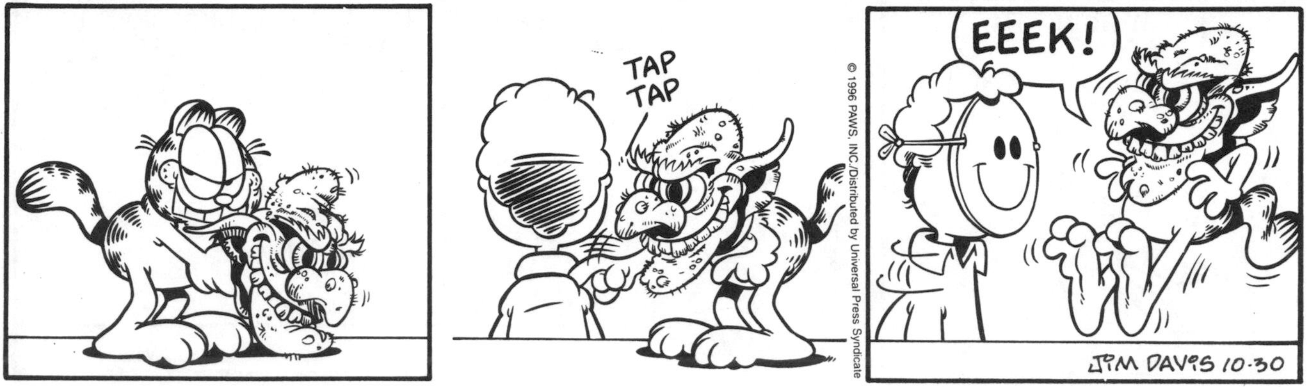
TAP
TAP
© 1996 PAWS, INC./Distributed by Universal Press Syndicate
EEEK!
JIM DAVIS 10-30

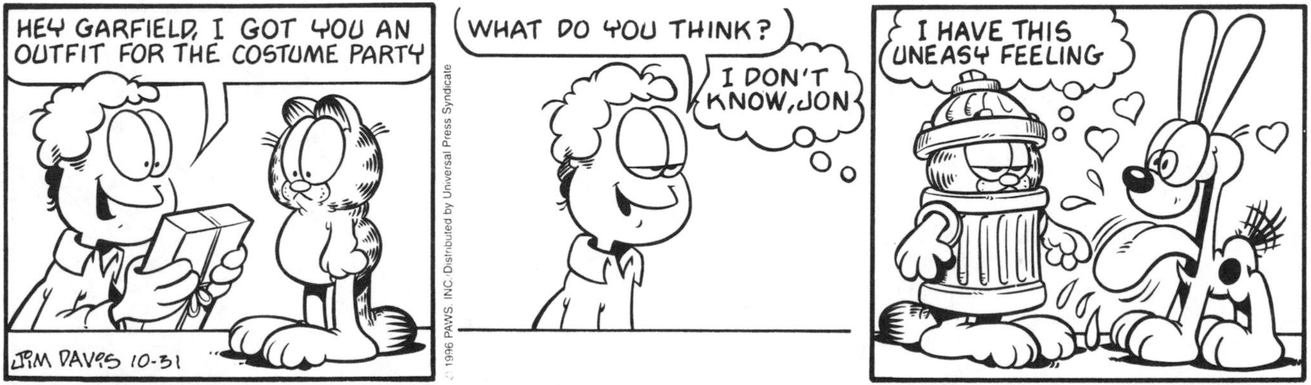
HEY GARFIELD, I GOT YOU AN OUTFIT FOR THE COSTUME PARTY
JIM DAVIS 10-31
© 1996 PAWS, INC./Distributed by Universal Press Syndicate
WHAT DO YOU THINK?
I DON'T KNOW, JON
I HAVE THIS UNEASY FEELING

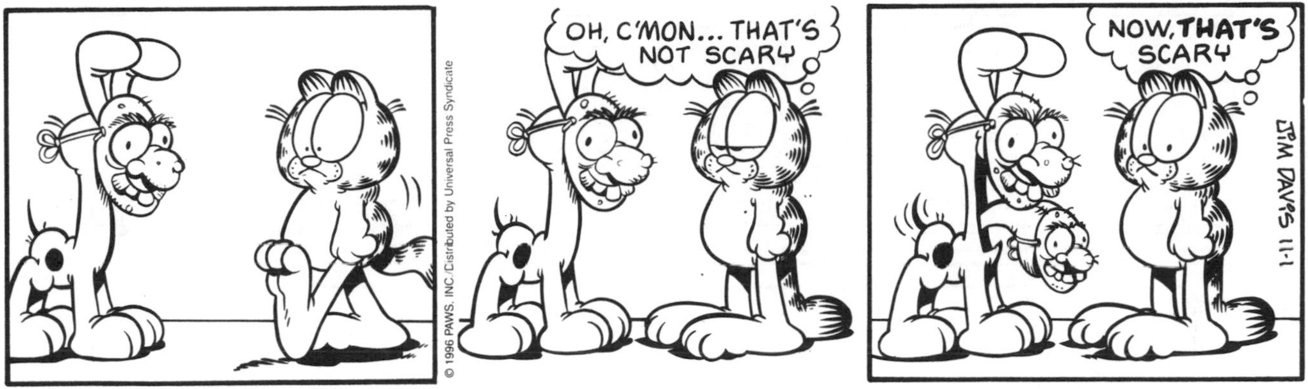
© 1996 PAWS, INC./Distributed by Universal Press Syndicate
OH, C'MON... THAT'S NOT SCARY
NOW, THAT'S SCARY
JIM DAVIS 11-1

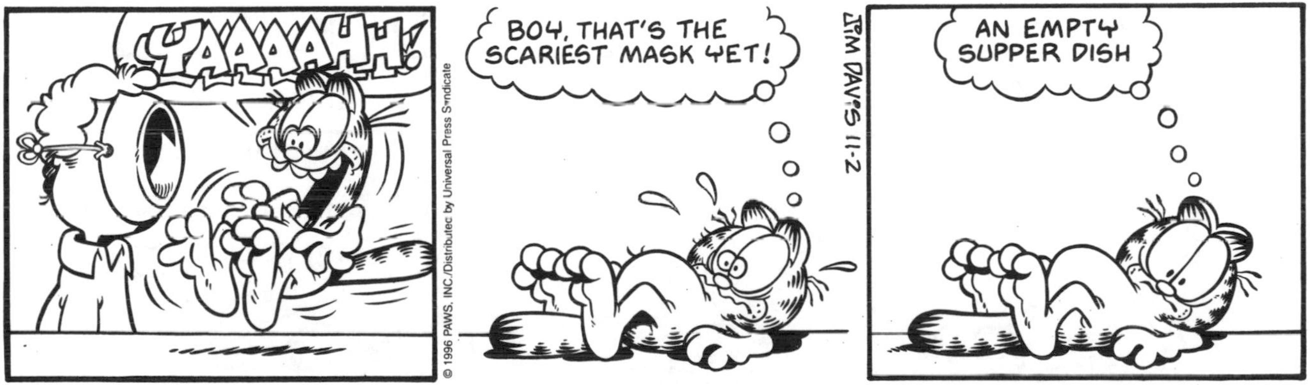
YAAAAHH!
© 1996 PAWS, INC./Distributed by Universal Press Syndicate
BOY, THAT'S THE SCARIEST MASK YET!
JIM DAVIS 11-2
AN EMPTY SUPPER DISH

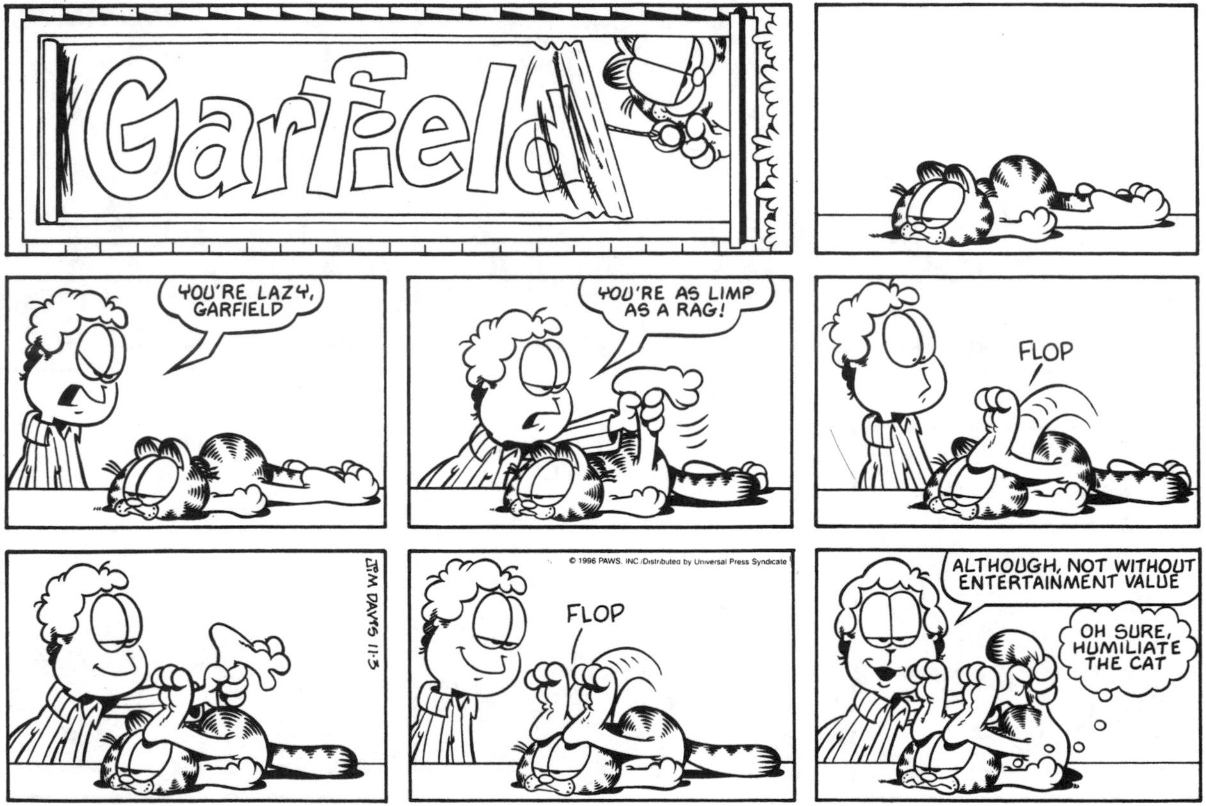
Garfield
YOU'RE LAZY, GARFIELD
YOU'RE AS LIMP AS A RAG!
FLOP
JIM DAVIS 11-3
© 1996 PAWS, INC./Distributed by Universal Press Syndicate
FLOP
ALTHOUGH, NOT WITHOUT ENTERTAINMENT VALUE
OH SURE, HUMILIATE THE CAT

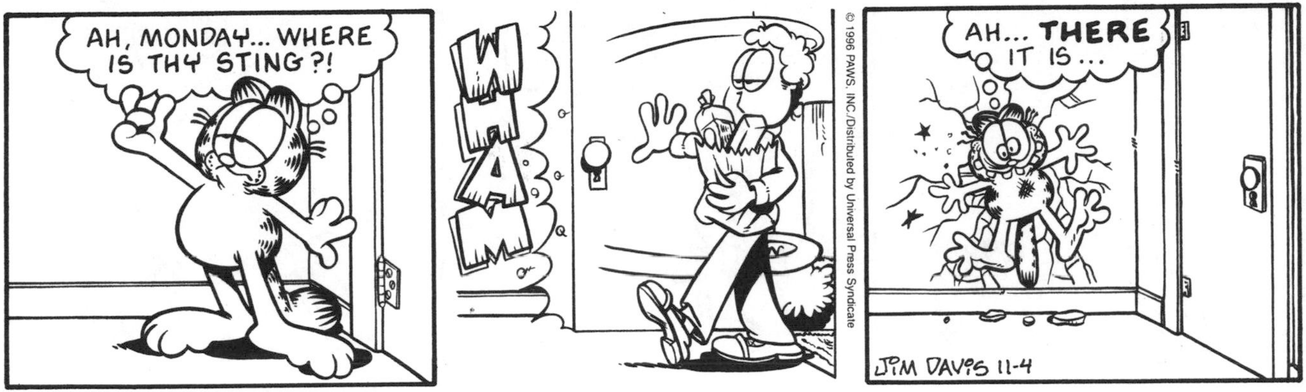
AH, MONDAY... WHERE IS THY STING?!
WHAM
AH... THERE IT IS...
JIM DAVIS 11-4

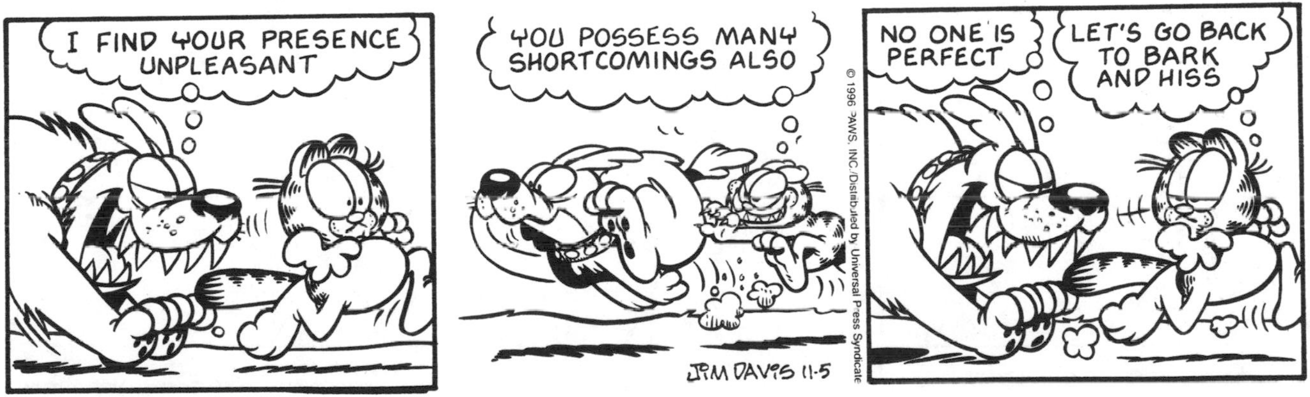
I FIND YOUR PRESENCE UNPLEASANT
YOU POSSESS MANY SHORTCOMINGS ALSO
NO ONE IS PERFECT
LET'S GO BACK TO BARK AND HISS
JIM DAVIS 11-5

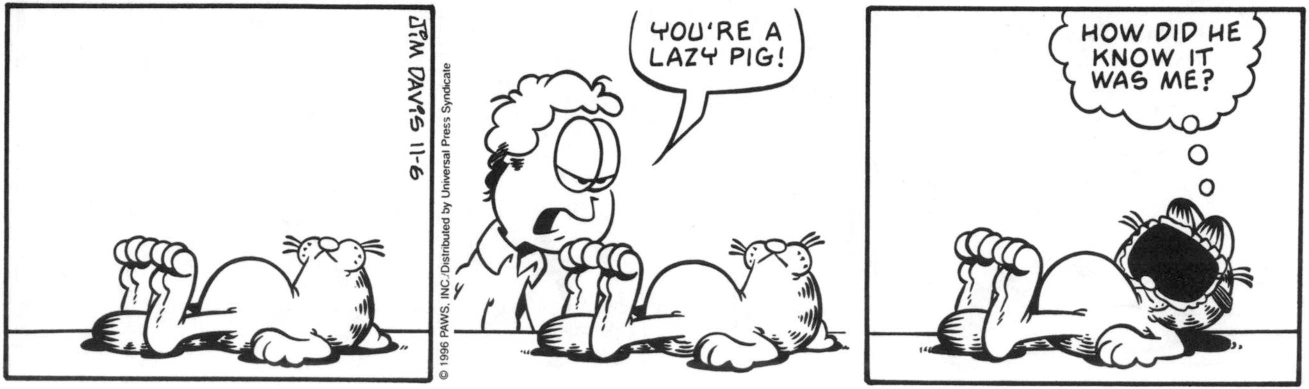
JIM DAVIS 11-6
© 1996 PAWS, INC./Distributed by Universal Press Syndicate
YOU'RE A LAZY PIG!
HOW DID HE KNOW IT WAS ME?

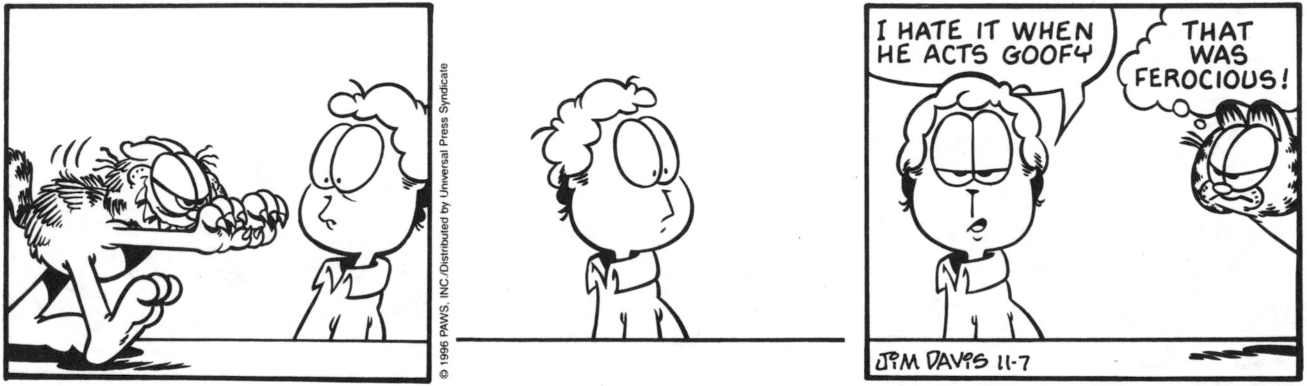
© 1996 PAWS, INC./Distributed by Universal Press Syndicate
I HATE IT WHEN HE ACTS GOOFY
THAT WAS FEROCIOUS!
JIM DAVIS 11-7

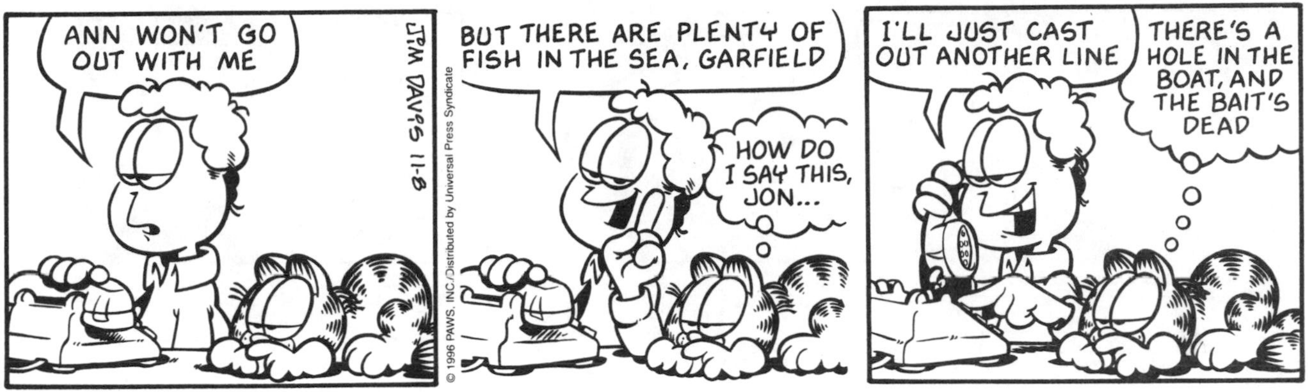
ANN WON'T GO OUT WITH ME
JPM DAVPS 11-8
© 1996 PAWS, INC./Distributed by Universal Press Syndicate
BUT THERE ARE PLENTY OF FISH IN THE SEA, GARFIELD
HOW DO I SAY THIS, JON...
I'LL JUST CAST OUT ANOTHER LINE
THERE'S A HOLE IN THE BOAT, AND THE BAIT'S DEAD

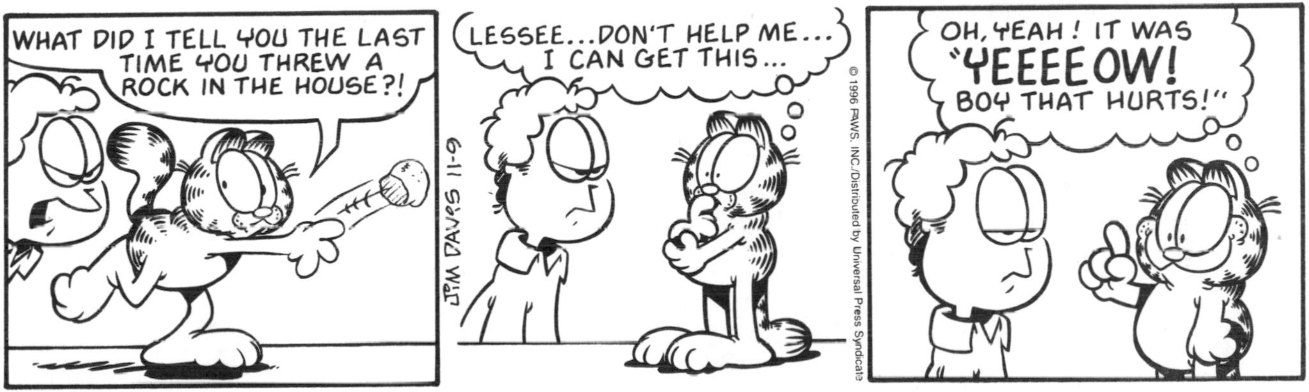
WHAT DID I TELL YOU THE LAST TIME YOU THREW A ROCK IN THE HOUSE?!
JPM DAVPS 11-9
LESSEE...DON'T HELP ME... I CAN GET THIS...
© 1996 PAWS, INC./Distributed by Universal Press Syndicate
OH, YEAH! IT WAS "YEEEEOW! BOY THAT HURTS!"

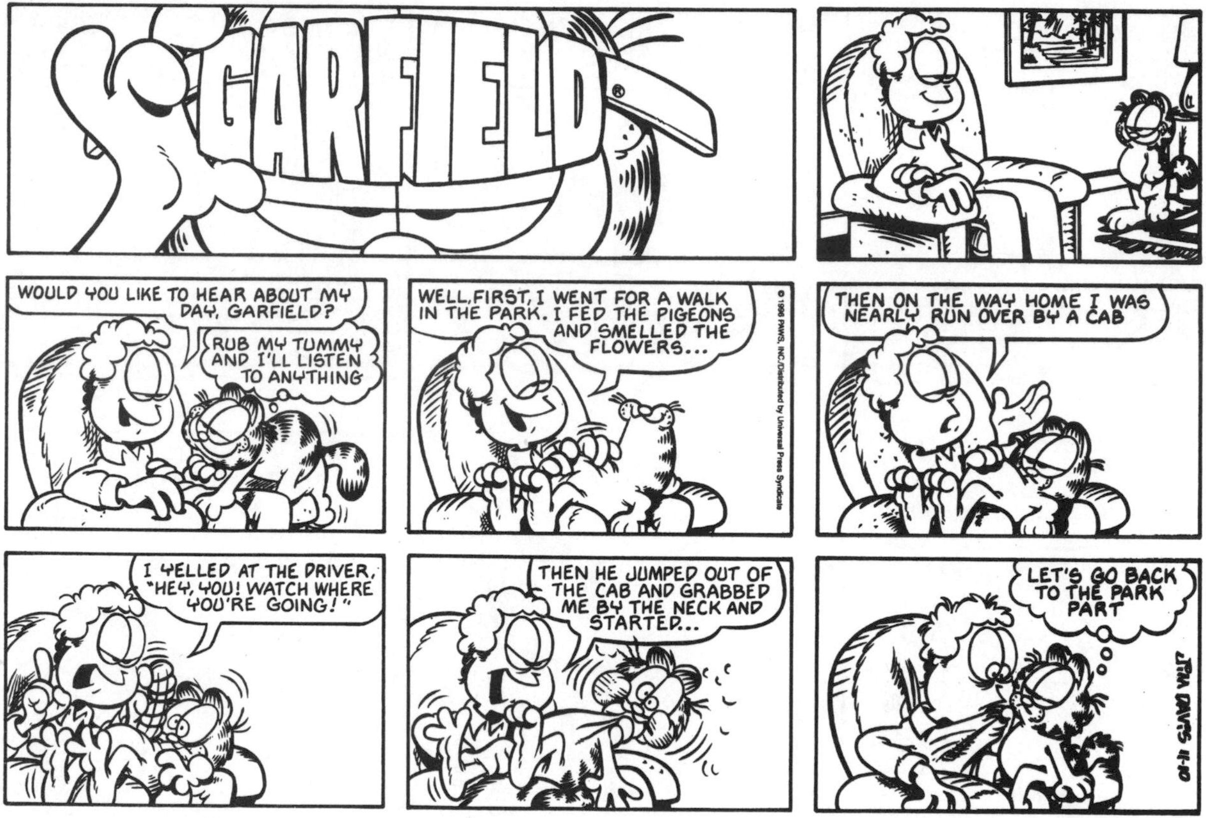
GARFIELD®
WOULD YOU LIKE TO HEAR ABOUT MY DAY, GARFIELD?
RUB MY TUMMY AND I'LL LISTEN TO ANYTHING
WELL, FIRST, I WENT FOR A WALK IN THE PARK. I FED THE PIGEONS AND SMELLED THE FLOWERS...
© 1996 PAWS, INC./Distributed by Universal Press Syndicate
THEN ON THE WAY HOME I WAS NEARLY RUN OVER BY A CAB
I YELLED AT THE DRIVER, "HEY, YOU! WATCH WHERE YOU'RE GOING!"
THEN HE JUMPED OUT OF THE CAB AND GRABBED ME BY THE NECK AND STARTED...
LET'S GO BACK TO THE PARK PART
JIM DAVIS 11-10

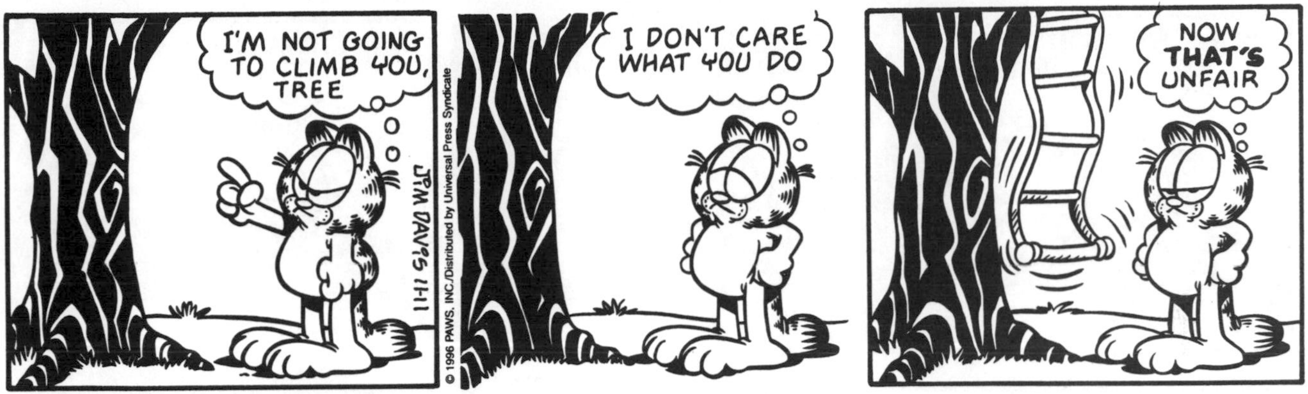
I'M NOT GOING TO CLIMB YOU, TREE
JIM DAVIS 11-11
© 1996 PAWS, INC./Distributed by Universal Press Syndicate
I DON'T CARE WHAT YOU DO
NOW THAT'S UNFAIR

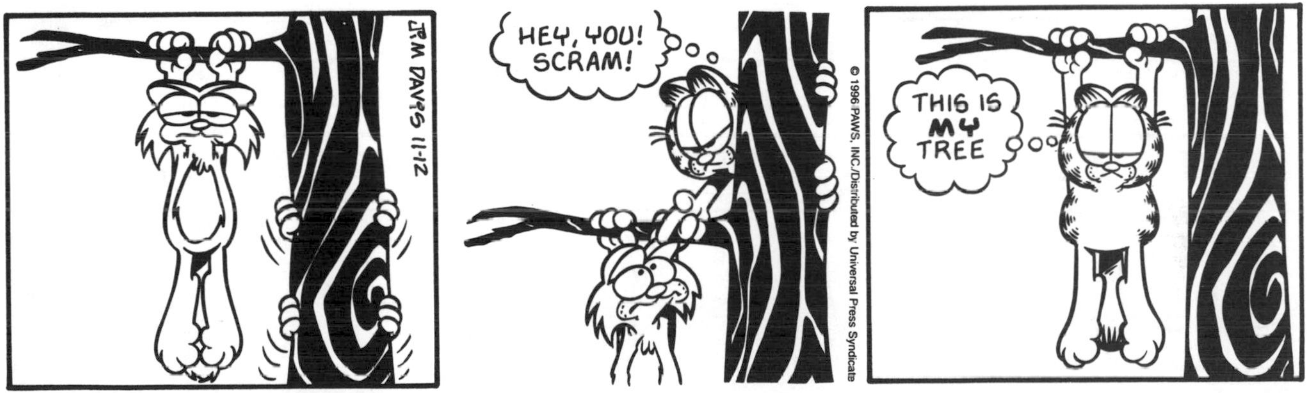
JIM DAVIS 11-12
HEY, YOU! SCRAM!
© 1996 PAWS, INC./Distributed by Universal Press Syndicate
THIS IS MY TREE

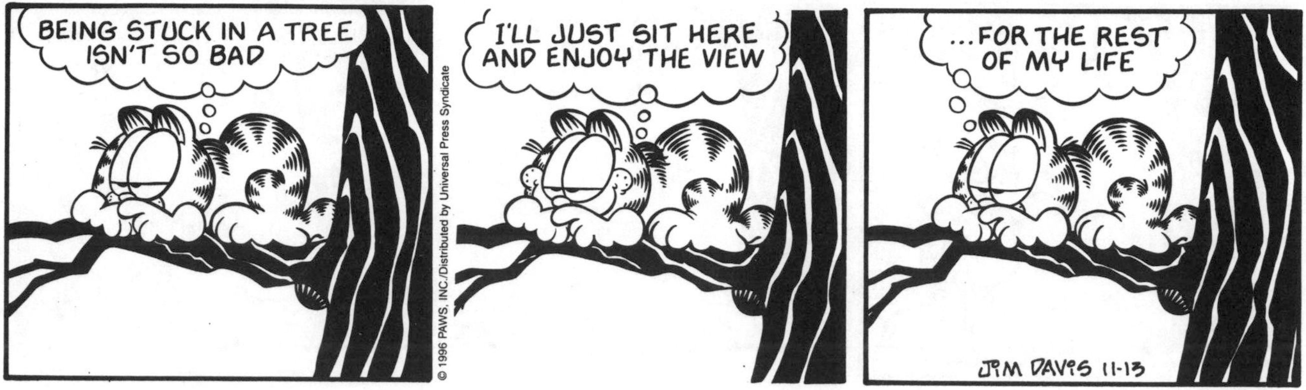
BEING STUCK IN A TREE ISN'T SO BAD
© 1996 PAWS, INC./Distributed by Universal Press Syndicate
I'LL JUST SIT HERE AND ENJOY THE VIEW
...FOR THE REST OF MY LIFE
JIM DAVIS 11-13

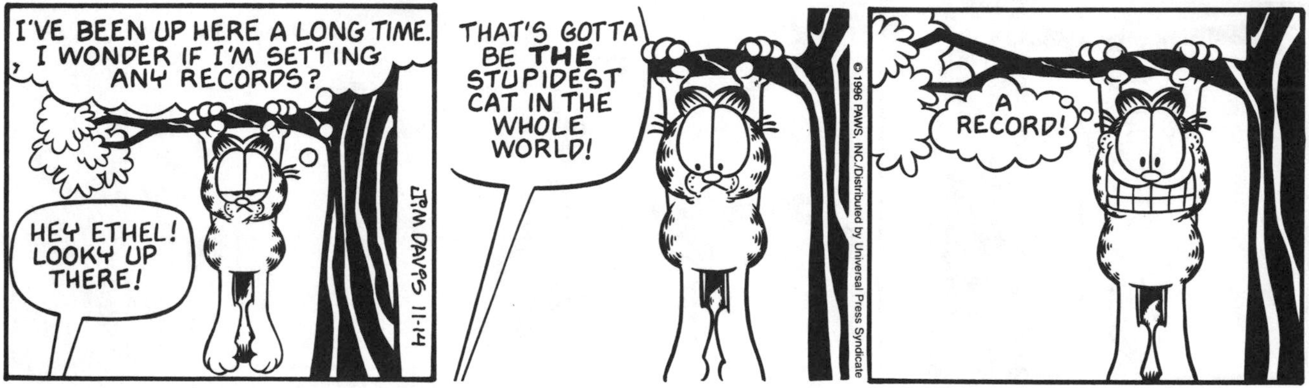
I'VE BEEN UP HERE A LONG TIME. I WONDER IF I'M SETTING ANY RECORDS?
HEY ETHEL! LOOKY UP THERE!
JIM DAVIS 11-14
THAT'S GOTTA BE **THE** STUPIDEST CAT IN THE WHOLE WORLD!
© 1996 PAWS, INC./Distributed by Universal Press Syndicate
A RECORD!

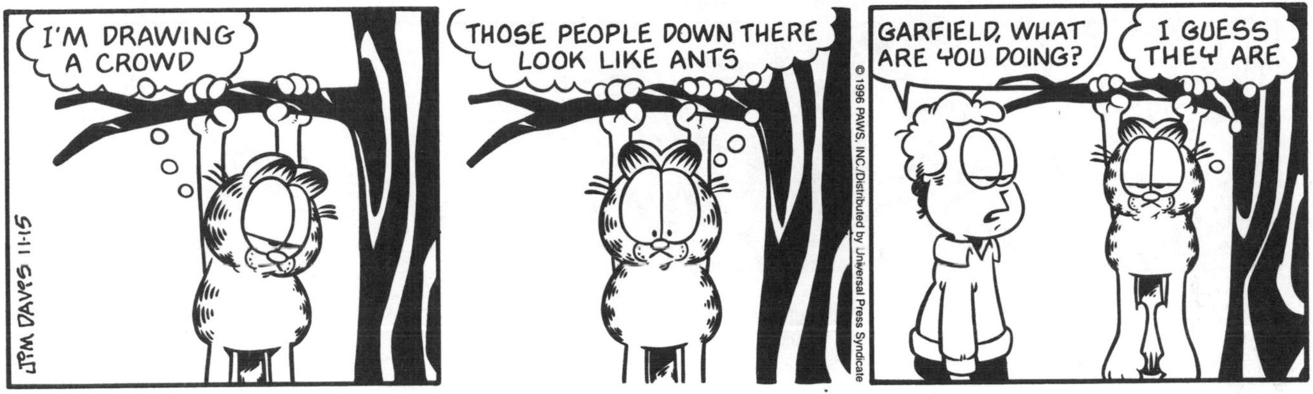
I'M DRAWING A CROWD
JIM DAVIS 11-15
THOSE PEOPLE DOWN THERE LOOK LIKE ANTS
GARFIELD, WHAT ARE YOU DOING?
I GUESS THEY ARE

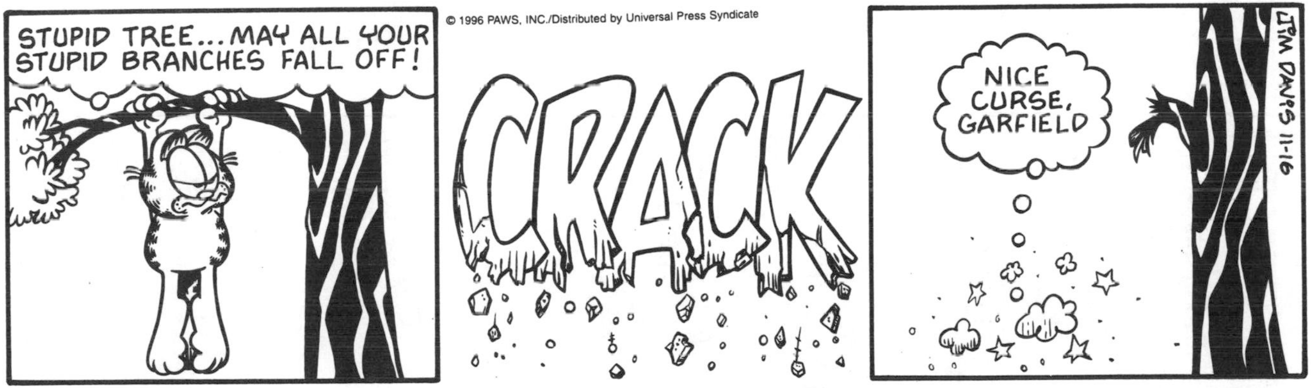
STUPID TREE... MAY ALL YOUR STUPID BRANCHES FALL OFF!
CRACK
NICE CURSE, GARFIELD
JIM DAVIS 11-16

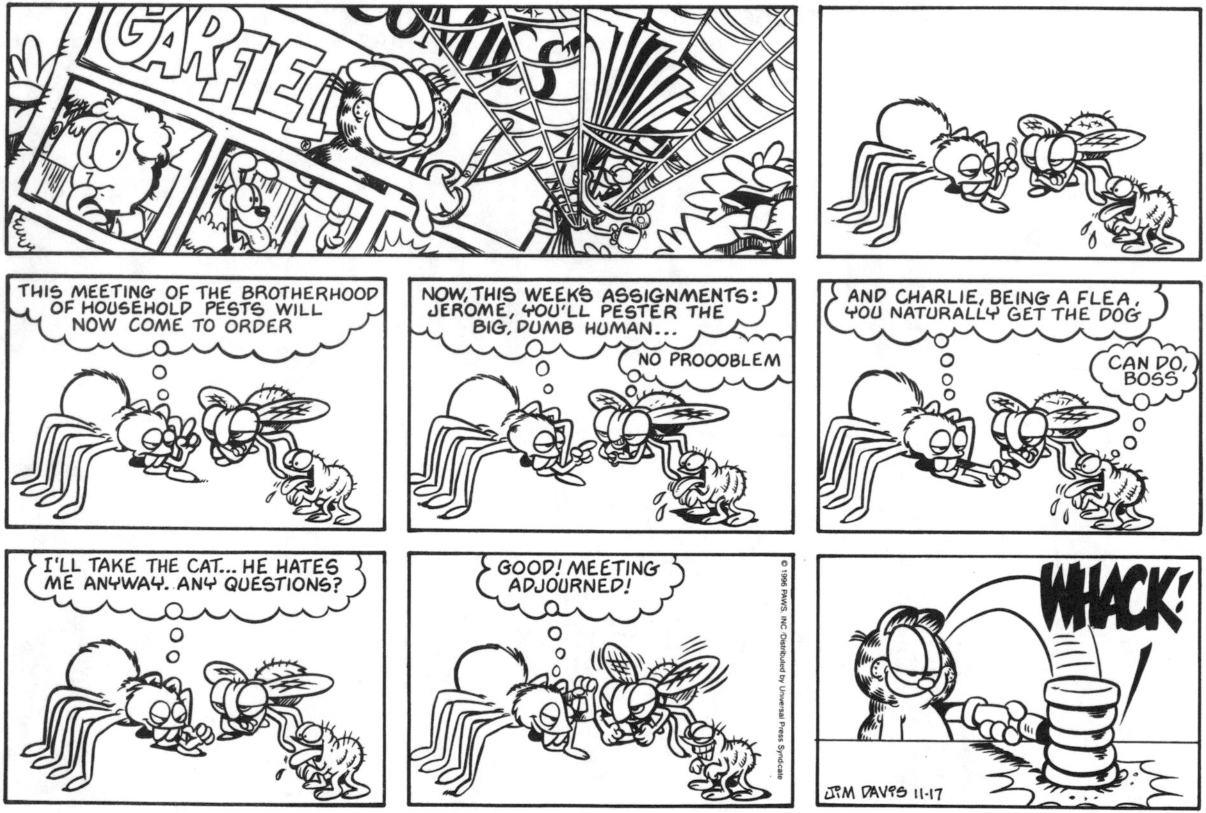
GARFIELD
COMICS
THIS MEETING OF THE BROTHERHOOD OF HOUSEHOLD PESTS WILL NOW COME TO ORDER
NOW, THIS WEEK'S ASSIGNMENTS: JEROME, YOU'LL PESTER THE BIG, DUMB HUMAN...
NO PROOOBLEM
AND CHARLIE, BEING A FLEA, YOU NATURALLY GET THE DOG
CAN DO, BOSS
I'LL TAKE THE CAT... HE HATES ME ANYWAY. ANY QUESTIONS?
GOOD! MEETING ADJOURNED!
© 1996 PAWS, INC./Distributed by Universal Press Syndicate
WHACK!
JIM DAVIS 11-17

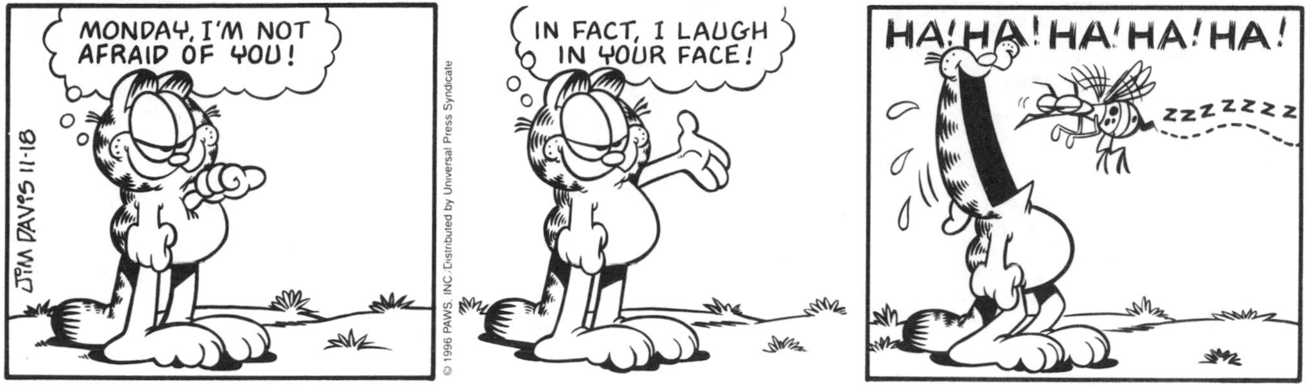
MONDAY, I'M NOT AFRAID OF YOU!
JIM DAVIS 11-18
IN FACT, I LAUGH IN YOUR FACE!
HA! HA! HA! HA! HA!
ZZZZZZZ
© 1996 PAWS, INC./Distributed by Universal Press Syndicate

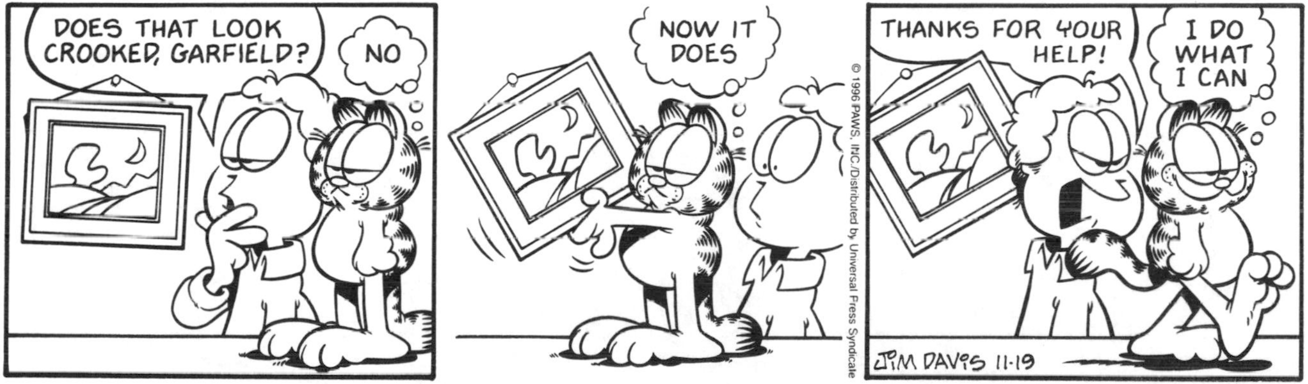
DOES THAT LOOK CROOKED, GARFIELD?
NO
NOW IT DOES
THANKS FOR YOUR HELP!
I DO WHAT I CAN
JIM DAVIS 11-19
© 1996 PAWS, INC./Distributed by Universal Press Syndicate

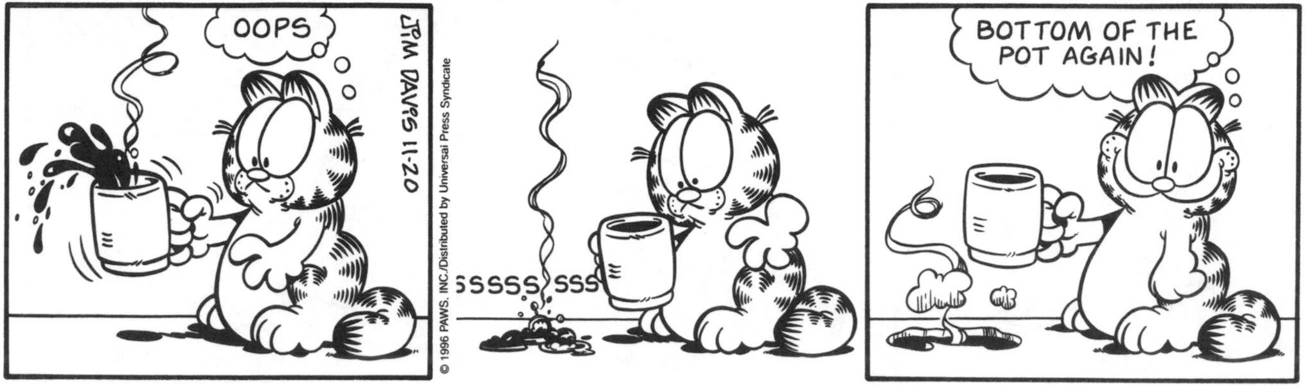
OOPS
JIM DAVIS 11-20
© 1996 PAWS, INC./Distributed by Universal Press Syndicate
SSSSS SSS
BOTTOM OF THE POT AGAIN!

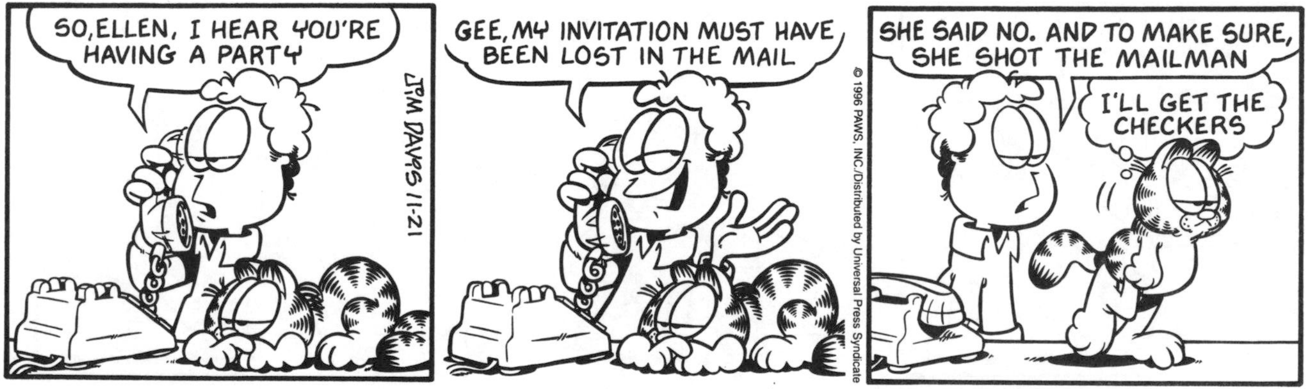
SO, ELLEN, I HEAR YOU'RE HAVING A PARTY
JIM DAVIS 11-21
GEE, MY INVITATION MUST HAVE BEEN LOST IN THE MAIL
© 1996 PAWS, INC./Distributed by Universal Press Syndicate
SHE SAID NO. AND TO MAKE SURE, SHE SHOT THE MAILMAN
I'LL GET THE CHECKERS

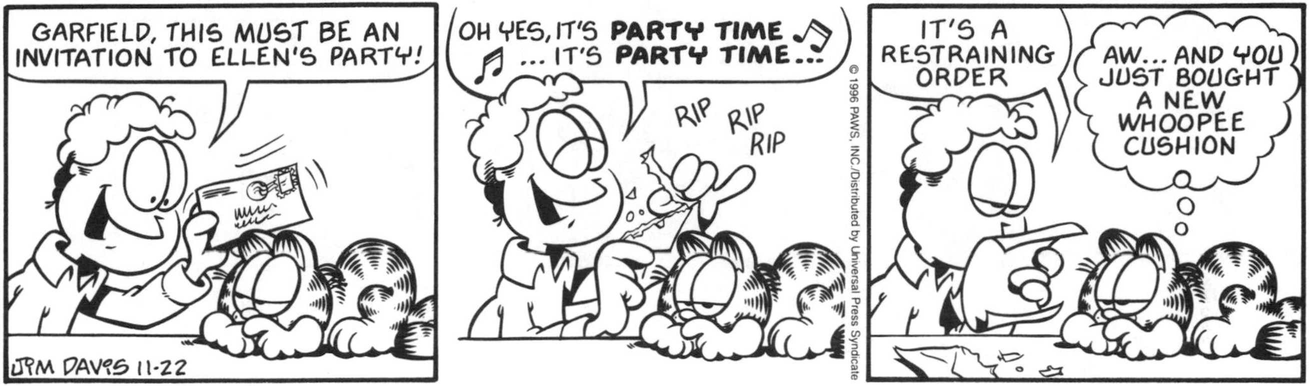
GARFIELD, THIS MUST BE AN INVITATION TO ELLEN'S PARTY!
JIM DAVIS 11-22
OH YES, IT'S **PARTY TIME** ... IT'S **PARTY TIME**...
RIP RIP RIP
© 1996 PAWS, INC./Distributed by Universal Press Syndicate
IT'S A RESTRAINING ORDER
AW... AND YOU JUST BOUGHT A NEW WHOOPEE CUSHION

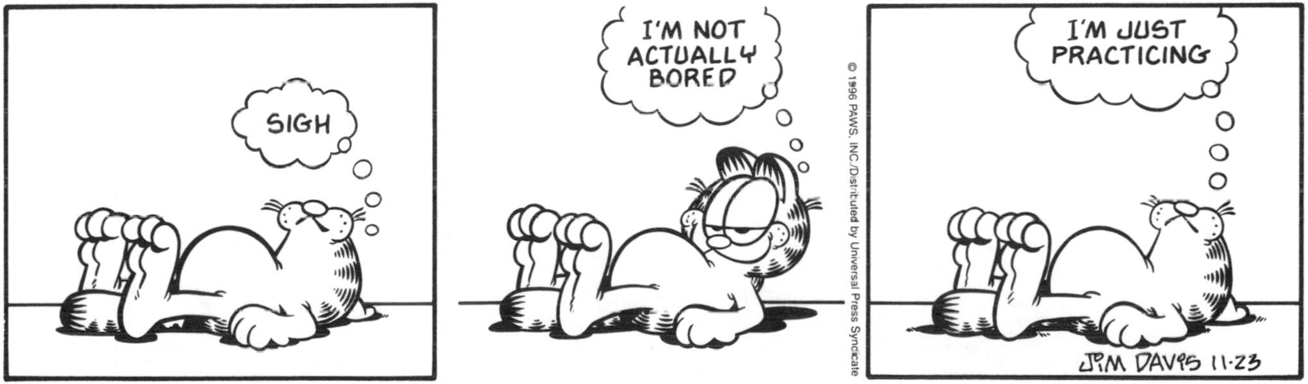
SIGH
I'M NOT ACTUALLY BORED
© 1996 PAWS, INC./Distributed by Universal Press Syndicate
I'M JUST PRACTICING
JIM DAVIS 11-23

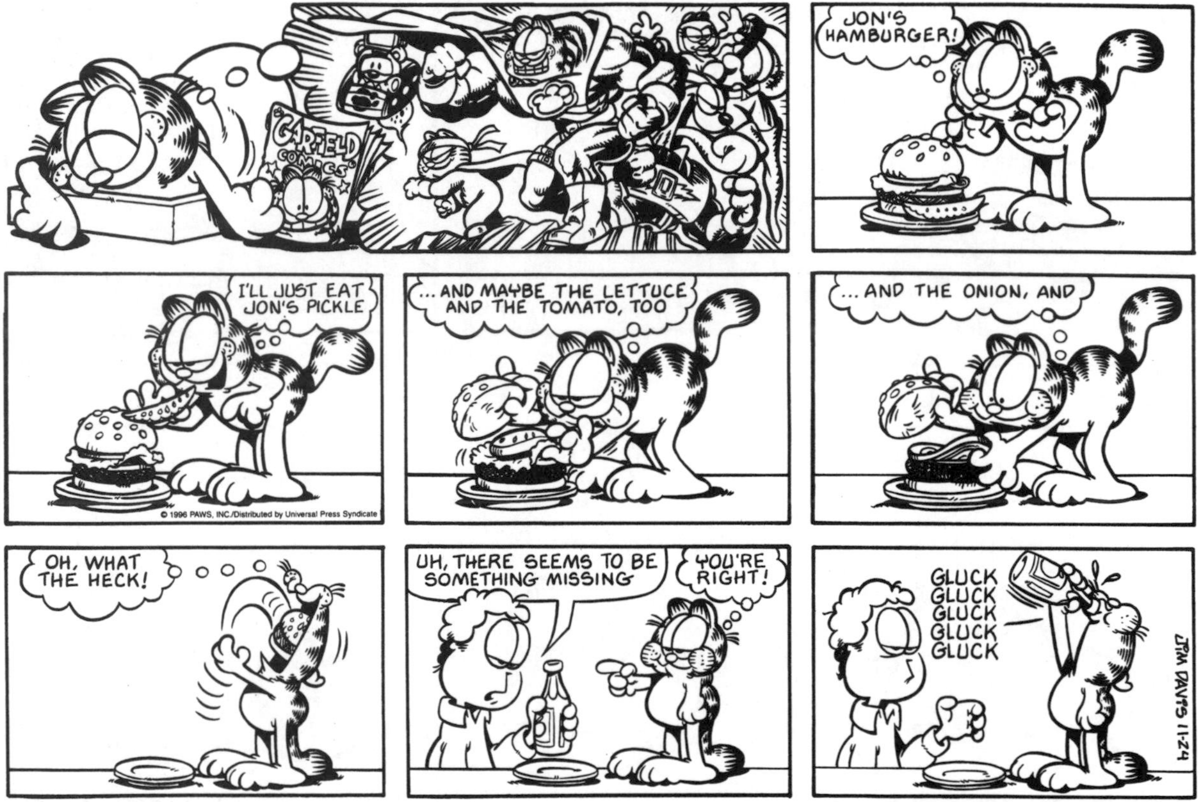
GARFIELD COMICS
JON'S HAMBURGER!
I'LL JUST EAT JON'S PICKLE
© 1996 PAWS, INC./Distributed by Universal Press Syndicate
...AND MAYBE THE LETTUCE AND THE TOMATO, TOO
...AND THE ONION, AND
OH, WHAT THE HECK!
UH, THERE SEEMS TO BE SOMETHING MISSING
YOU'RE RIGHT!
GLUCK GLUCK GLUCK GLUCK GLUCK
JIM DAVIS 11-24

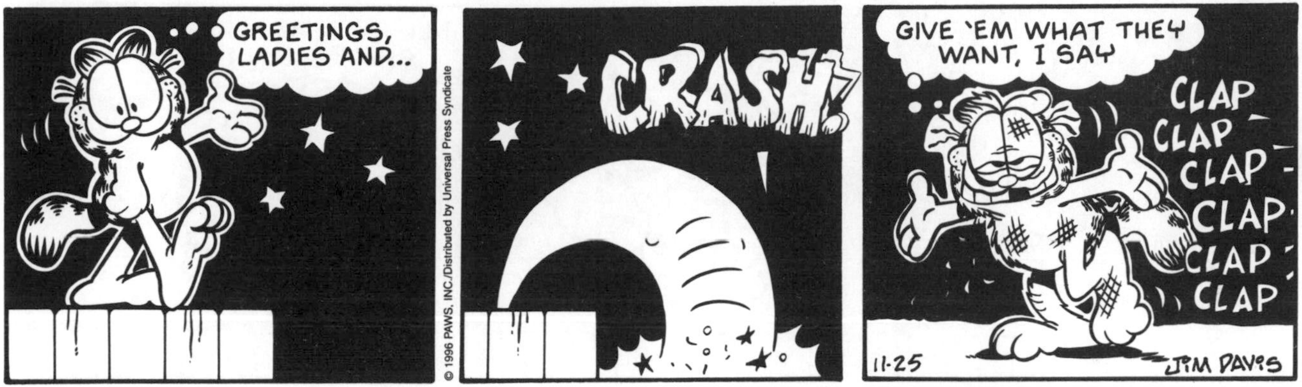
GREETINGS, LADIES AND...
CRASH!
GIVE 'EM WHAT THEY WANT, I SAY
CLAP CLAP CLAP CLAP CLAP CLAP
11-25
JIM DAVIS
© 1996 PAWS, INC./Distributed by Universal Press Syndicate

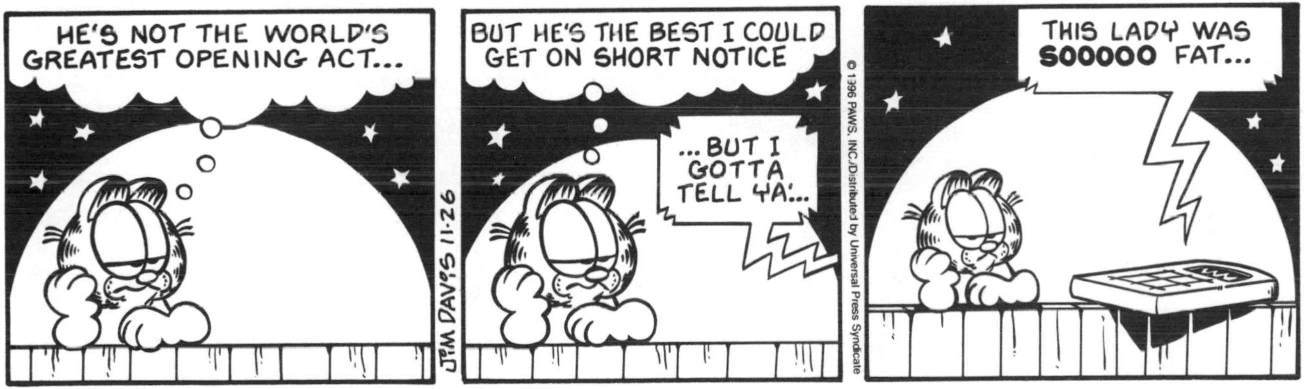
HE'S NOT THE WORLD'S GREATEST OPENING ACT...
JIM DAVIS 11-26
BUT HE'S THE BEST I COULD GET ON SHORT NOTICE
...BUT I GOTTA TELL YA'...
© 1996 PAWS, INC./Distributed by Universal Press Syndicate
THIS LADY WAS SOOOOO FAT...

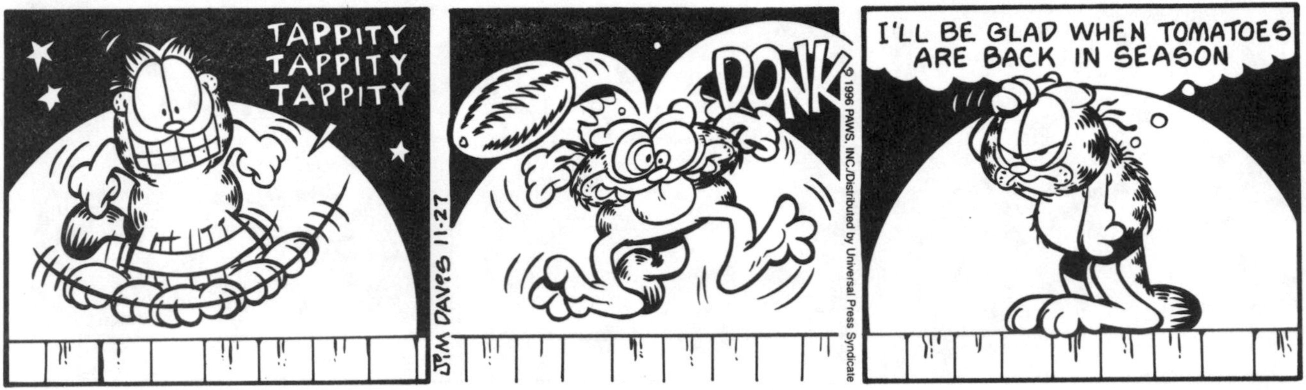
TAPPITY
TAPPITY
TAPPITY
JPM DAVPS 11-27
DONK
© 1996 PAWS, INC./Distributed by Universal Press Syndicate
I'LL BE GLAD WHEN TOMATOES ARE BACK IN SEASON

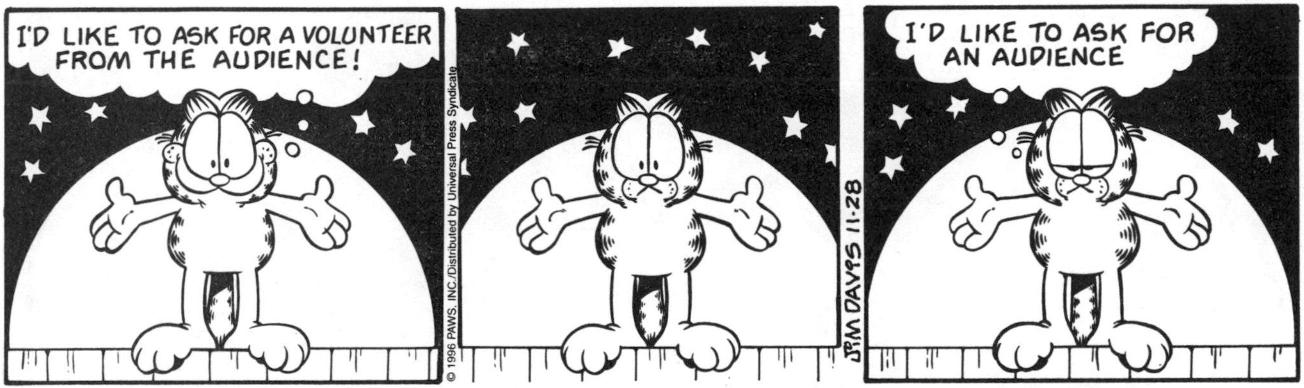
I'D LIKE TO ASK FOR A VOLUNTEER FROM THE AUDIENCE!
© 1996 PAWS, INC./Distributed by Universal Press Syndicate
JPM DAVPS 11-28
I'D LIKE TO ASK FOR AN AUDIENCE

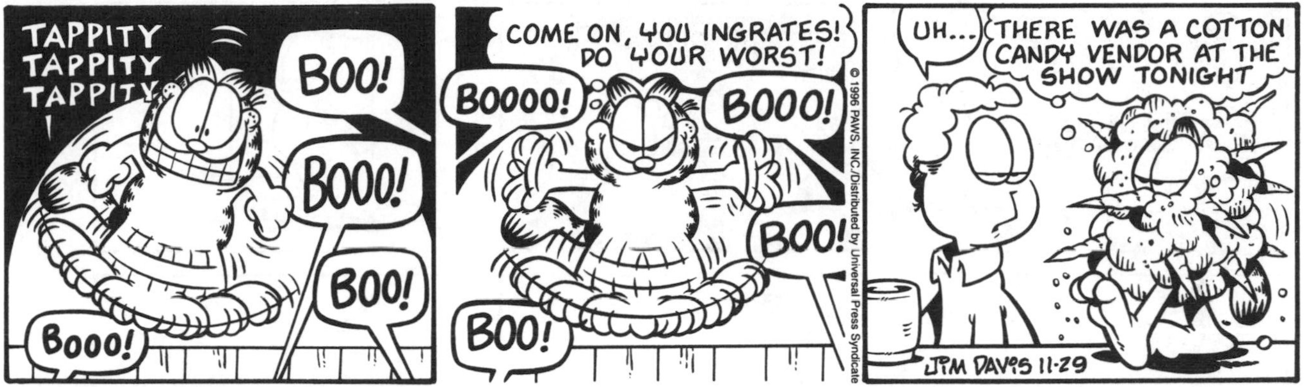
TAPPITY
TAPPITY
TAPPITY
BOO!
BOOO!
BOO!
Booo!
COME ON, YOU INGRATES! DO YOUR WORST!
BOOOOO!
BOOO!
BOO!
BOO!
© 1996 PAWS, INC./Distributed by Universal Press Syndicate
UH...
THERE WAS A COTTON CANDY VENDOR AT THE SHOW TONIGHT
JIM DAVIS 11-29

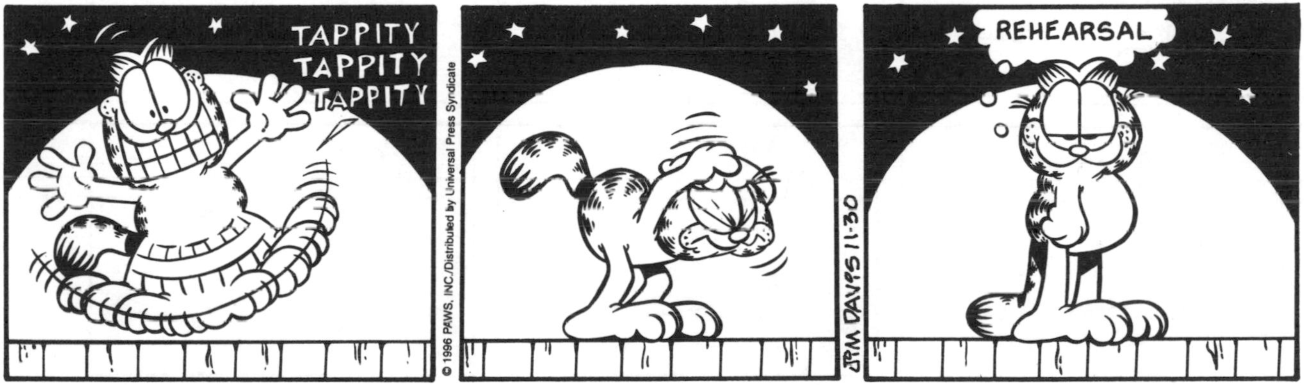
TAPPITY
TAPPITY
TAPPITY
© 1996 PAWS, INC./Distributed by Universal Press Syndicate
JIM DAVIS 11-30
REHEARSAL

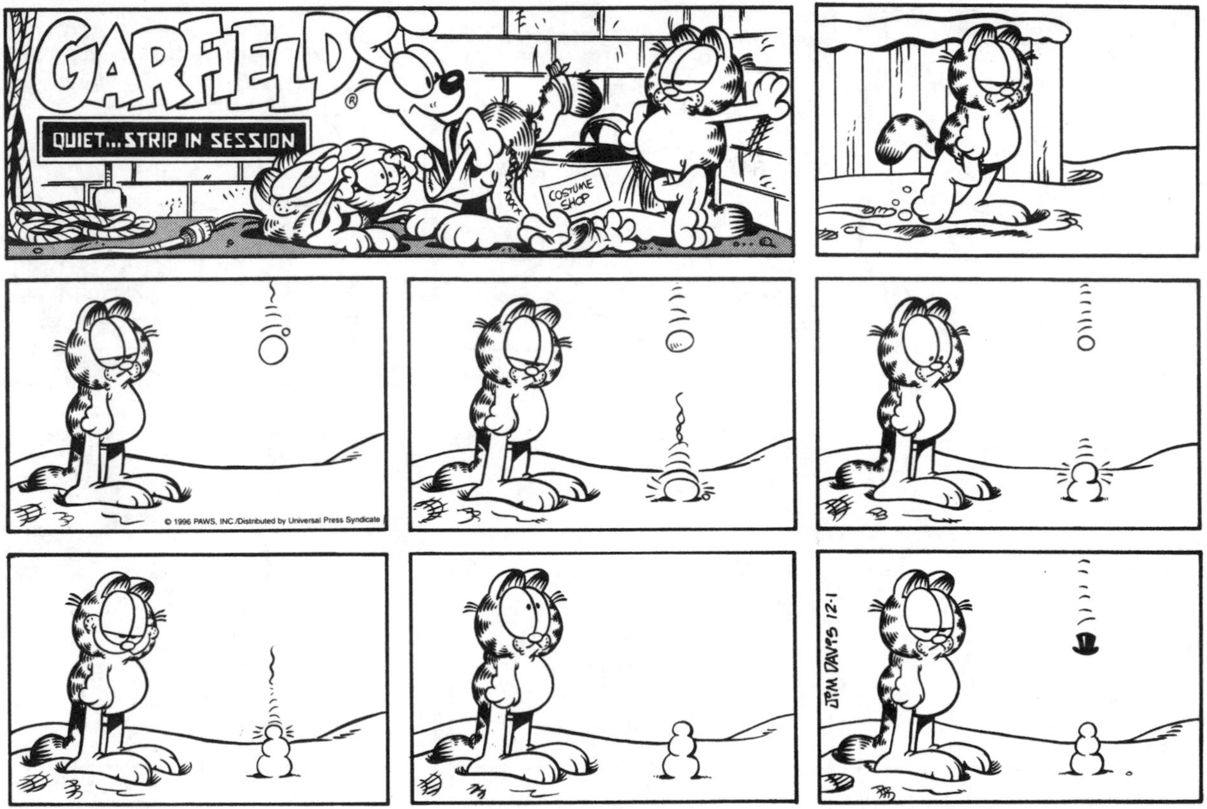
GARFIELD
QUIET...STRIP IN SESSION
COSTUME SHOP
© 1996 PAWS, INC./Distributed by Universal Press Syndicate
JIM DAVIS 12-1

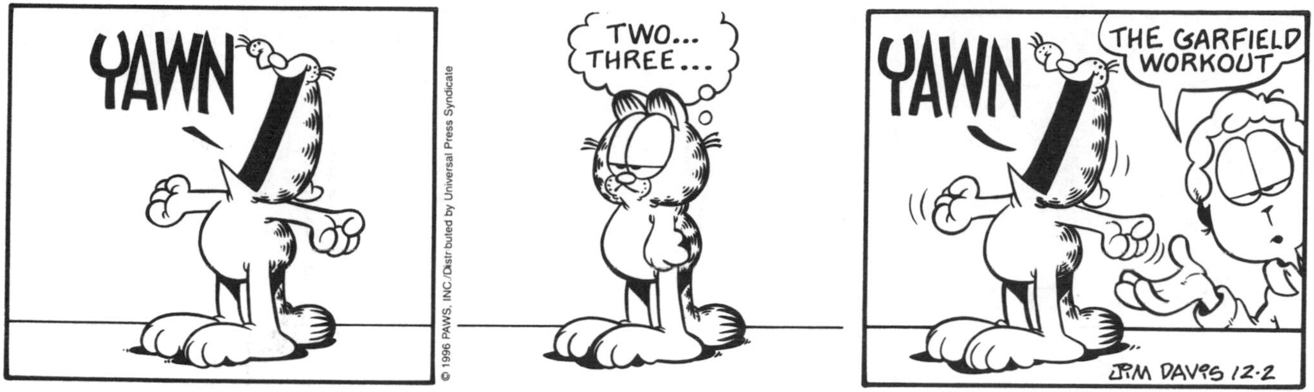
YAWN
TWO... THREE...
YAWN
THE GARFIELD WORKOUT
JIM DAVIS 12-2
© 1996 PAWS, INC./Distributed by Universal Press Syndicate

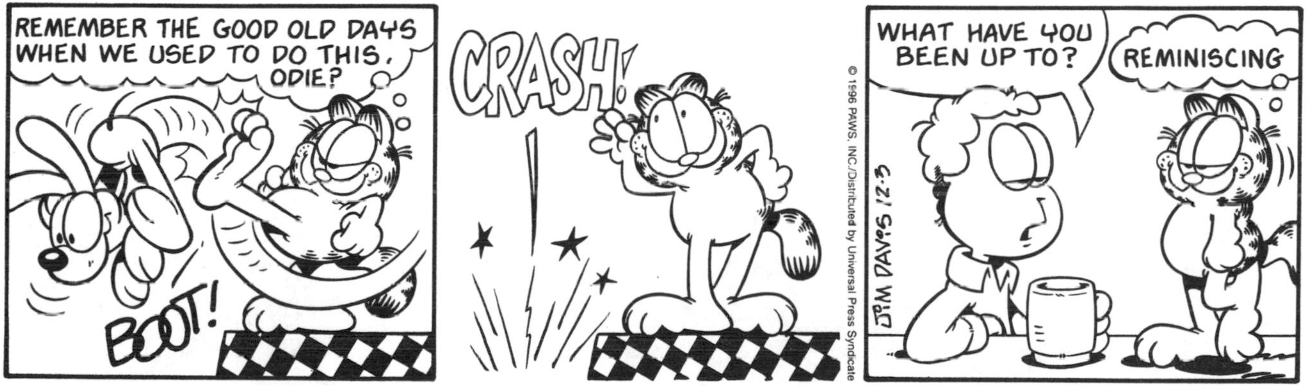
REMEMBER THE GOOD OLD DAYS WHEN WE USED TO DO THIS, ODIE?
BOOT!
CRASH!
WHAT HAVE YOU BEEN UP TO?
REMINISCING
JIM DAVIS 12-3
© 1996 PAWS, INC./Distributed by Universal Press Syndicate

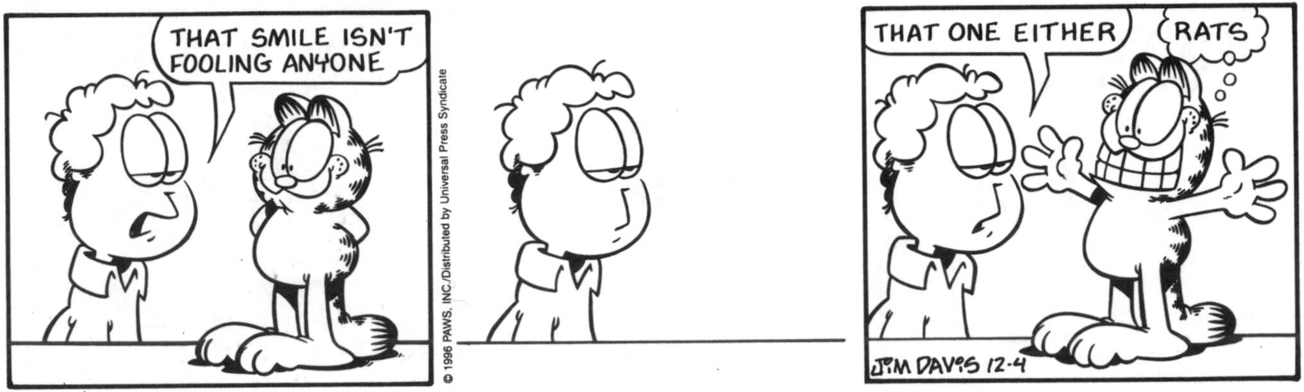
THAT SMILE ISN'T FOOLING ANYONE
THAT ONE EITHER
RATS
JIM DAVIS 12-4

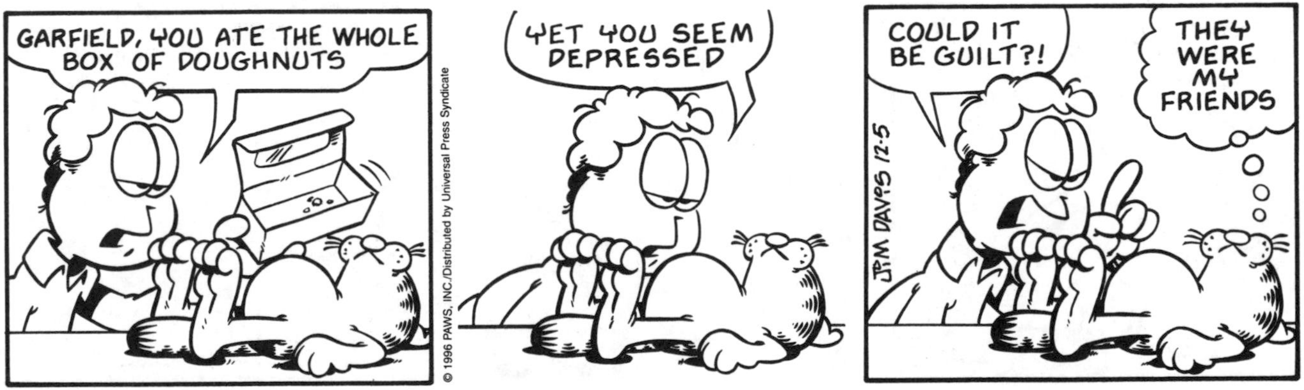
GARFIELD, YOU ATE THE WHOLE BOX OF DOUGHNUTS
YET YOU SEEM DEPRESSED
COULD IT BE GUILT?!
THEY WERE MY FRIENDS
JIM DAVIS 12-5

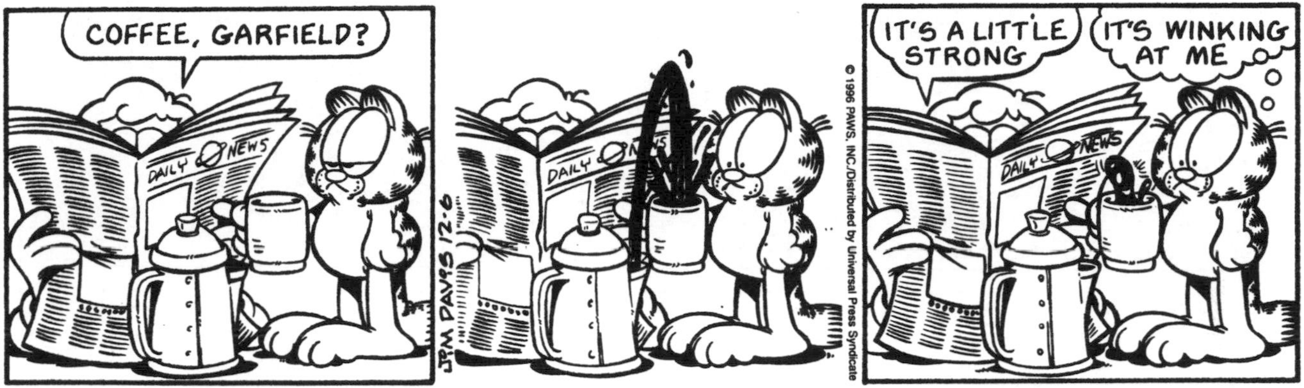
COFFEE, GARFIELD?
JIM DAVIS 12-6
IT'S A LITTLE STRONG
IT'S WINKING AT ME
© 1996 PAWS, INC/Distributed by Universal Press Syndicate

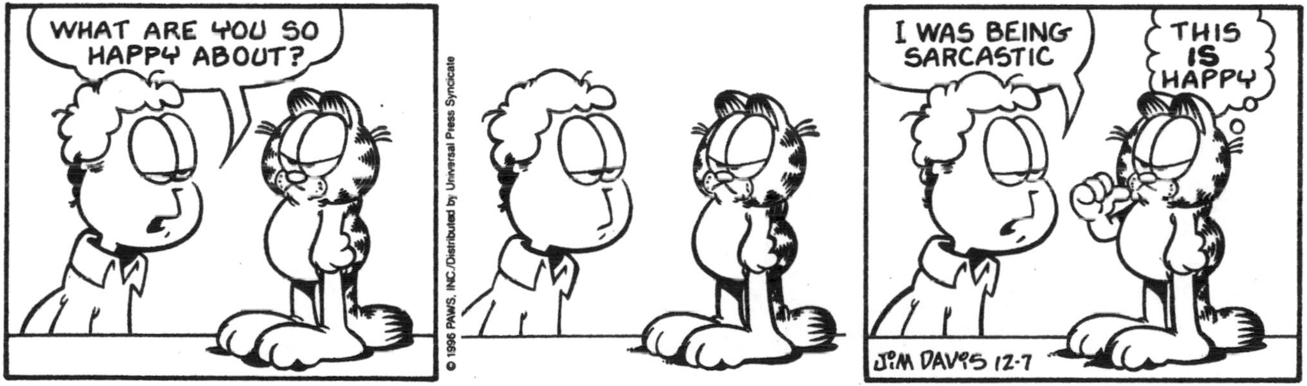
WHAT ARE YOU SO HAPPY ABOUT?
© 1996 PAWS, INC./Distributed by Universal Press Syndicate
I WAS BEING SARCASTIC
THIS **IS** HAPPY
JIM DAVIS 12-7

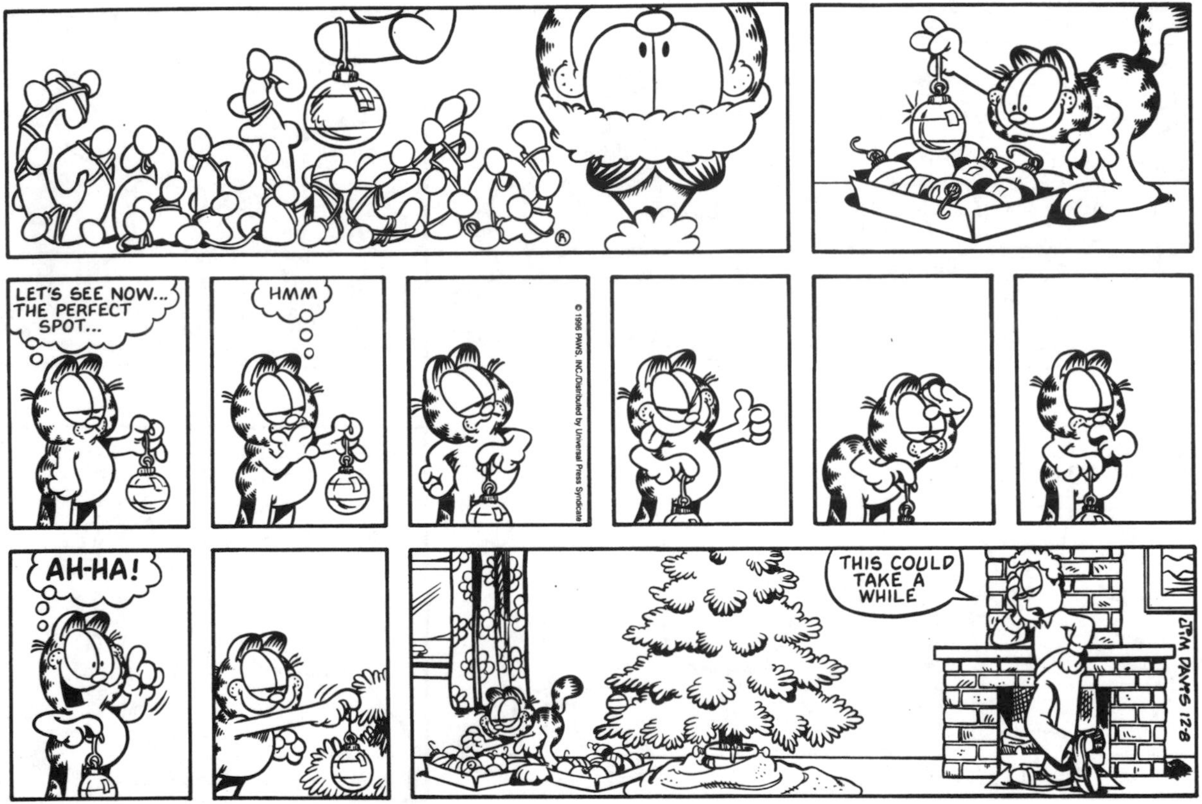
Garfield®
LET'S SEE NOW... THE PERFECT SPOT...
HMM
© 1996 PAWS, INC./Distributed by Universal Press Syndicate
AH-HA!
THIS COULD TAKE A WHILE
JIM DAVIS 12-8

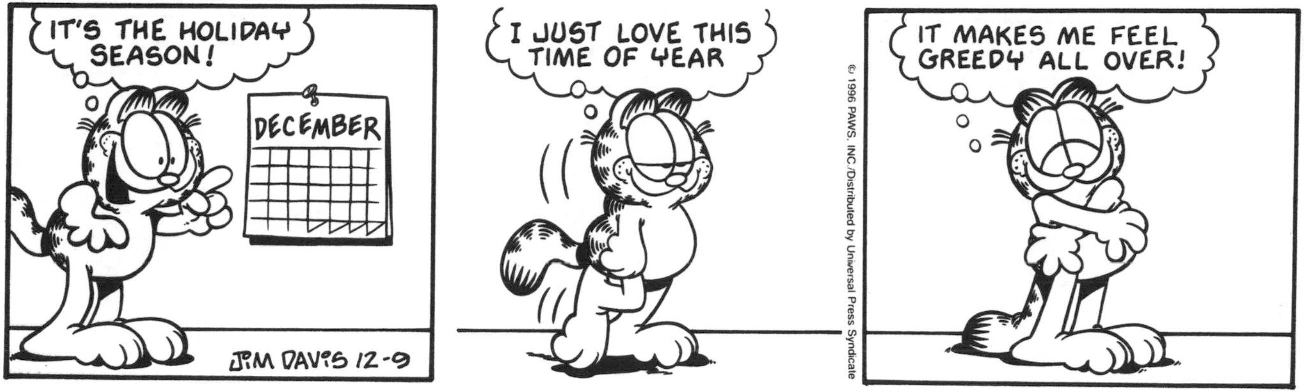
IT'S THE HOLIDAY SEASON!
DECEMBER
JIM DAVIS 12-9
I JUST LOVE THIS TIME OF YEAR
© 1996 PAWS, INC./Distributed by Universal Press Syndicate
IT MAKES ME FEEL GREEDY ALL OVER!

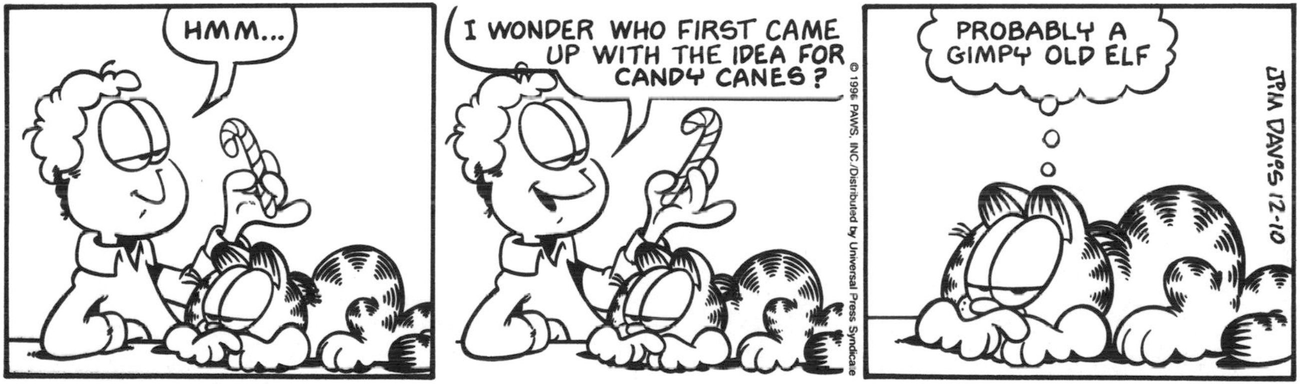
HMM...
I WONDER WHO FIRST CAME UP WITH THE IDEA FOR CANDY CANES?
© 1996 PAWS, INC./Distributed by Universal Press Syndicate
PROBABLY A GIMPY OLD ELF
JIM DAVIS 12-10

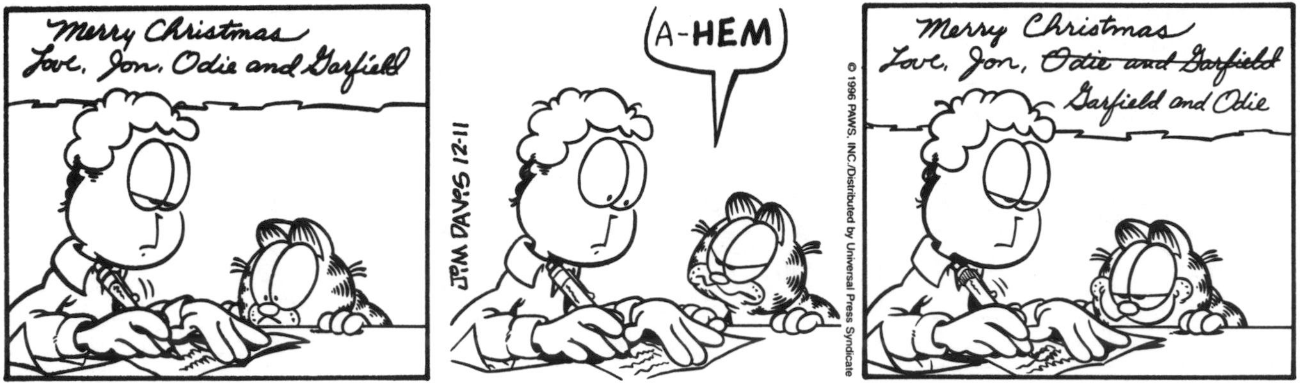
Merry Christmas
Love, Jon, Odie and Garfield
JIM DAVIS 12-11
A-HEM
© 1996 PAWS, INC./Distributed by Universal Press Syndicate
Merry Christmas
Love, Jon, ~~Odie and Garfield~~
Garfield and Odie

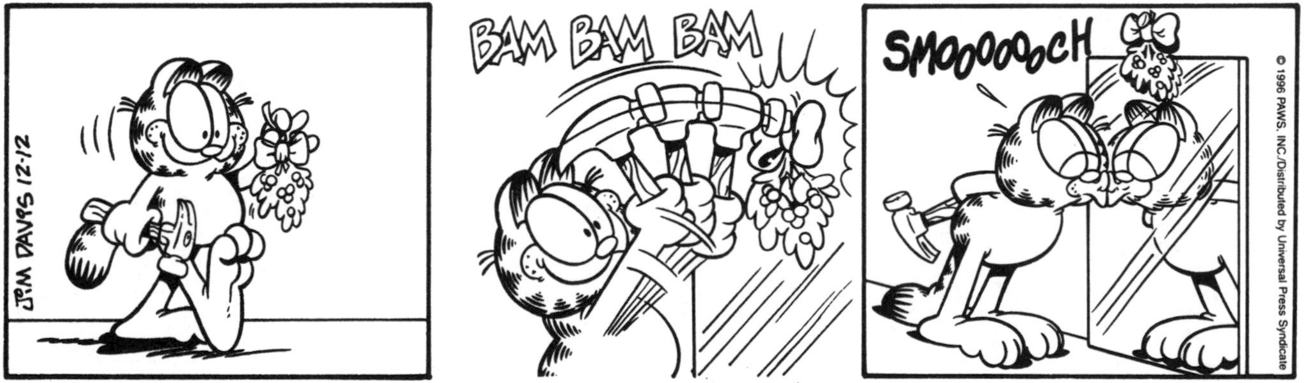
JIM DAVIS 12-12
BAM BAM BAM
SMOOOOOOCH
© 1996 PAWS, INC./Distributed by Universal Press Syndicate

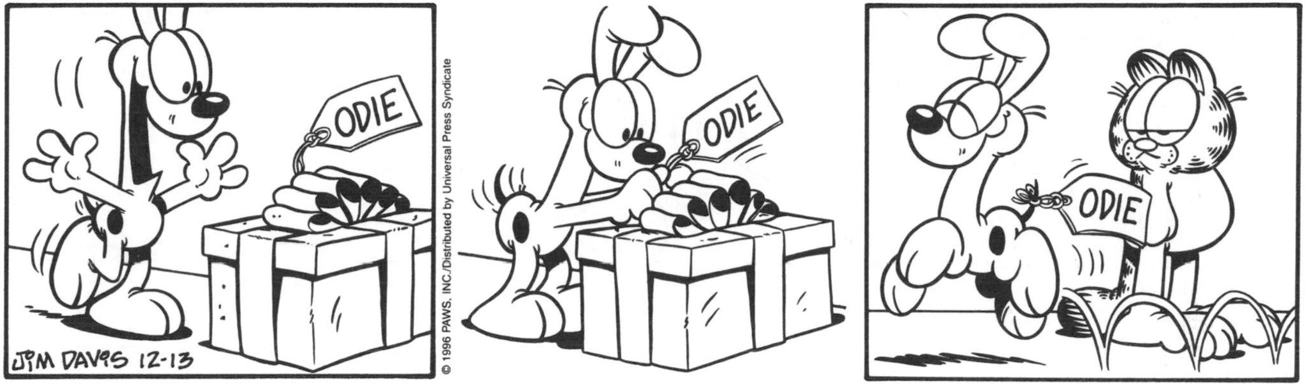
ODIE
JIM DAVIS 12-13
© 1996 PAWS, INC./Distributed by Universal Press Syndicate
ODIE
ODIE

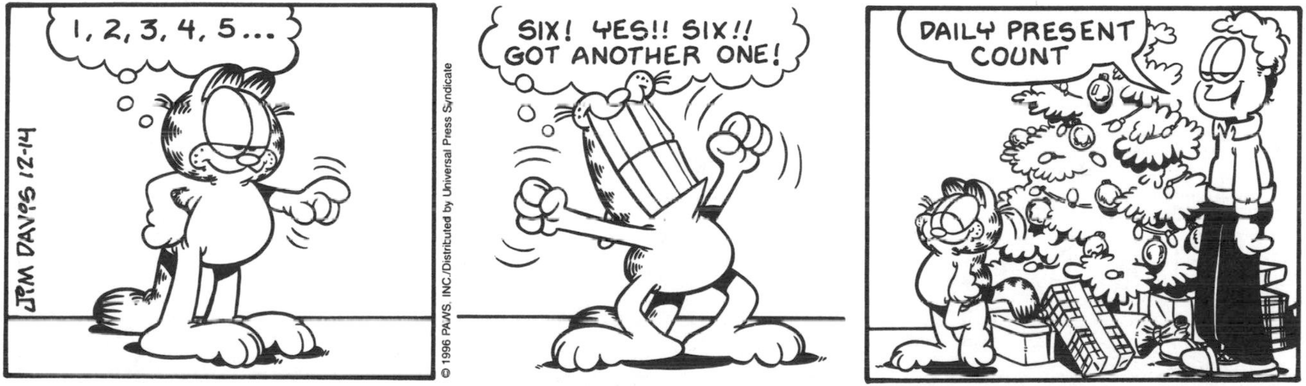
1, 2, 3, 4, 5...
JIM DAVIS 12-14
© 1996 PAWS, INC./Distributed by Universal Press Syndicate
SIX! YES!! SIX!!
GOT ANOTHER ONE!
DAILY PRESENT COUNT

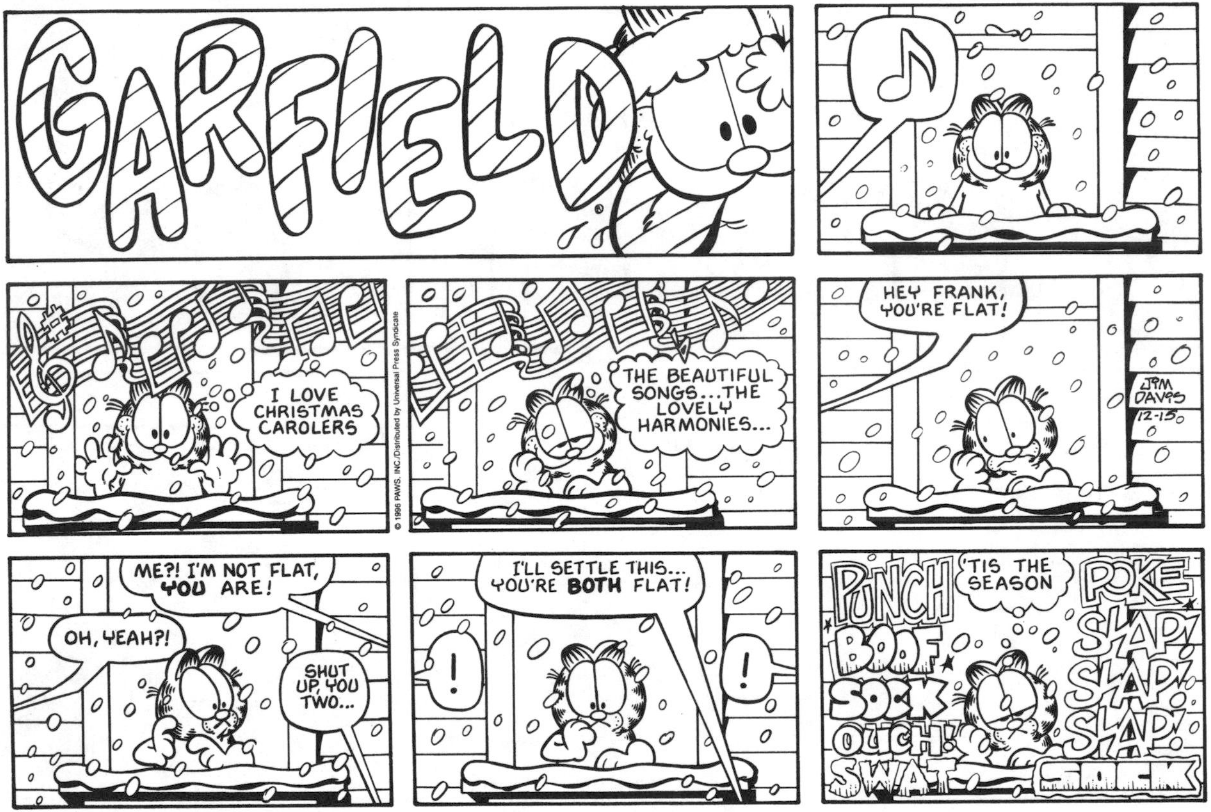
GARFIELD
HEY FRANK, YOU'RE FLAT!
JIM DAVIS 12-15
I LOVE CHRISTMAS CAROLERS
THE BEAUTIFUL SONGS...THE LOVELY HARMONIES...
© 1996 PAWS, INC./Distributed by Universal Press Syndicate
ME?! I'M NOT FLAT, YOU ARE!
OH, YEAH?!
SHUT UP, YOU TWO...
I'LL SETTLE THIS... YOU'RE BOTH FLAT!
!
!
PUNCH
'TIS THE SEASON
POKE
BOOF
SLAP!
SOCK
SLAP!
OUCH!
SLAP!
SWAT
SOCK

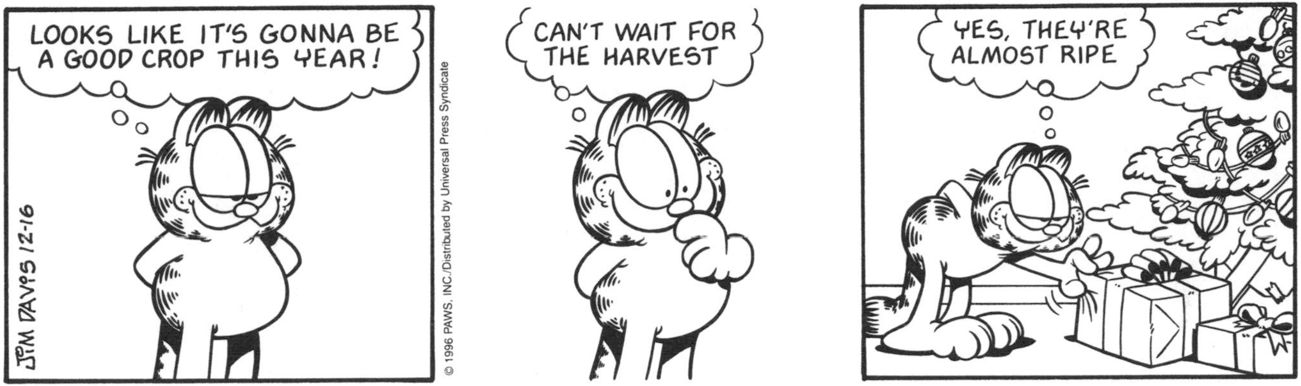
LOOKS LIKE IT'S GONNA BE A GOOD CROP THIS YEAR!
JIM DAVIS 12-16
© 1996 PAWS, INC./Distributed by Universal Press Syndicate
CAN'T WAIT FOR THE HARVEST
YES, THEY'RE ALMOST RIPE

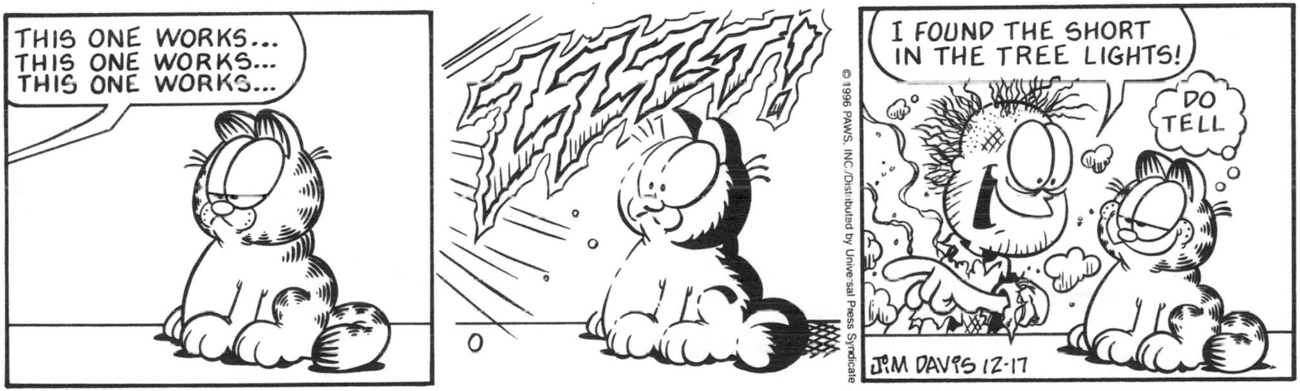
THIS ONE WORKS... THIS ONE WORKS... THIS ONE WORKS...
ZZZZZT!
© 1996 PAWS, INC./Distributed by Universal Press Syndicate
I FOUND THE SHORT IN THE TREE LIGHTS!
DO TELL
JIM DAVIS 12-17

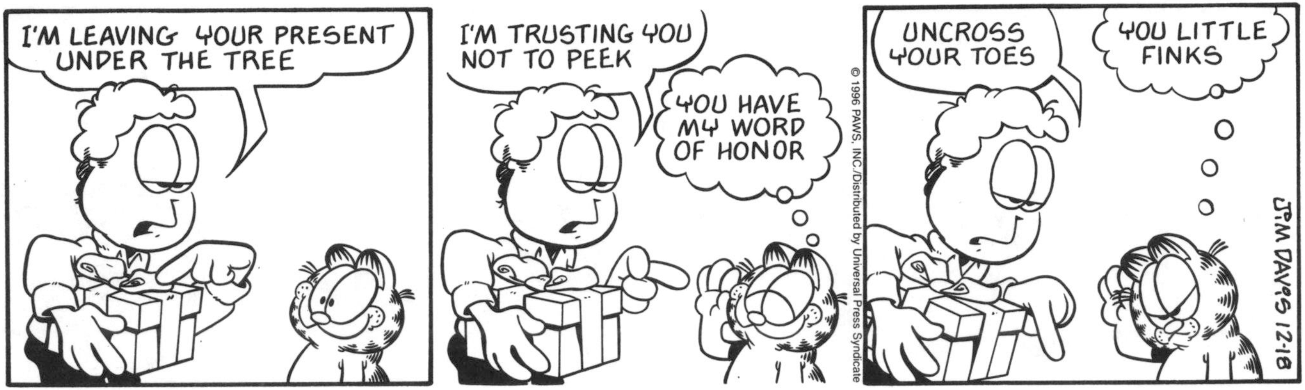
I'M LEAVING YOUR PRESENT UNDER THE TREE
I'M TRUSTING YOU NOT TO PEEK
YOU HAVE MY WORD OF HONOR
UNCROSS YOUR TOES
YOU LITTLE FINKS
JIM DAVIS 12-18
© 1996 PAWS, INC./Distributed by Universal Press Syndicate

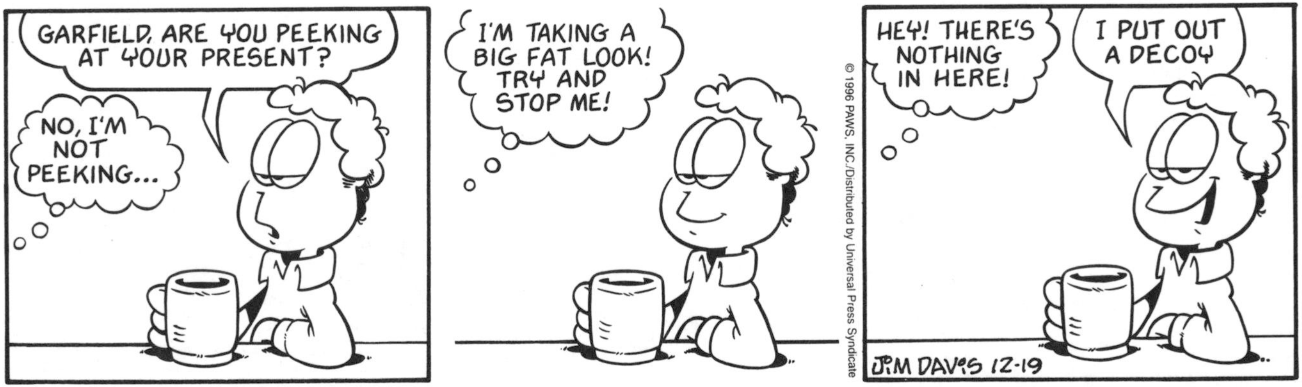
GARFIELD, ARE YOU PEEKING AT YOUR PRESENT?
NO, I'M NOT PEEKING...
I'M TAKING A BIG FAT LOOK! TRY AND STOP ME!
HEY! THERE'S NOTHING IN HERE!
I PUT OUT A DECOY
JIM DAVIS 12-19
© 1996 PAWS, INC./Distributed by Universal Press Syndicate

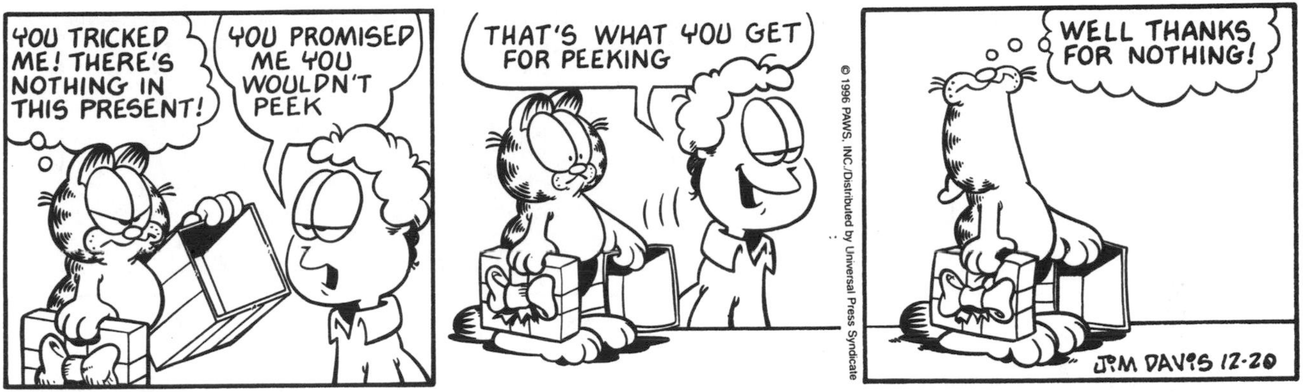
YOU TRICKED ME! THERE'S NOTHING IN THIS PRESENT!
YOU PROMISED ME YOU WOULDN'T PEEK
THAT'S WHAT YOU GET FOR PEEKING
WELL THANKS FOR NOTHING!
JIM DAVIS 12-20

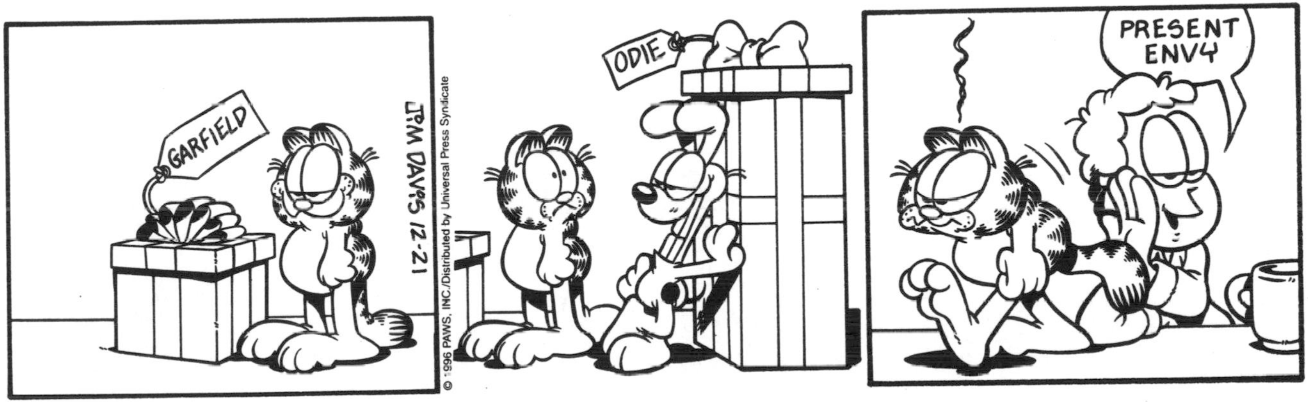
GARFIELD
JIM DAVIS 12-21
ODIE
PRESENT ENVY

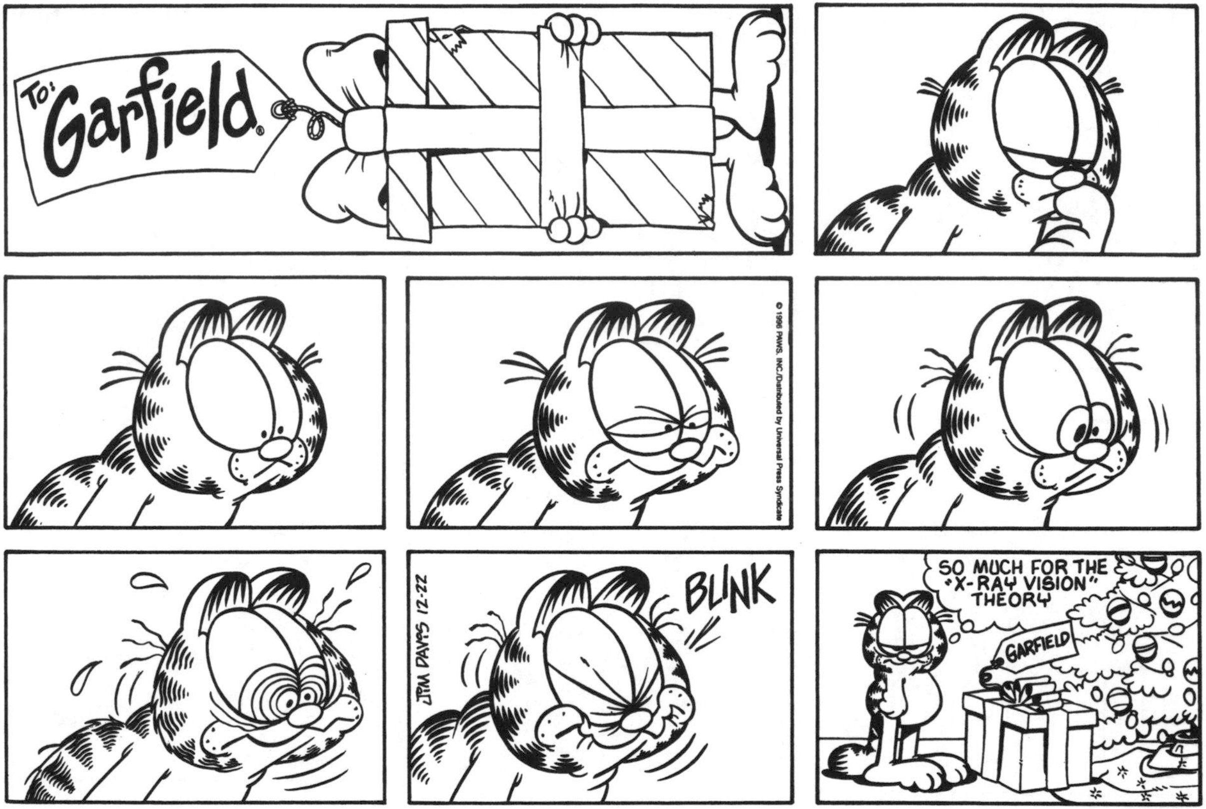
To: Garfield
© 1996 PAWS, INC./Distributed by Universal Press Syndicate
JIM DAVIS 12-22
BLINK
SO MUCH FOR THE "X-RAY VISION" THEORY
GARFIELD

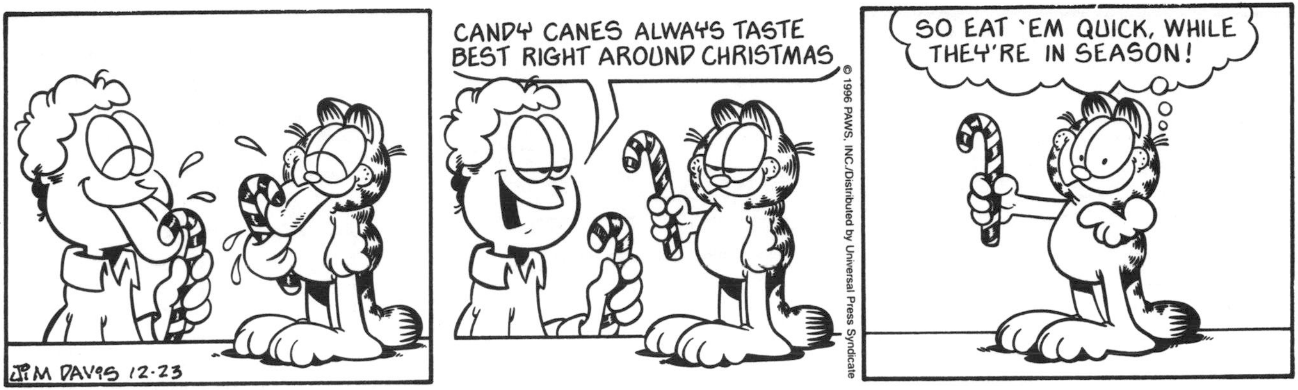
JIM DAVIS 12-23
CANDY CANES ALWAYS TASTE BEST RIGHT AROUND CHRISTMAS
© 1996 PAWS, INC./Distributed by Universal Press Syndicate
SO EAT 'EM QUICK, WHILE THEY'RE IN SEASON!

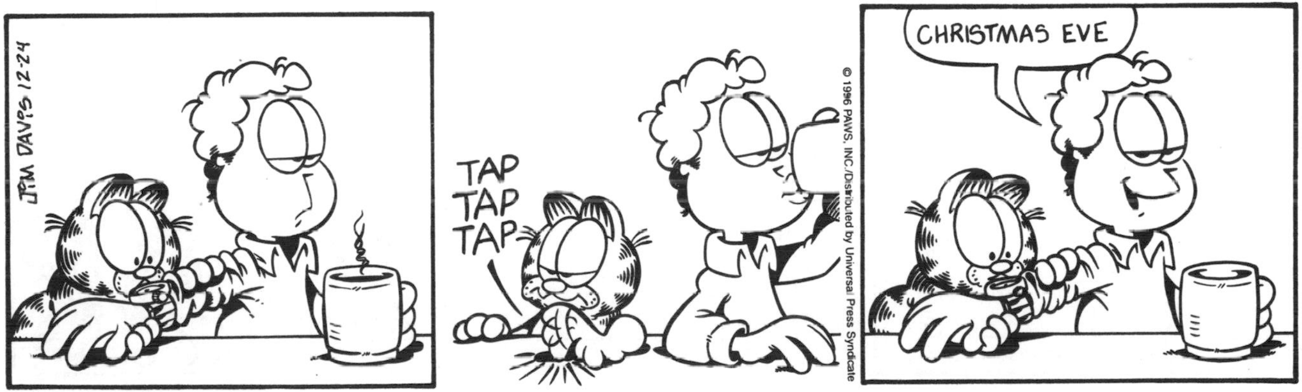
JIM DAVIS 12-24
TAP
TAP
TAP
© 1996 PAWS, INC./Distributed by Universal Press Syndicate
CHRISTMAS EVE

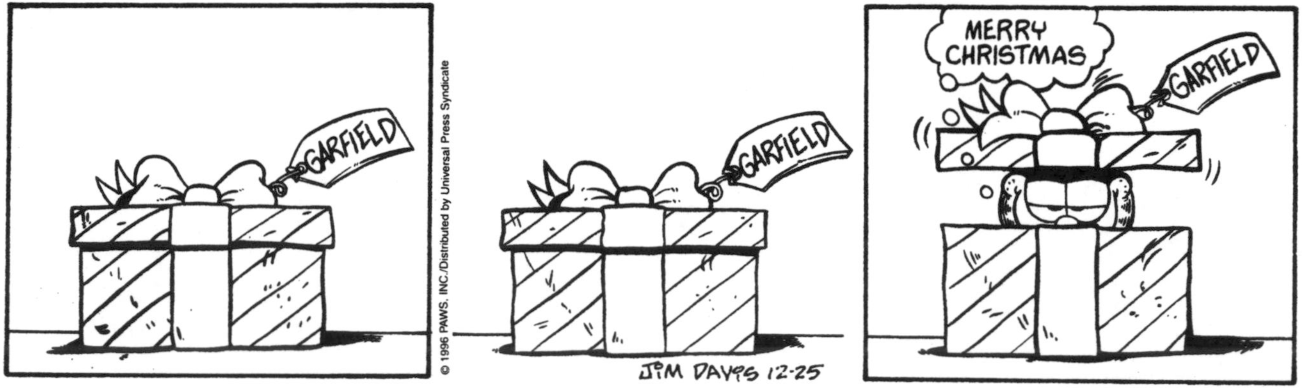
GARFIELD
GARFIELD
JIM DAVIS 12-25
MERRY CHRISTMAS
GARFIELD

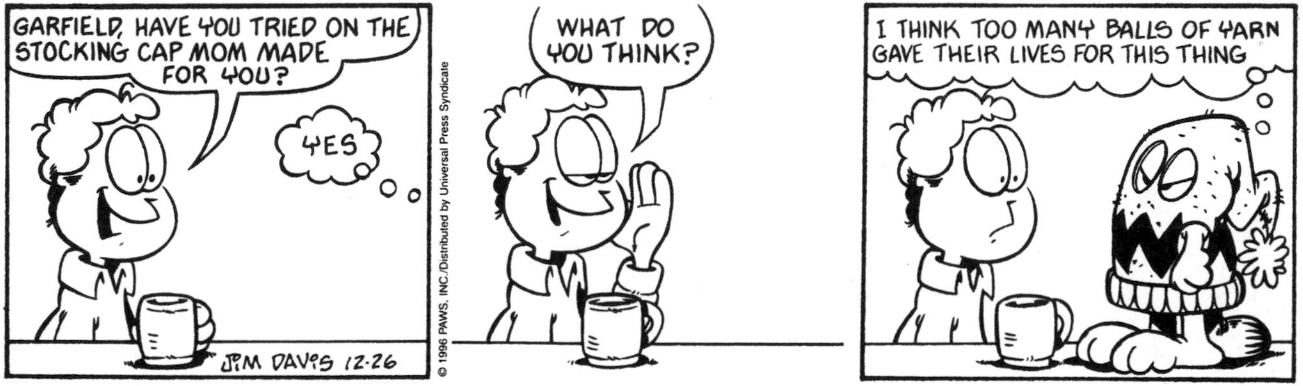
GARFIELD, HAVE YOU TRIED ON THE STOCKING CAP MOM MADE FOR YOU?
YES
JIM DAVIS 12-26
WHAT DO YOU THINK?
I THINK TOO MANY BALLS OF YARN GAVE THEIR LIVES FOR THIS THING

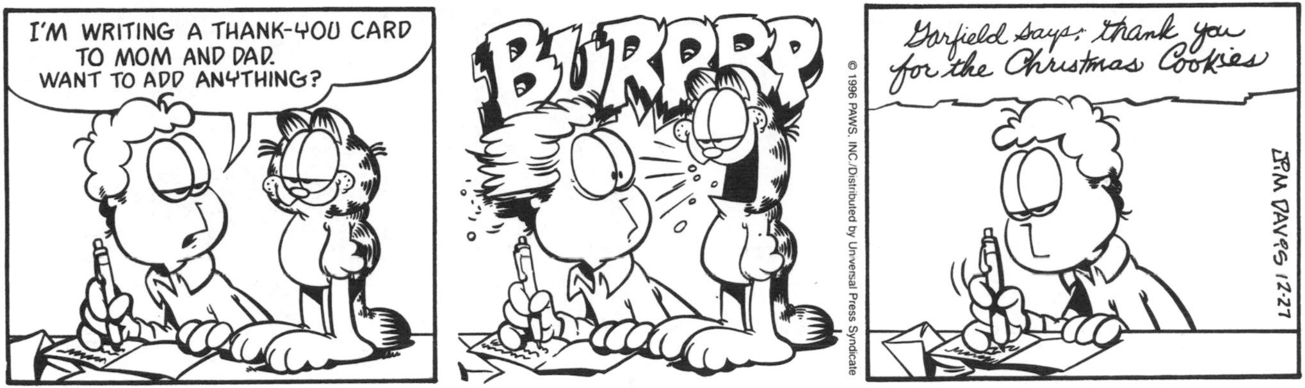
I'M WRITING A THANK-YOU CARD TO MOM AND DAD. WANT TO ADD ANYTHING?
BURPRP
© 1996 PAWS, INC./Distributed by Universal Press Syndicate
Garfield says: thank you for the Christmas Cookies
JPM DAVIS 12-27

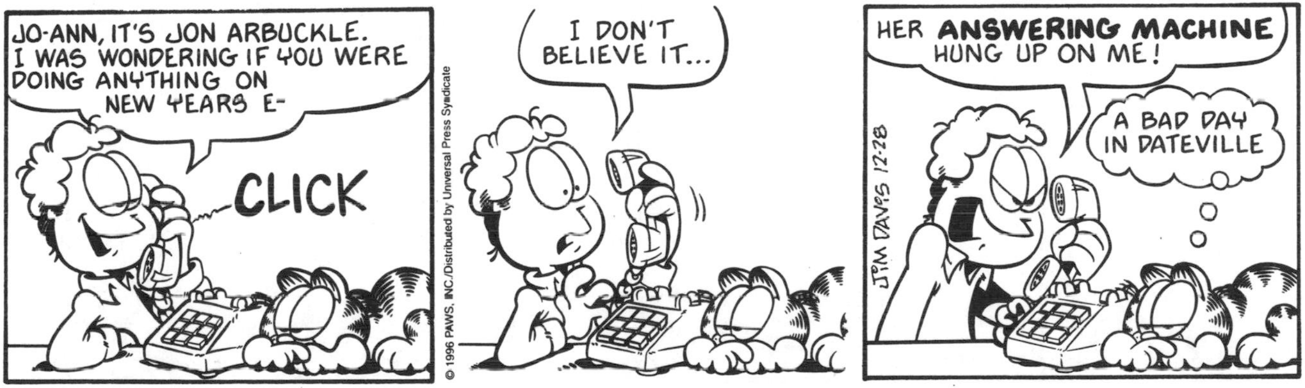
JO-ANN, IT'S JON ARBUCKLE. I WAS WONDERING IF YOU WERE DOING ANYTHING ON NEW YEARS E-
CLICK
© 1996 PAWS, INC./Distributed by Universal Press Syndicate
I DON'T BELIEVE IT...
HER **ANSWERING MACHINE** HUNG UP ON ME!
A BAD DAY IN DATEVILLE
JPM DAVIS 12-28

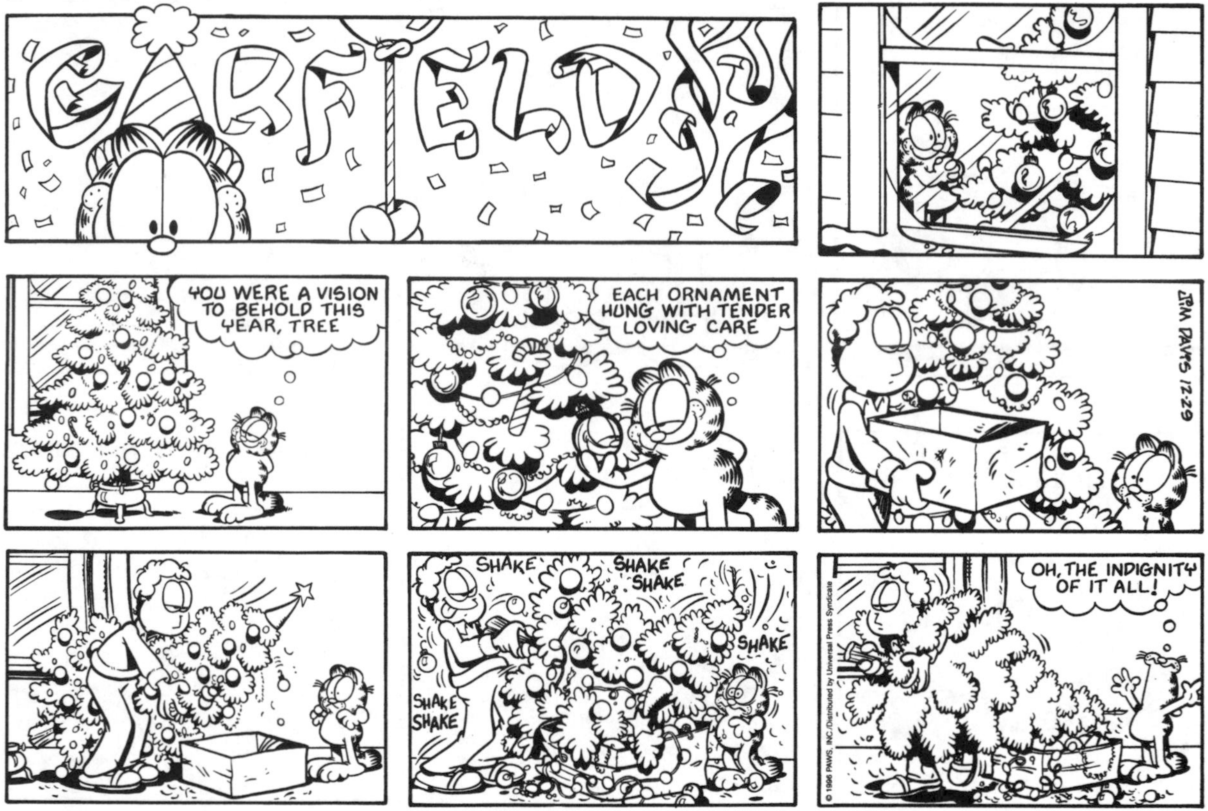
GARFIELD
YOU WERE A VISION TO BEHOLD THIS YEAR, TREE
EACH ORNAMENT HUNG WITH TENDER LOVING CARE
JPM DAVIS 12-29
SHAKE
SHAKE SHAKE
SHAKE
SHAKE SHAKE
OH, THE INDIGNITY OF IT ALL!
© 1996 PAWS, INC./Distributed by Universal Press Syndicate

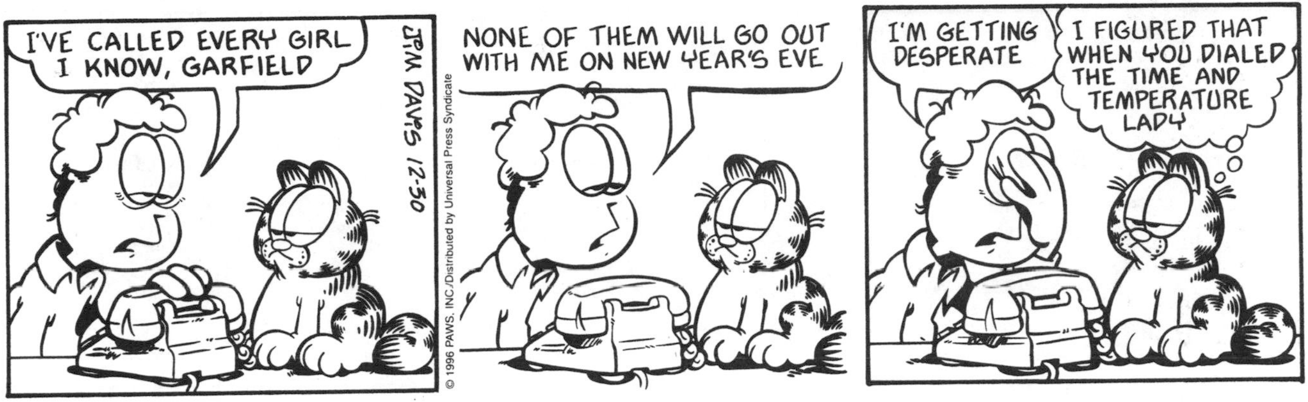
I'VE CALLED EVERY GIRL I KNOW, GARFIELD
JIM DAVIS 12-30
© 1996 PAWS, INC./Distributed by Universal Press Syndicate
NONE OF THEM WILL GO OUT WITH ME ON NEW YEAR'S EVE
I'M GETTING DESPERATE
I FIGURED THAT WHEN YOU DIALED THE TIME AND TEMPERATURE LADY

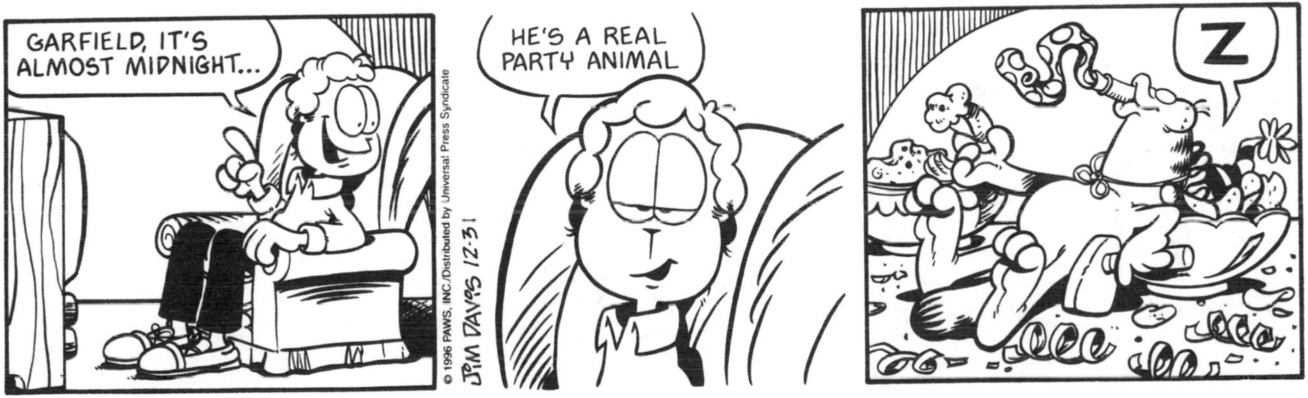
GARFIELD, IT'S ALMOST MIDNIGHT...
© 1996 PAWS, INC./Distributed by Universal Press Syndicate
JIM DAVIS 12-31
HE'S A REAL PARTY ANIMAL
Z

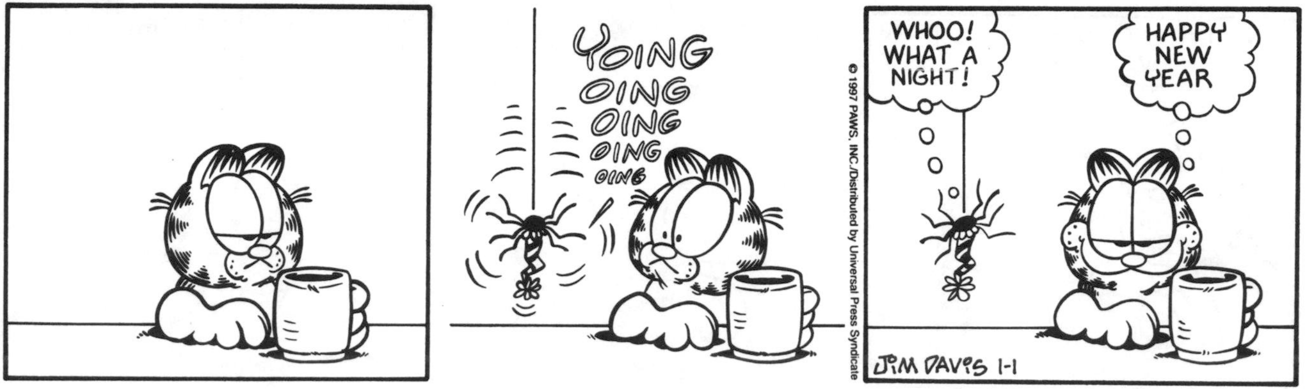
YOING OING OING OING OING
WHOO! WHAT A NIGHT!
HAPPY NEW YEAR
© 1997 PAWS, INC./Distributed by Universal Press Syndicate
JIM DAVIS 1-1

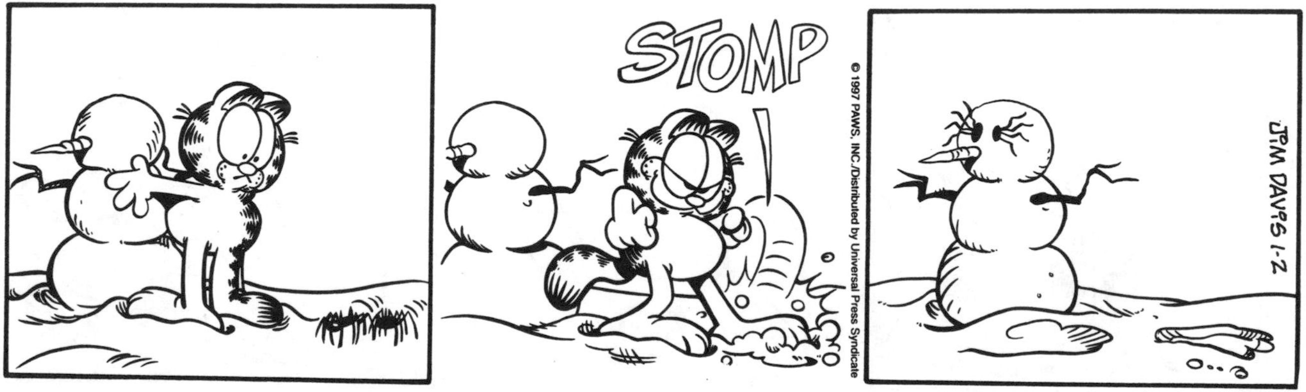
STOMP
© 1997 PAWS, INC./Distributed by Universal Press Syndicate
JIM DAVIS 1-2

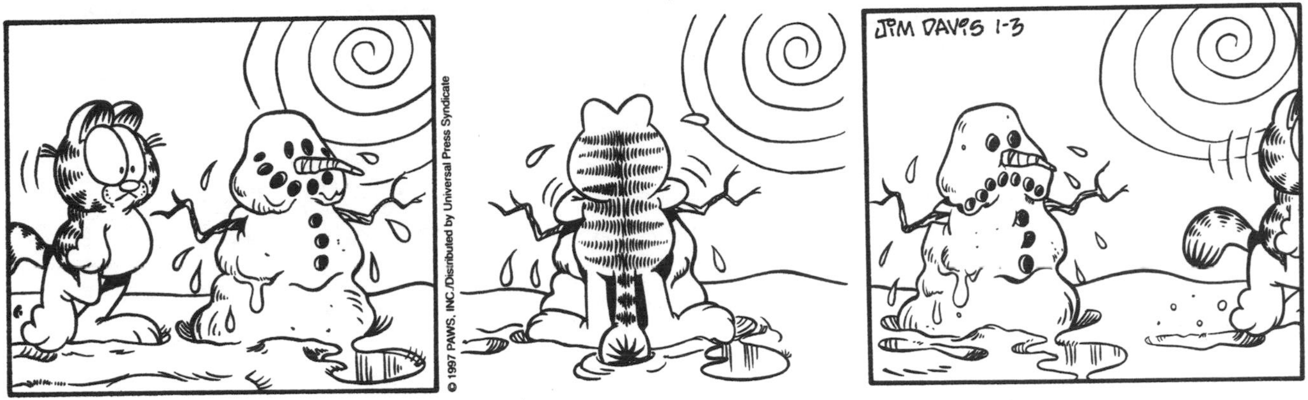
© 1997 PAWS, INC./Distributed by Universal Press Syndicate
JIM DAVIS 1-3

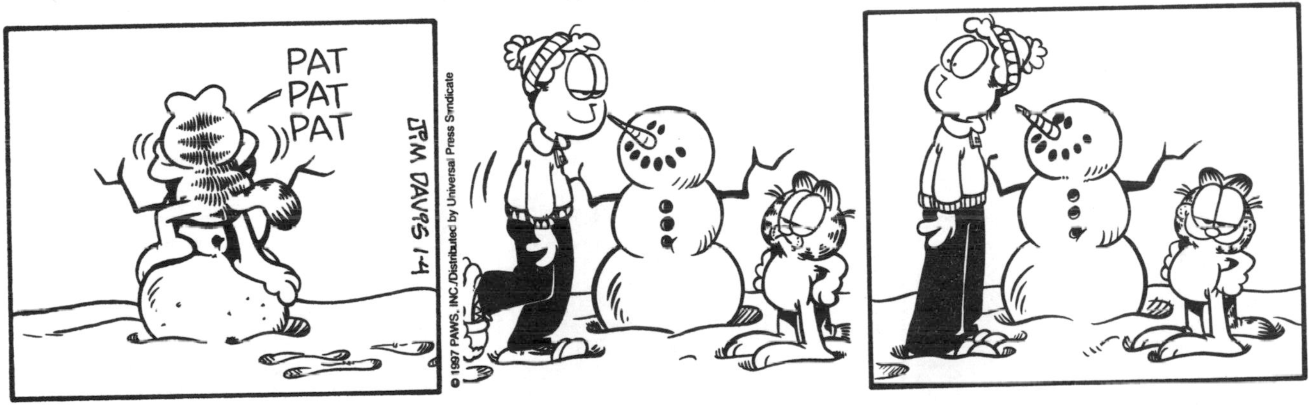
PAT
PAT
PAT
JIM DAVIS 1-4
© 1997 PAWS, INC./Distributed by Universal Press Syndicate

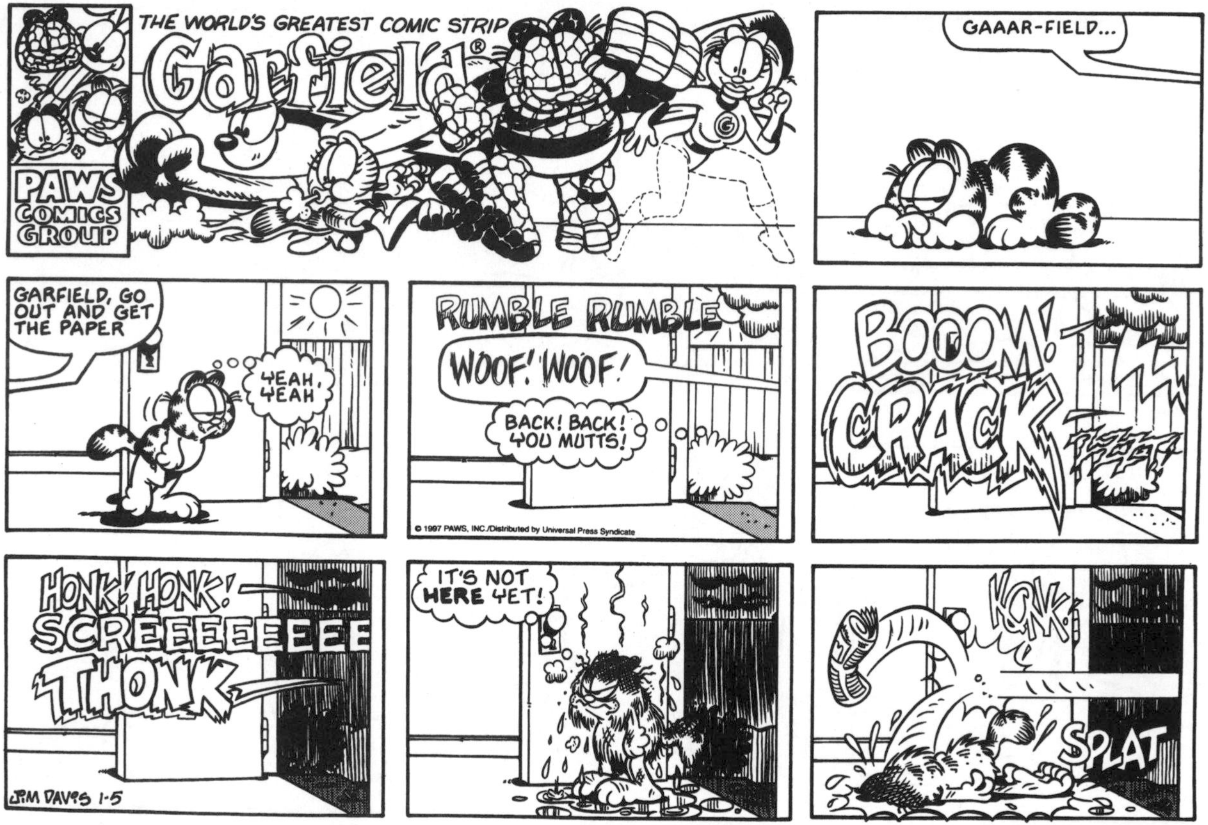
THE WORLD'S GREATEST COMIC STRIP
Garfield®
PAWS COMICS GROUP
GAAAR-FIELD...
GARFIELD, GO OUT AND GET THE PAPER
YEAH, YEAH
RUMBLE RUMBLE
WOOF! WOOF!
BACK! BACK! YOU MUTTS!
© 1997 PAWS, INC./Distributed by Universal Press Syndicate
BOOOM!
CRACK
HONK! HONK!
SCREEEEEEEEE
THONK
JIM DAVIS 1-5
IT'S NOT **HERE** YET!
KONK!
SPLAT

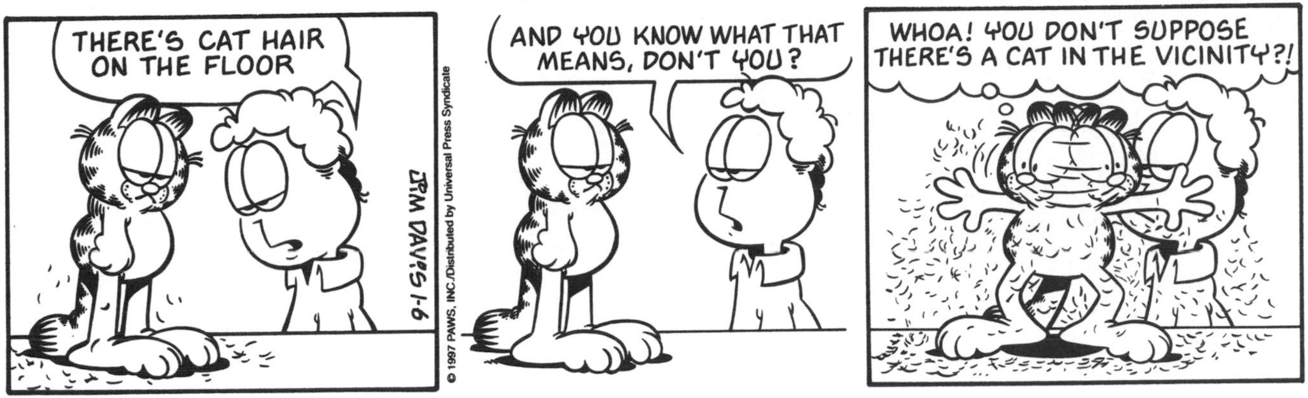
THERE'S CAT HAIR ON THE FLOOR
AND YOU KNOW WHAT THAT MEANS, DON'T YOU?
WHOA! YOU DON'T SUPPOSE THERE'S A CAT IN THE VICINITY?!
JIM DAVIS 1-6

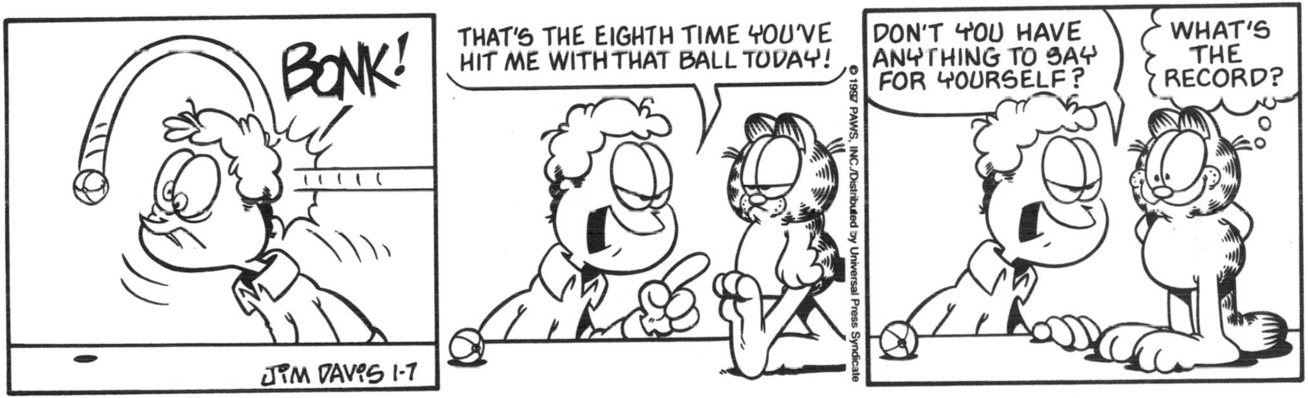
BONK!
JIM DAVIS 1-7
THAT'S THE EIGHTH TIME YOU'VE HIT ME WITH THAT BALL TODAY!
DON'T YOU HAVE ANYTHING TO SAY FOR YOURSELF?
WHAT'S THE RECORD?

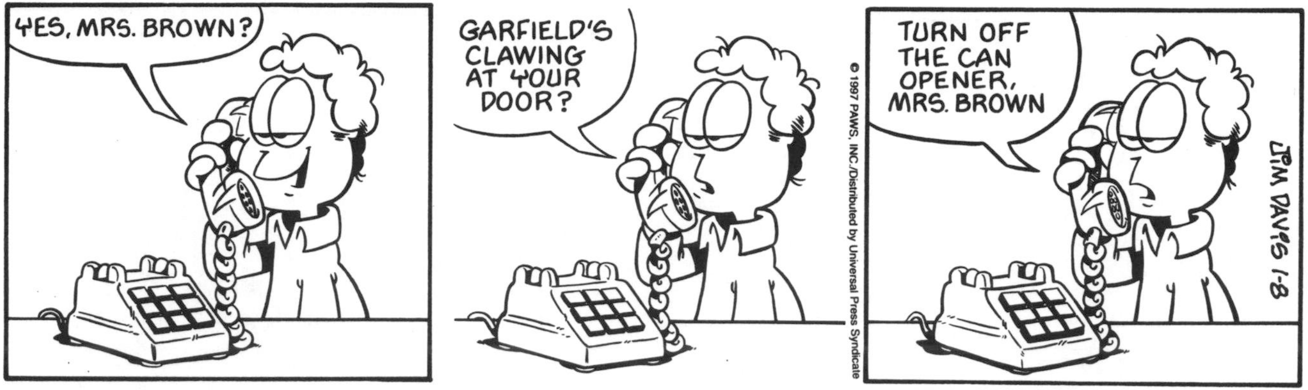
YES, MRS. BROWN?
GARFIELD'S CLAWING AT YOUR DOOR?
TURN OFF THE CAN OPENER, MRS. BROWN
JIM DAVIS 1-8
© 1997 PAWS, INC./Distributed by Universal Press Syndicate

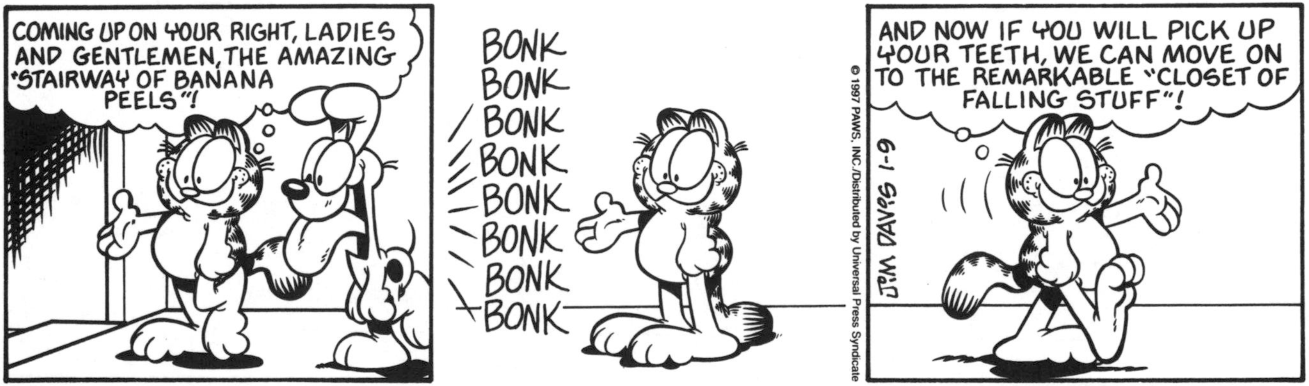
COMING UP ON YOUR RIGHT, LADIES AND GENTLEMEN, THE AMAZING "STAIRWAY OF BANANA PEELS"!
BONK
BONK
BONK
BONK
BONK
BONK
BONK
BONK
AND NOW IF YOU WILL PICK UP YOUR TEETH, WE CAN MOVE ON TO THE REMARKABLE "CLOSET OF FALLING STUFF"!
JIM DAVIS 1-9
© 1997 PAWS, INC./Distributed by Universal Press Syndicate

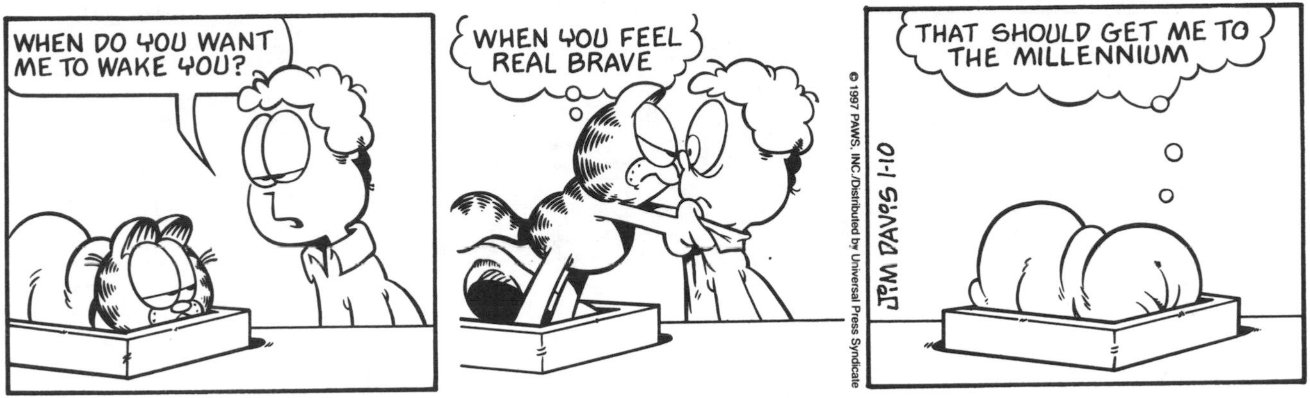
WHEN DO YOU WANT ME TO WAKE YOU?
WHEN YOU FEEL REAL BRAVE
THAT SHOULD GET ME TO THE MILLENNIUM
© 1997 PAWS, INC./Distributed by Universal Press Syndicate
JIM DAVIS 1-10

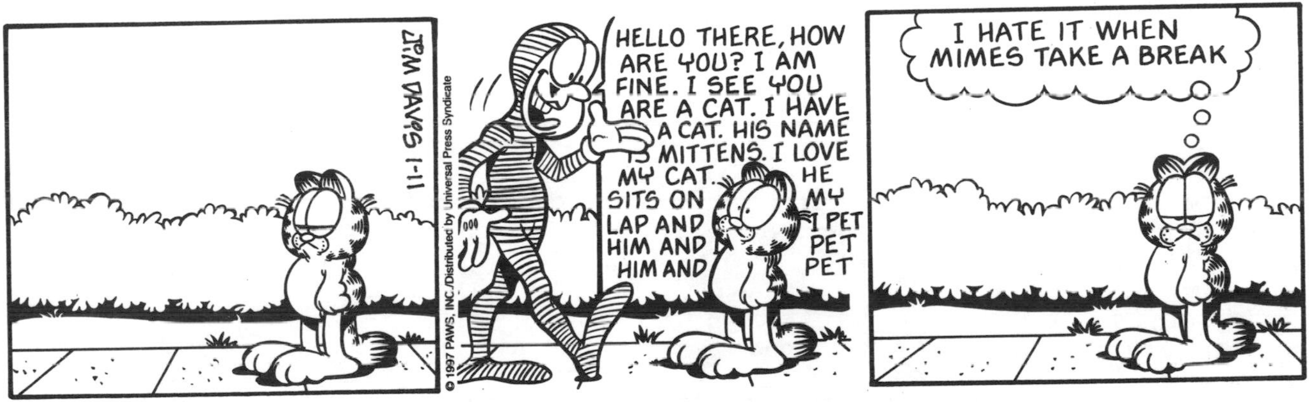
JIM DAVIS 1-11
© 1997 PAWS, INC./Distributed by Universal Press Syndicate
HELLO THERE, HOW
ARE YOU? I AM
FINE. I SEE YOU
ARE A CAT. I HAVE
A CAT. HIS NAME
MITTENS. I LOVE
MY CAT. HE
SITS ON MY
LAP AND I PET
HIM AND PET
HIM AND PET
I HATE IT WHEN MIMES TAKE A BREAK

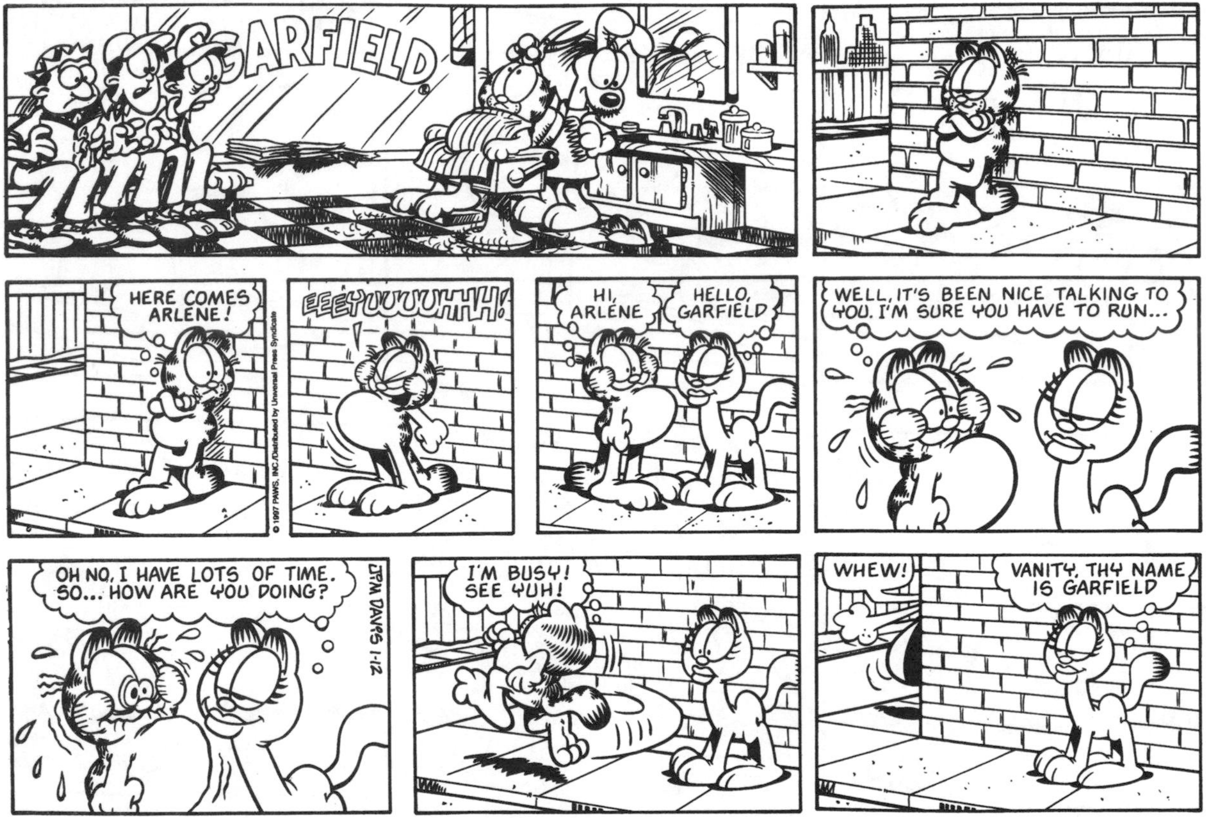
GARFIELD
HERE COMES ARLENE!
© 1997 PAWS, INC./Distributed by Universal Press Syndicate
EEEYUUUUHHH!
HI, ARLENE
HELLO, GARFIELD
WELL, IT'S BEEN NICE TALKING TO YOU. I'M SURE YOU HAVE TO RUN...
OH NO, I HAVE LOTS OF TIME. SO... HOW ARE YOU DOING?
JPM DAVIS 1-12
I'M BUSY! SEE YUH!
WHEW!
VANITY, THY NAME IS GARFIELD

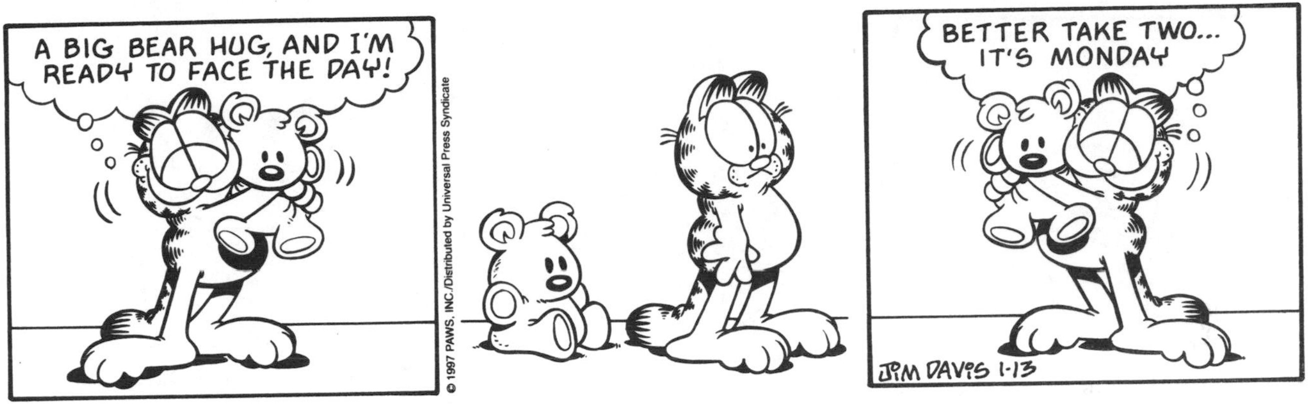
A BIG BEAR HUG, AND I'M READY TO FACE THE DAY!
BETTER TAKE TWO... IT'S MONDAY
JIM DAVIS 1-13

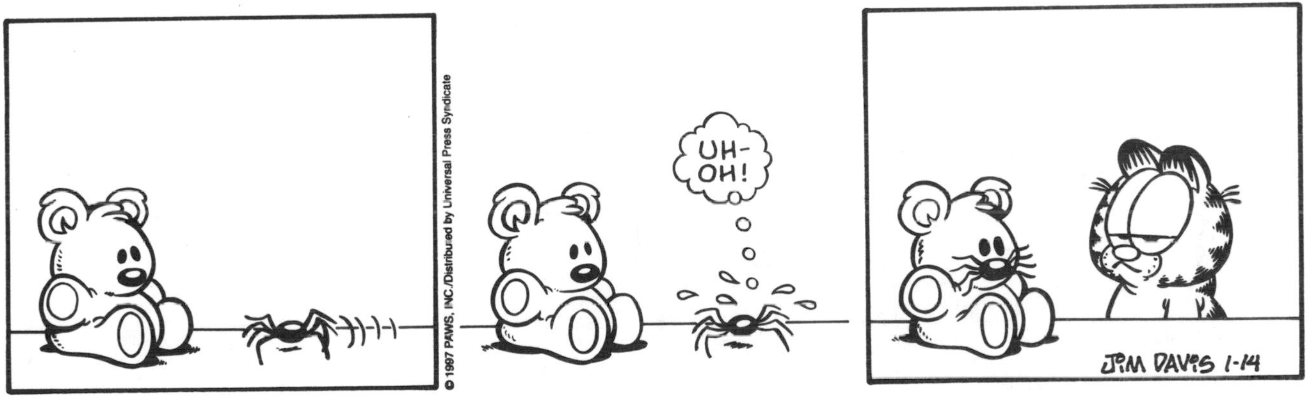
UH-OH!
JIM DAVIS 1-14

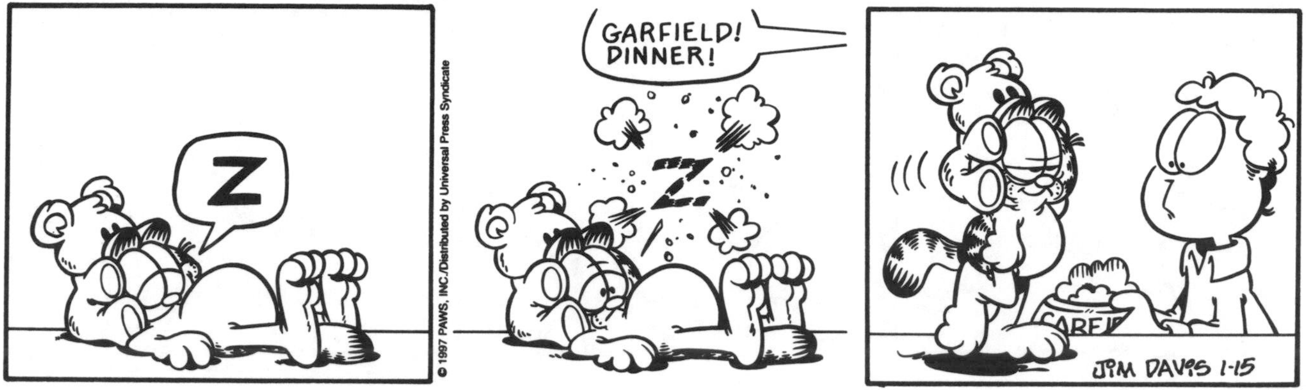
Z
GARFIELD! DINNER!
Z
© 1997 PAWS, INC./Distributed by Universal Press Syndicate
JIM DAVIS 1-15

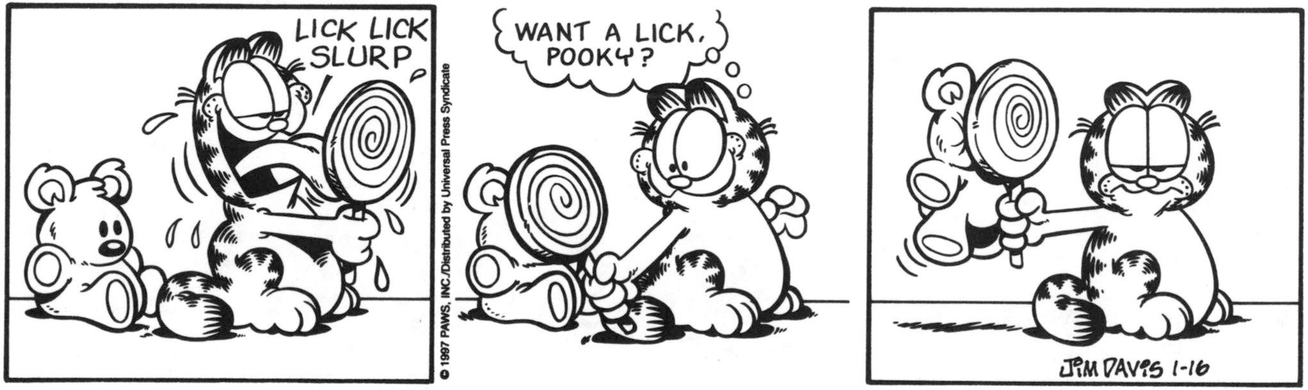
LICK LICK SLURP
WANT A LICK, POOKY?
© 1997 PAWS, INC./Distributed by Universal Press Syndicate
JIM DAVIS 1-16

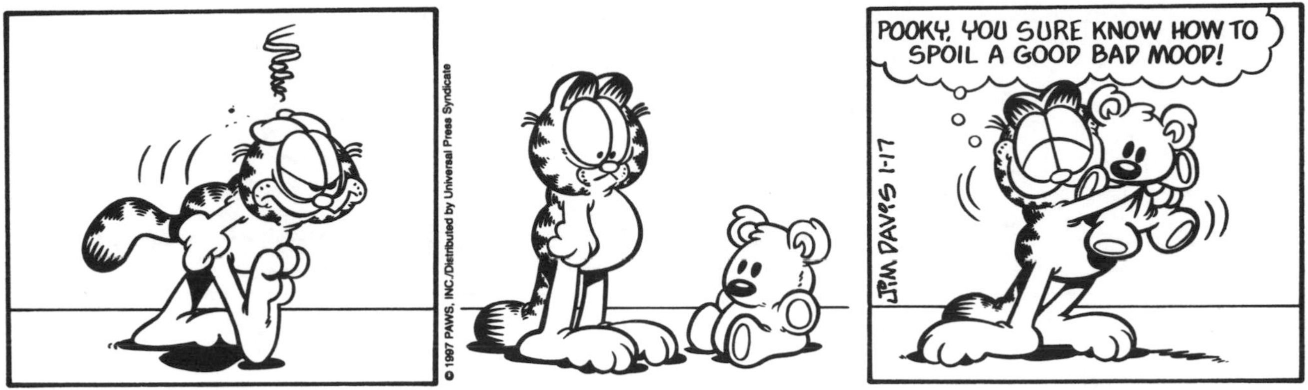
© 1997 PAWS, INC./Distributed by Universal Press Syndicate
POOKY, YOU SURE KNOW HOW TO SPOIL A GOOD BAD MOOD!
JIM DAVIS 1-17

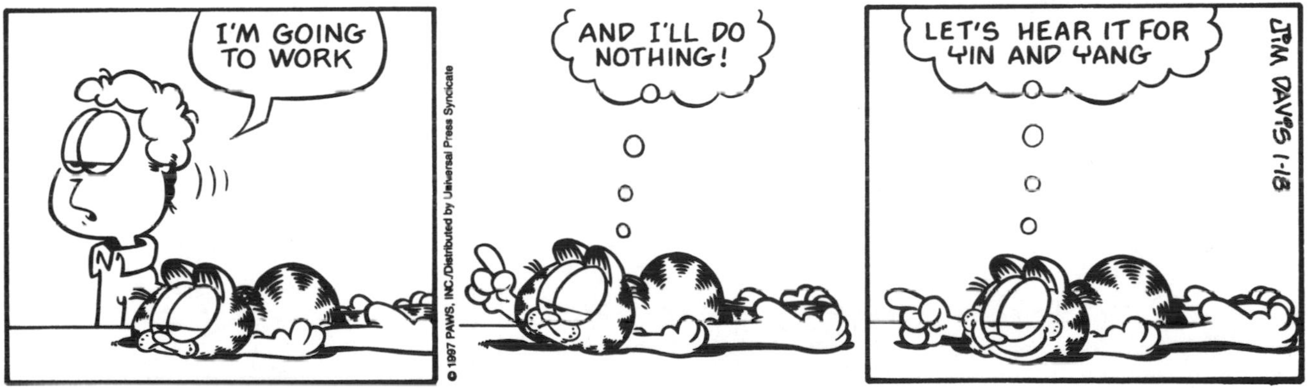
I'M GOING TO WORK
© 1997 PAWS, INC./Distributed by Universal Press Syndicate
AND I'LL DO NOTHING!
LET'S HEAR IT FOR YIN AND YANG
JIM DAVIS 1-18

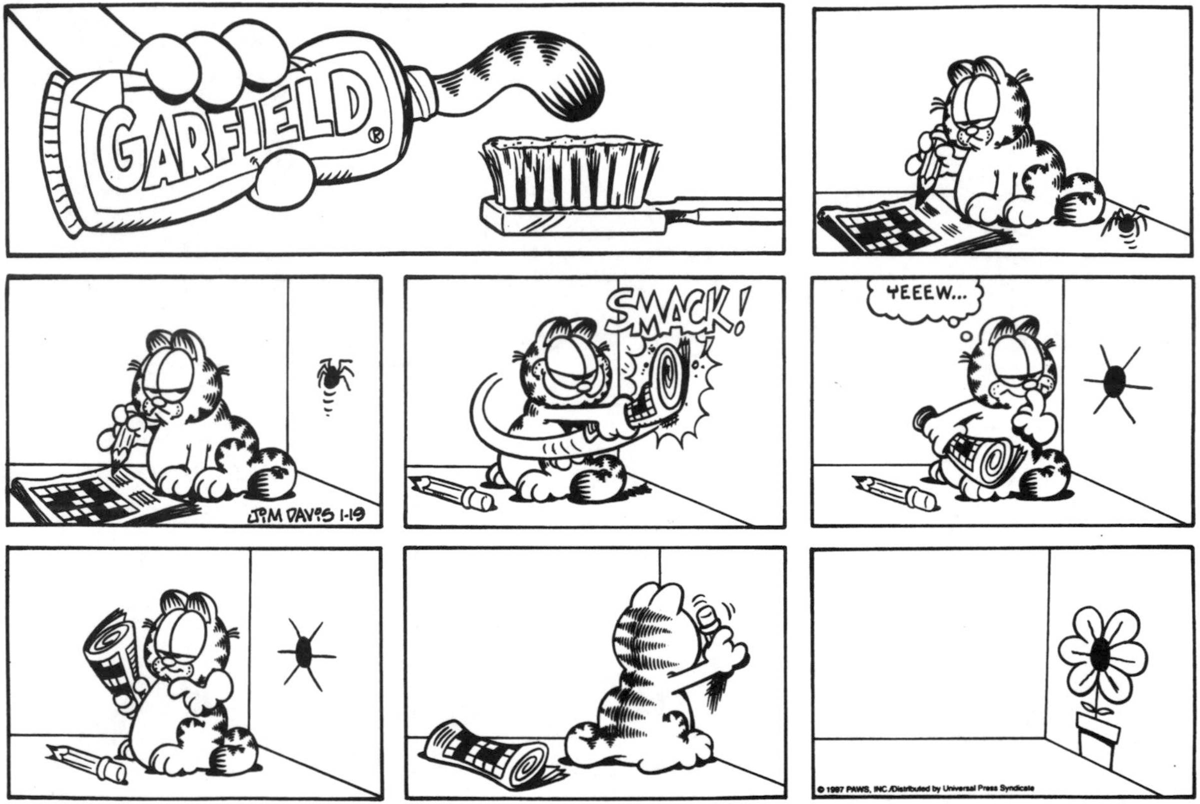
GARFIELD®
JIM DAVIS 1-19
SMACK!
YEEEW...
© 1997 PAWS, INC./Distributed by Universal Press Syndicate

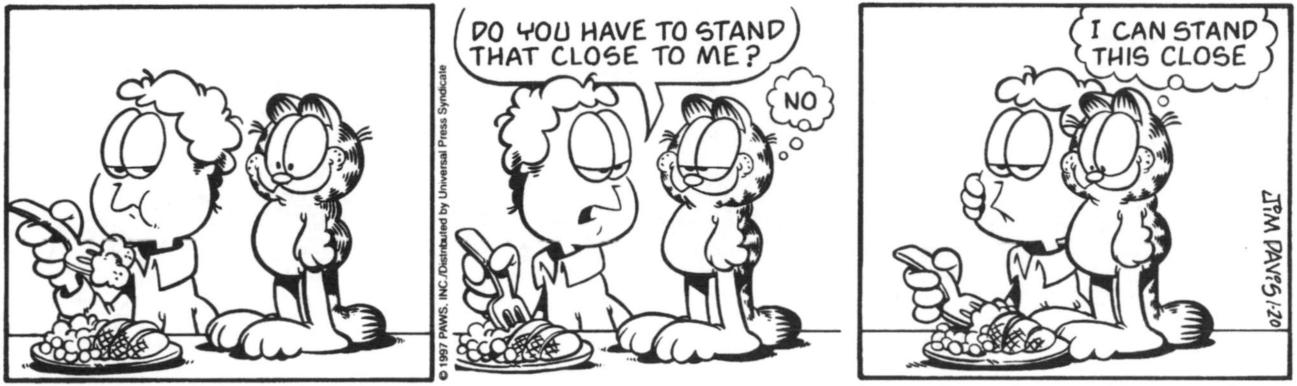
DO YOU HAVE TO STAND THAT CLOSE TO ME?
NO
I CAN STAND THIS CLOSE
© 1997 PAWS, INC./Distributed by Universal Press Syndicate
JIM DAVIS 1-20

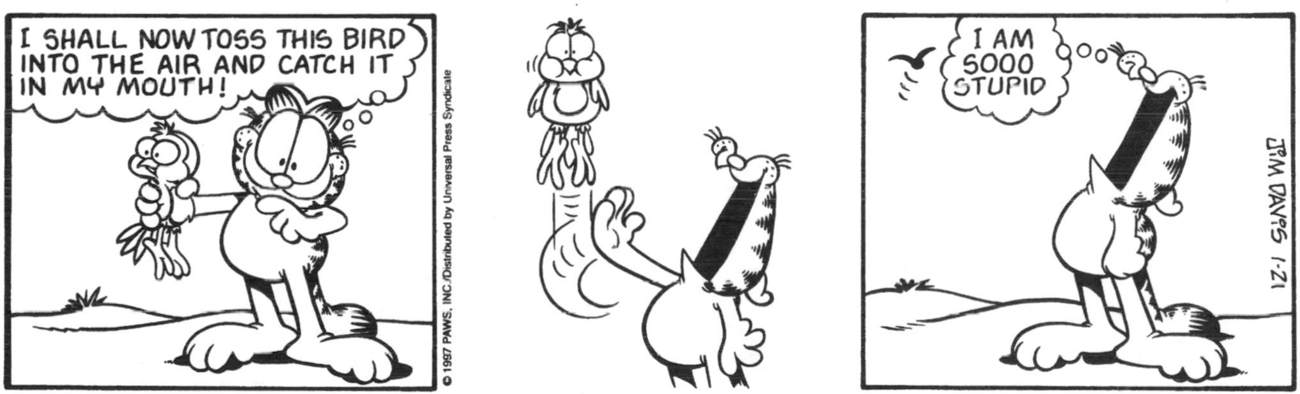
I SHALL NOW TOSS THIS BIRD INTO THE AIR AND CATCH IT IN MY MOUTH!
I AM SOOO STUPID
© 1997 PAWS, INC./Distributed by Universal Press Syndicate
JIM DAVIS 1-21

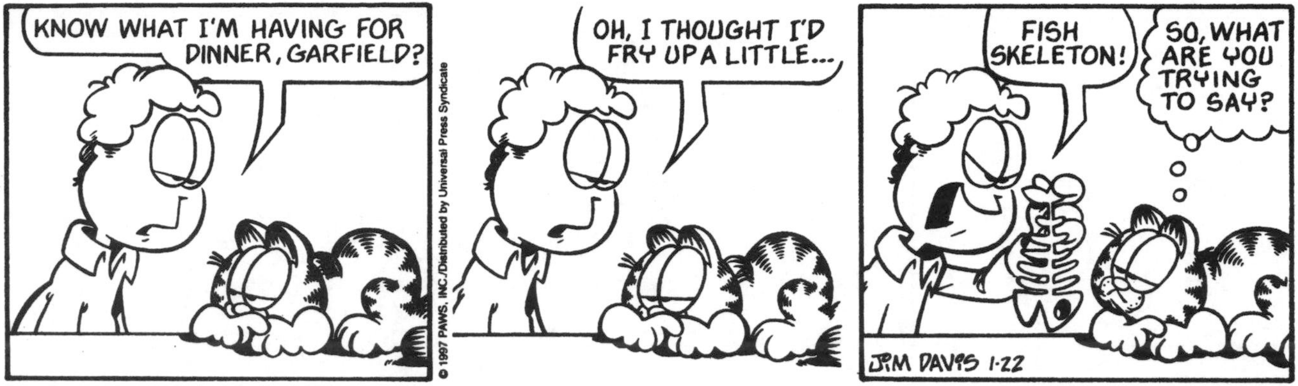
KNOW WHAT I'M HAVING FOR DINNER, GARFIELD?
© 1997 PAWS, INC./Distributed by Universal Press Syndicate
OH, I THOUGHT I'D FRY UP A LITTLE...
FISH SKELETON!
SO, WHAT ARE YOU TRYING TO SAY?
JIM DAVIS 1-22

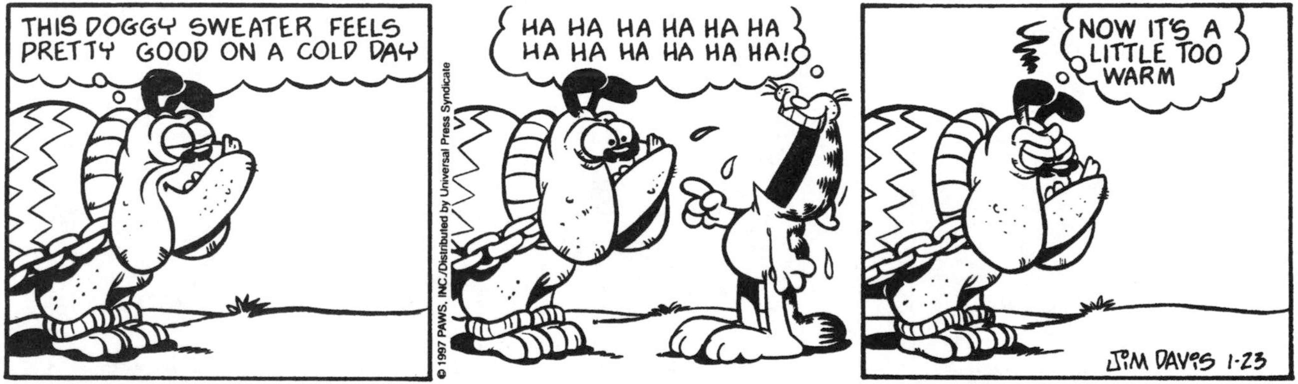
THIS DOGGY SWEATER FEELS PRETTY GOOD ON A COLD DAY
© 1997 PAWS, INC./Distributed by Universal Press Syndicate
HA HA HA HA HA HA HA HA HA HA HA HA!
NOW IT'S A LITTLE TOO WARM
JIM DAVIS 1-23

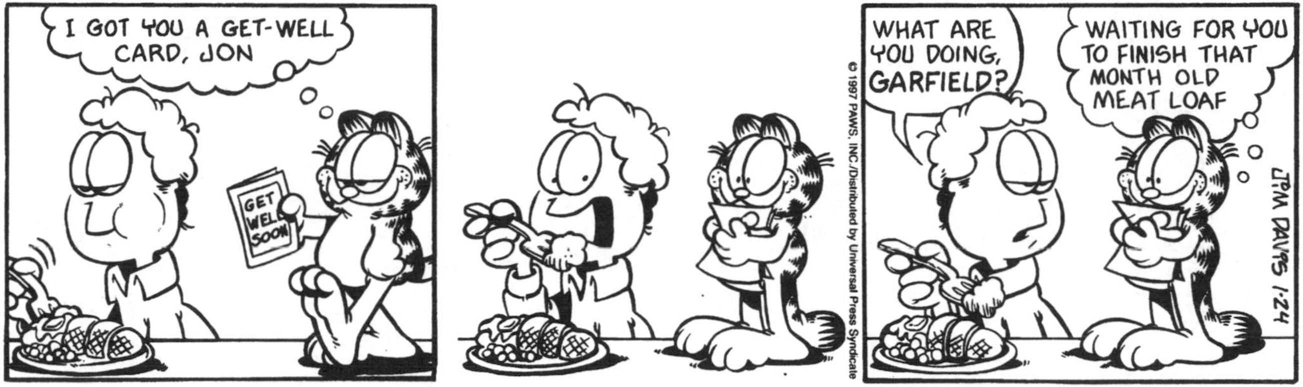
I GOT YOU A GET-WELL CARD, JON
GET WELL SOON
© 1997 PAWS, INC./Distributed by Universal Press Syndicate
WHAT ARE YOU DOING, GARFIELD?
WAITING FOR YOU TO FINISH THAT MONTH OLD MEAT LOAF
JIM DAVIS 1-24

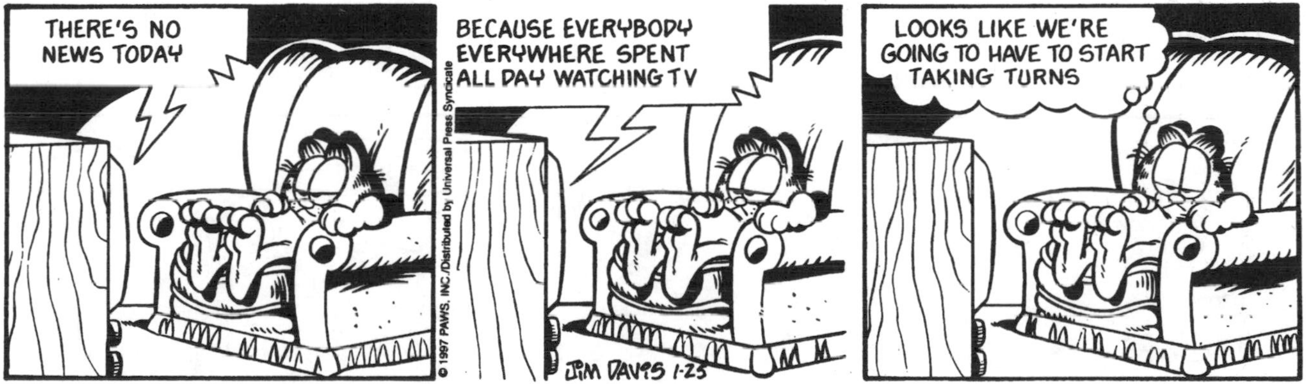
THERE'S NO NEWS TODAY
© 1997 PAWS, INC./Distributed by Universal Press Syndicate
BECAUSE EVERYBODY EVERYWHERE SPENT ALL DAY WATCHING TV
JIM DAVIS 1-25
LOOKS LIKE WE'RE GOING TO HAVE TO START TAKING TURNS

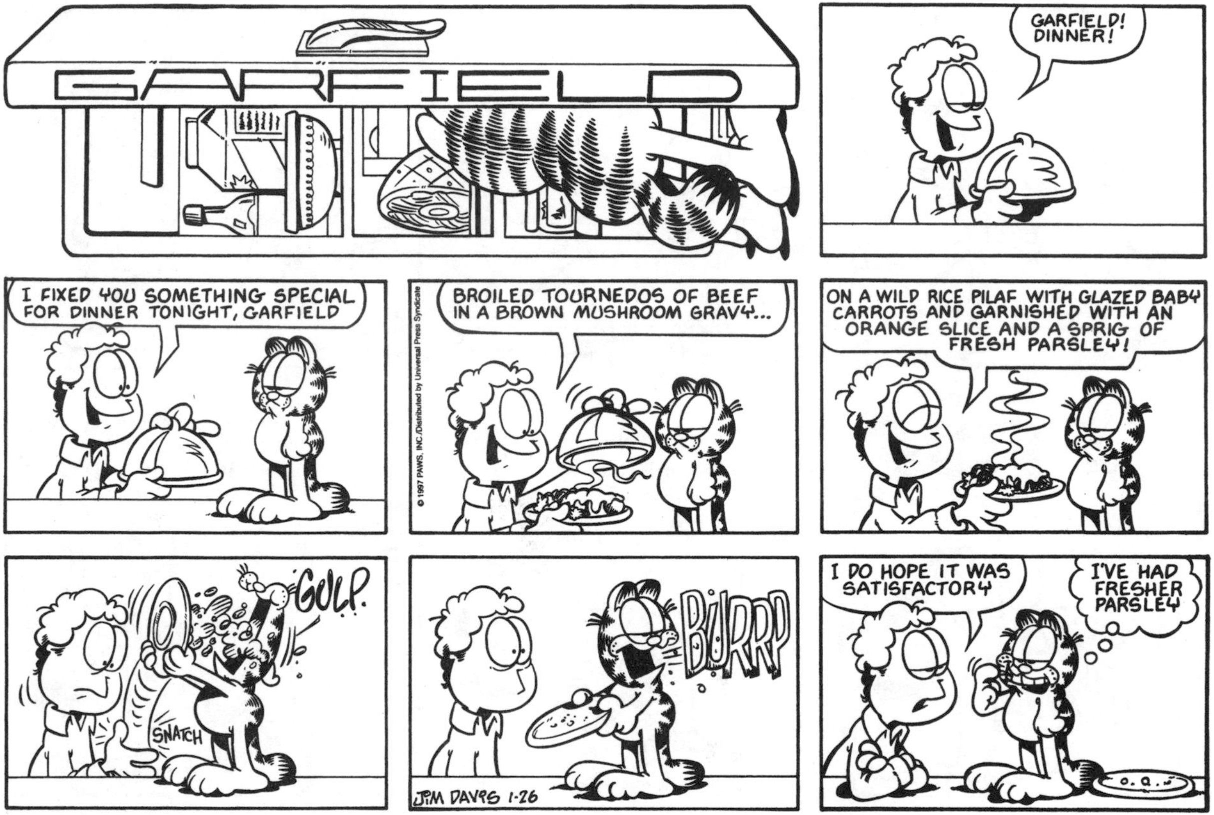
GARFIELD
GARFIELD! DINNER!
I FIXED YOU SOMETHING SPECIAL FOR DINNER TONIGHT, GARFIELD
© 1997 PAWS, INC./Distributed by Universal Press Syndicate
BROILED TOURNEDOS OF BEEF IN A BROWN MUSHROOM GRAVY...
ON A WILD RICE PILAF WITH GLAZED BABY CARROTS AND GARNISHED WITH AN ORANGE SLICE AND A SPRIG OF FRESH PARSLEY!
SNATCH
GULP
BURRP
JIM DAVIS 1-26
I DO HOPE IT WAS SATISFACTORY
I'VE HAD FRESHER PARSLEY

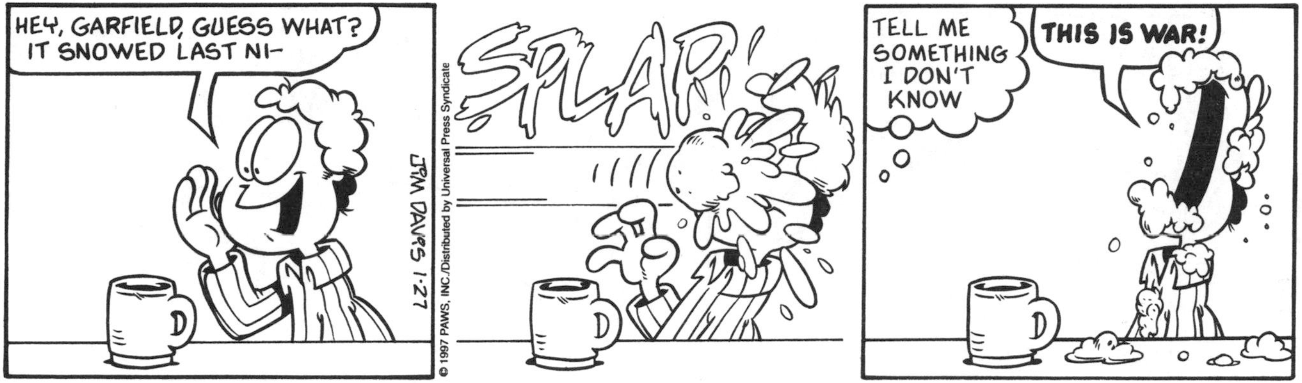
HEY, GARFIELD, GUESS WHAT? IT SNOWED LAST NI–
JIM DAVIS 1·27
© 1997 PAWS, INC./Distributed by Universal Press Syndicate
SPLAP!
TELL ME SOMETHING I DON'T KNOW
THIS IS WAR!

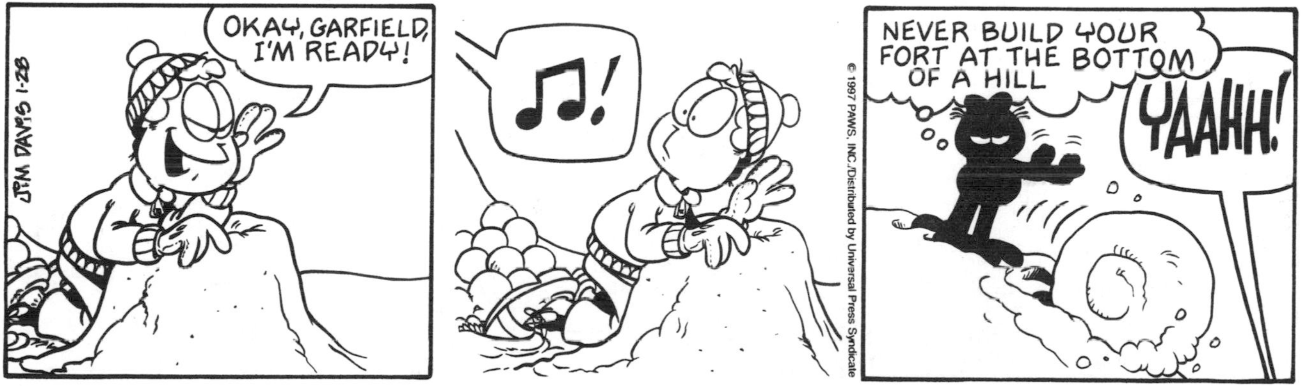
JIM DAVIS 1·28
OKAY, GARFIELD, I'M READY!
♫!
© 1997 PAWS, INC./Distributed by Universal Press Syndicate
NEVER BUILD YOUR FORT AT THE BOTTOM OF A HILL
YAAHH!

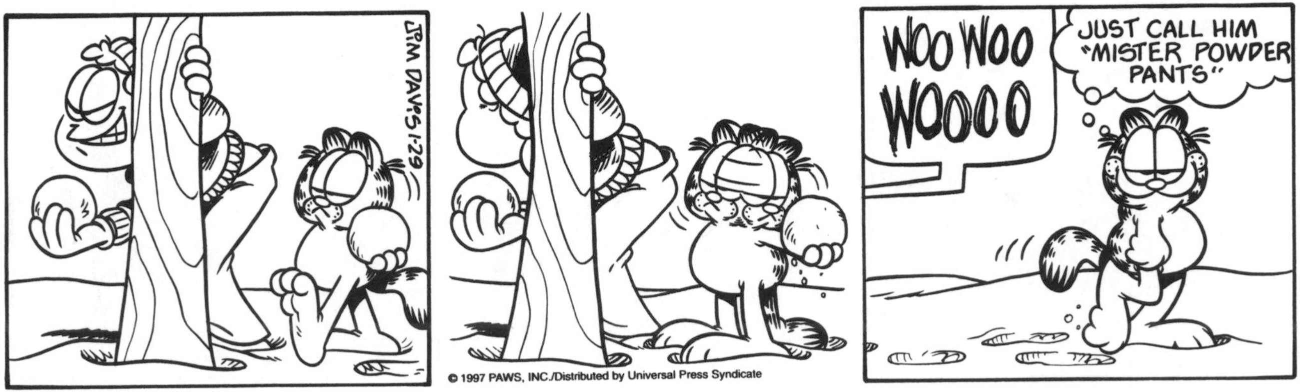
JIM DAVIS 1-29
WOO WOO WOOOO
JUST CALL HIM "MISTER POWDER PANTS"
© 1997 PAWS, INC./Distributed by Universal Press Syndicate

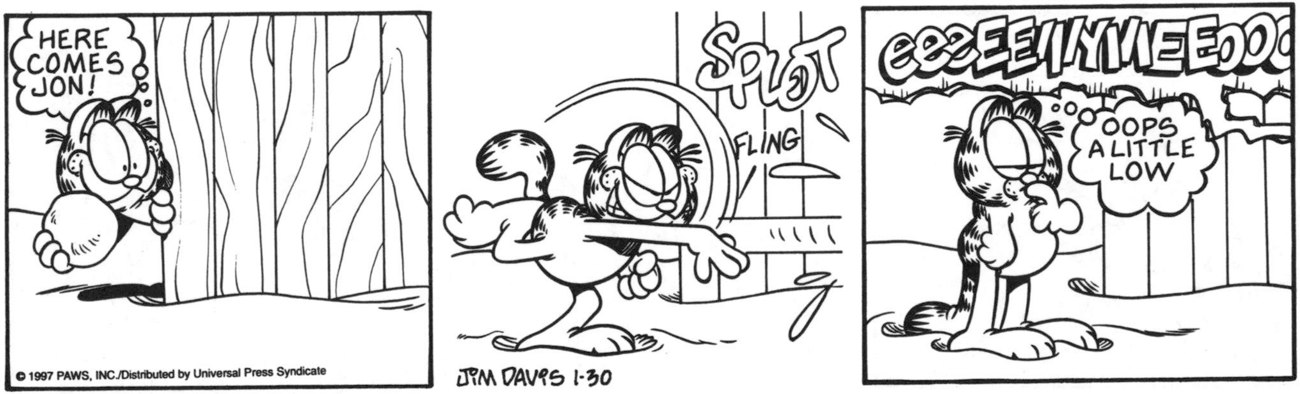
HERE COMES JON!
SPLOT
FLING
EEEEEIIIYYIIEEEOOO
OOPS A LITTLE LOW
© 1997 PAWS, INC./Distributed by Universal Press Syndicate
JIM DAVIS 1-30

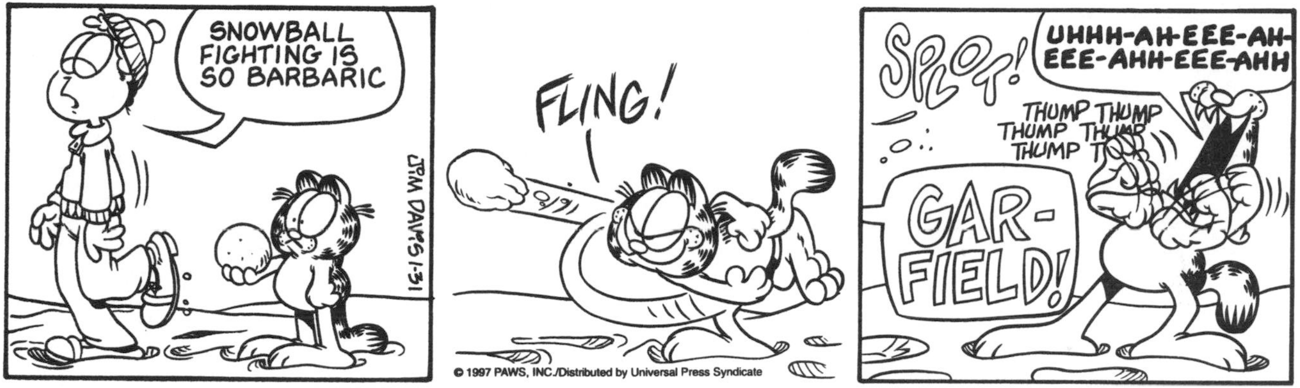
SNOWBALL FIGHTING IS SO BARBARIC
JIM DAVIS 1-31
FLING!
© 1997 PAWS, INC./Distributed by Universal Press Syndicate
SPLOT!
UHHH-AH-EEE-AH-EEE-AHH-EEE-AHH
THUMP THUMP THUMP
GAR-FIELD!

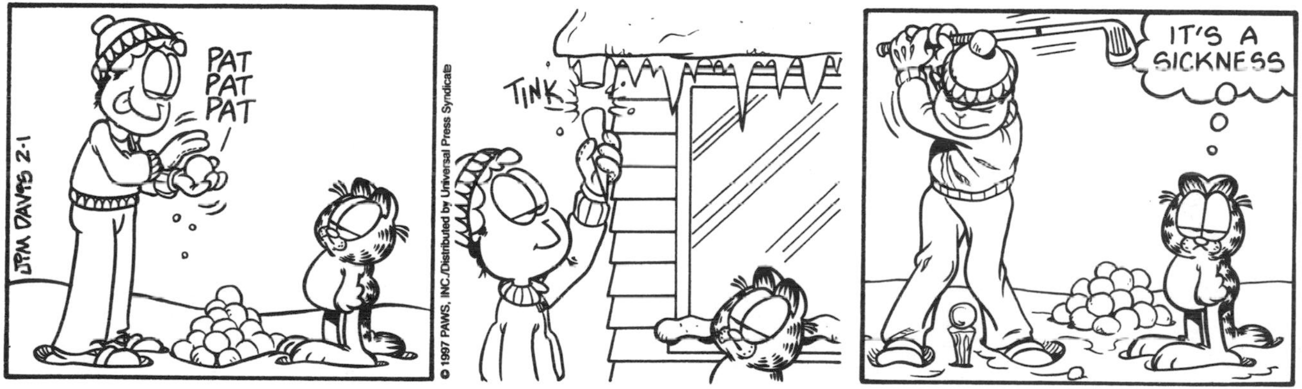
JIM DAVIS 2-1
PAT PAT PAT
© 1997 PAWS, INC./Distributed by Universal Press Syndicate
TINK
IT'S A SICKNESS

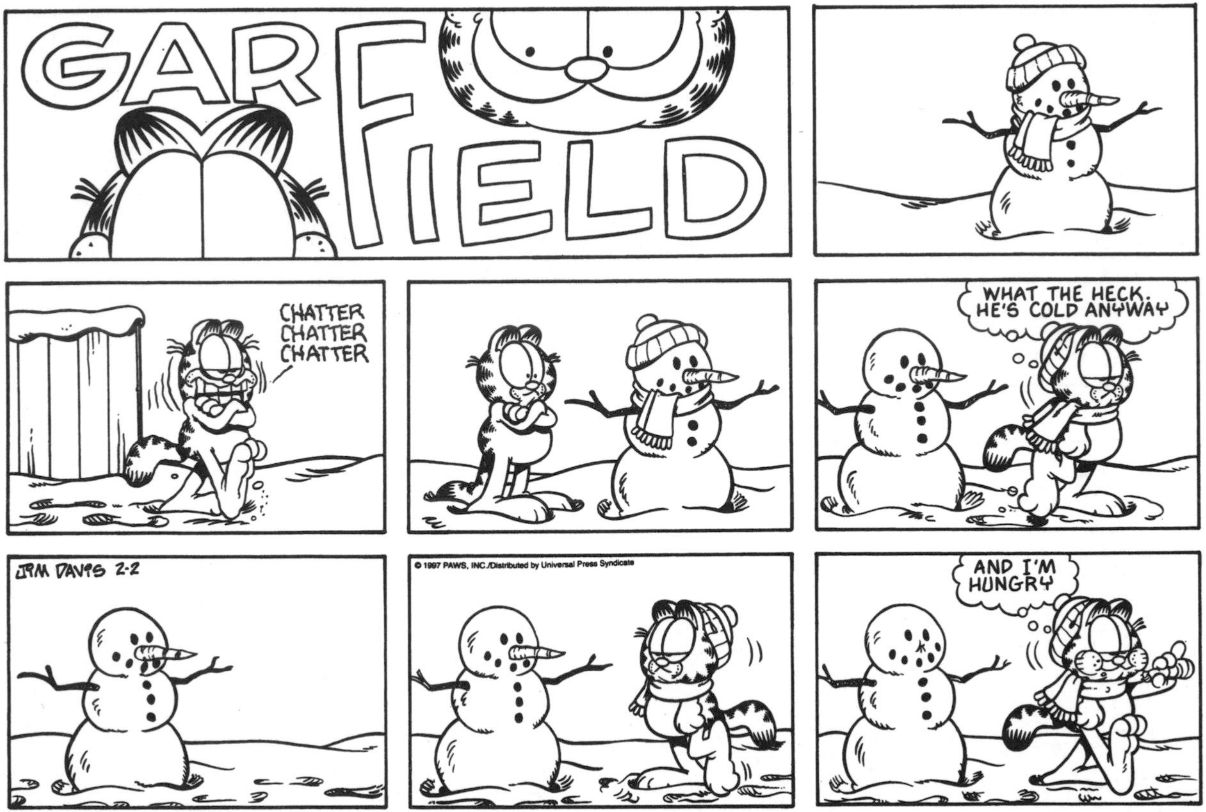
GARFIELD
CHATTER CHATTER CHATTER
WHAT THE HECK. HE'S COLD ANYWAY
JIM DAVIS 2-2
© 1997 PAWS, INC./Distributed by Universal Press Syndicate
AND I'M HUNGRY

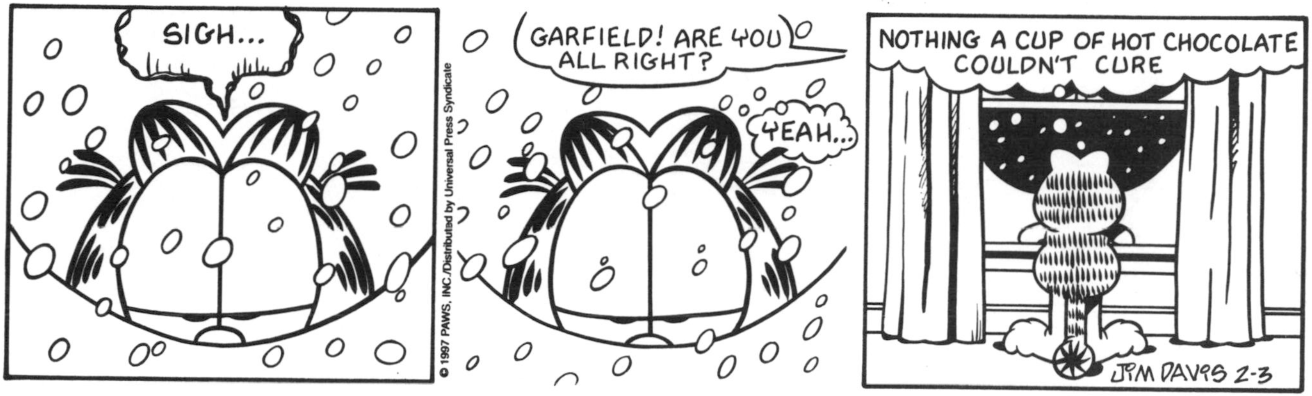
SIGH...
GARFIELD! ARE YOU ALL RIGHT?
YEAH...
NOTHING A CUP OF HOT CHOCOLATE COULDN'T CURE
JIM DAVIS 2-3

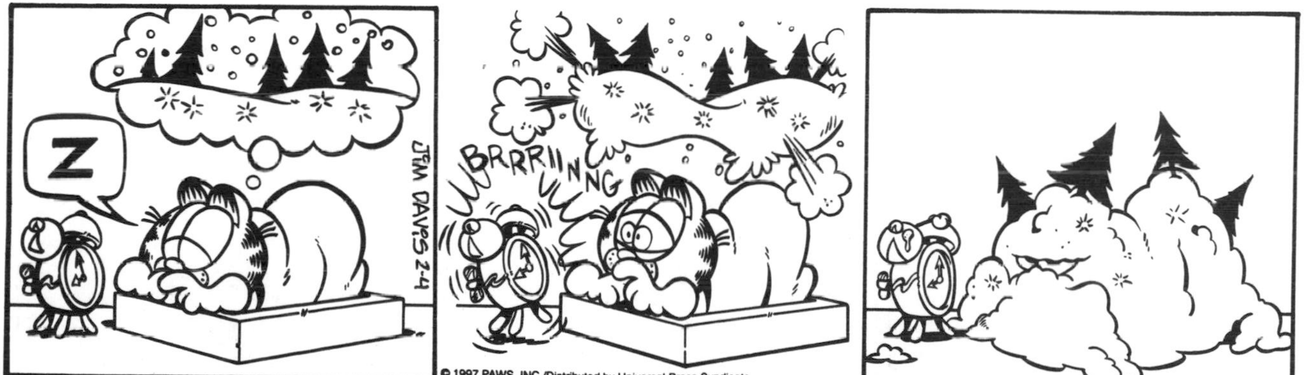
Z
JIM DAVIS 2-4
BRRRIINNG

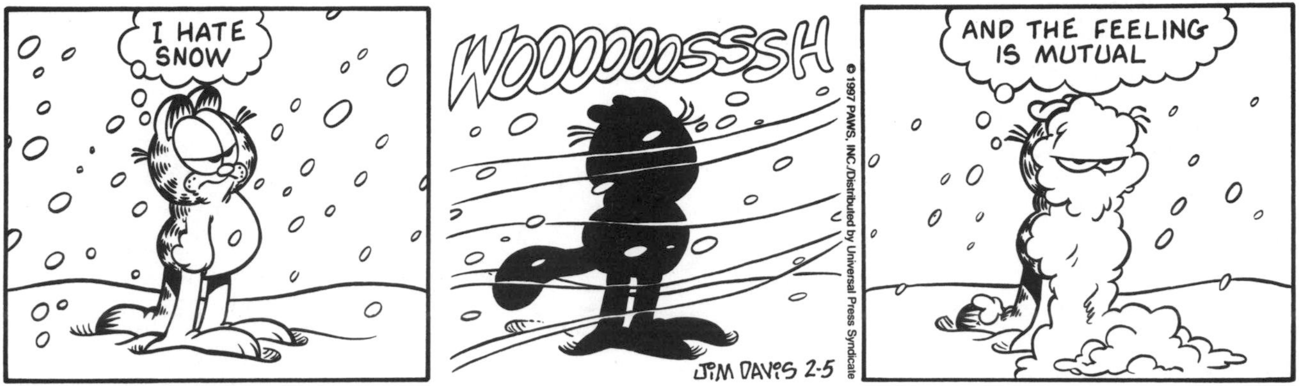
I HATE SNOW
WOOOOOOSSSSH
AND THE FEELING IS MUTUAL
© 1997 PAWS, INC./Distributed by Universal Press Syndicate
JIM DAVIS 2-5

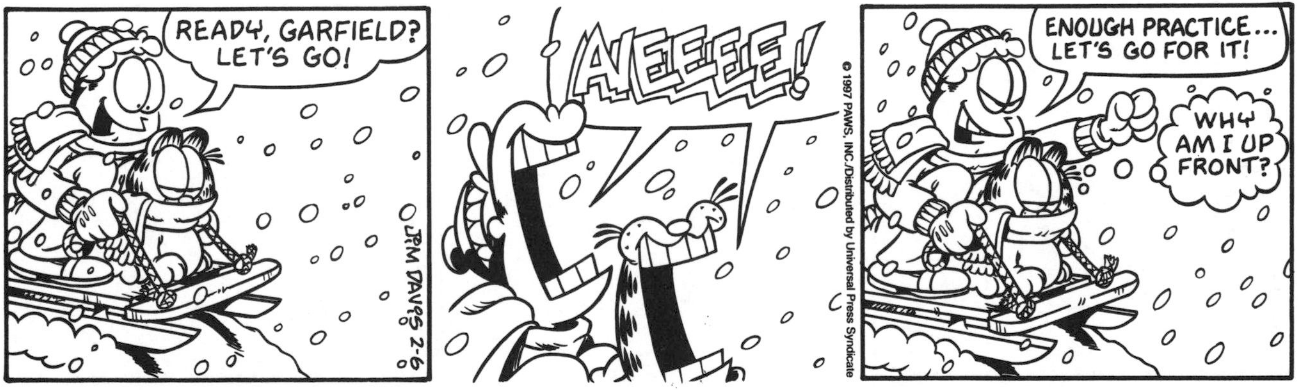
READY, GARFIELD? LET'S GO!
JIM DAVIS 2-6
AIEEEE!
© 1997 PAWS, INC./Distributed by Universal Press Syndicate
ENOUGH PRACTICE... LET'S GO FOR IT!
WHY AM I UP FRONT?

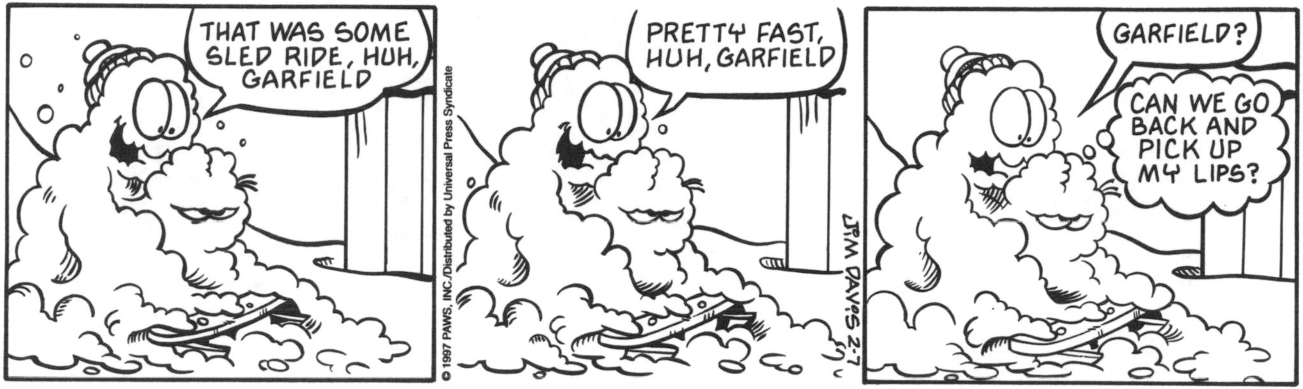
THAT WAS SOME SLED RIDE, HUH, GARFIELD
PRETTY FAST, HUH, GARFIELD
JIM DAVIS 2-7
GARFIELD?
CAN WE GO BACK AND PICK UP MY LIPS?

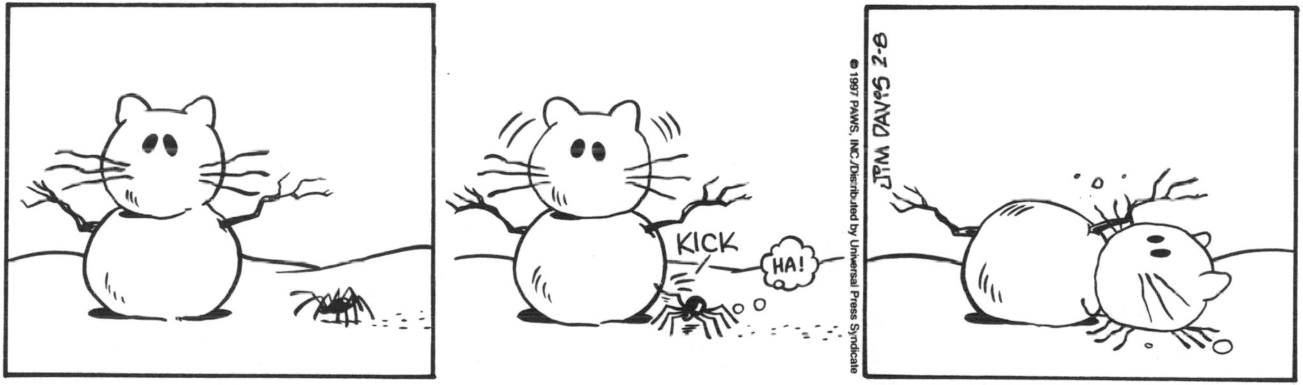
KICK
HA!
JIM DAVIS 2-8

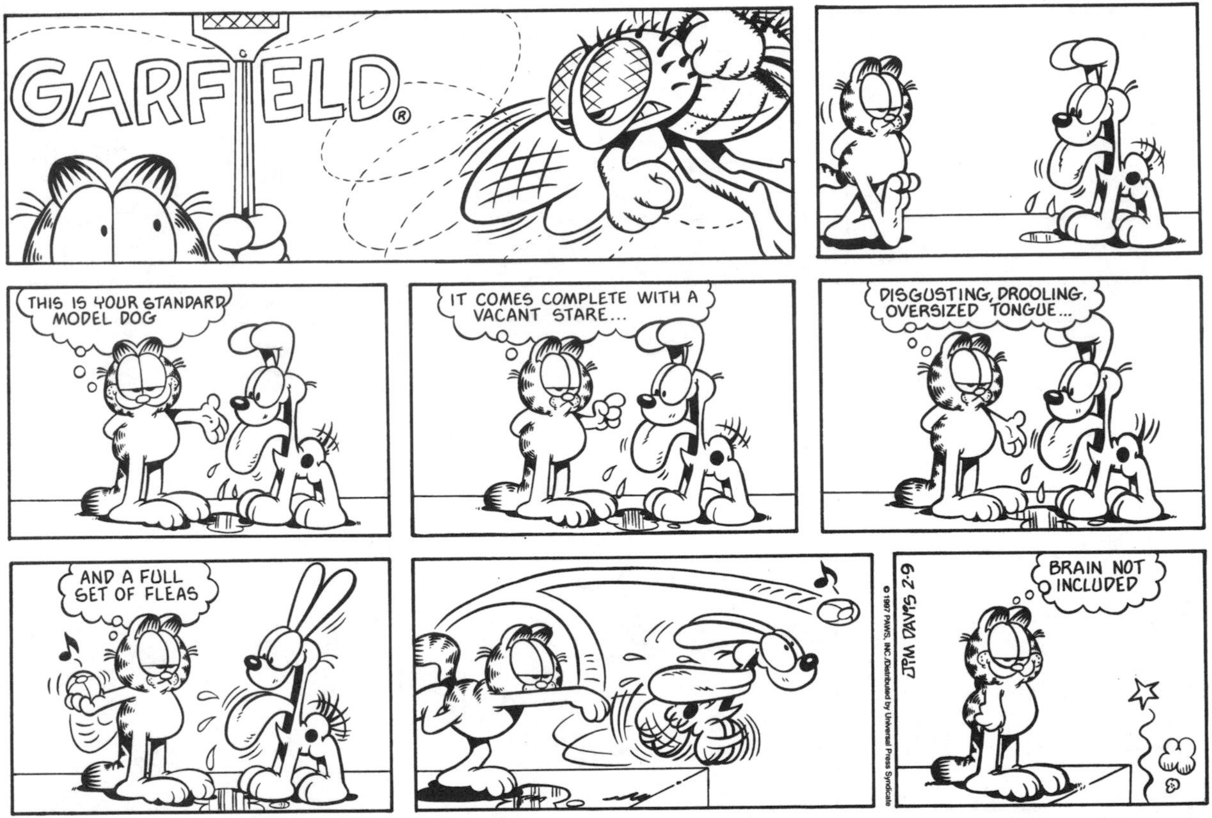
GARFIELD®
THIS IS YOUR STANDARD MODEL DOG
IT COMES COMPLETE WITH A VACANT STARE...
DISGUSTING, DROOLING, OVERSIZED TONGUE...
AND A FULL SET OF FLEAS
JPM DAVIS 2-9
© 1997 PAWS, INC./Distributed by Universal Press Syndicate
BRAIN NOT INCLUDED

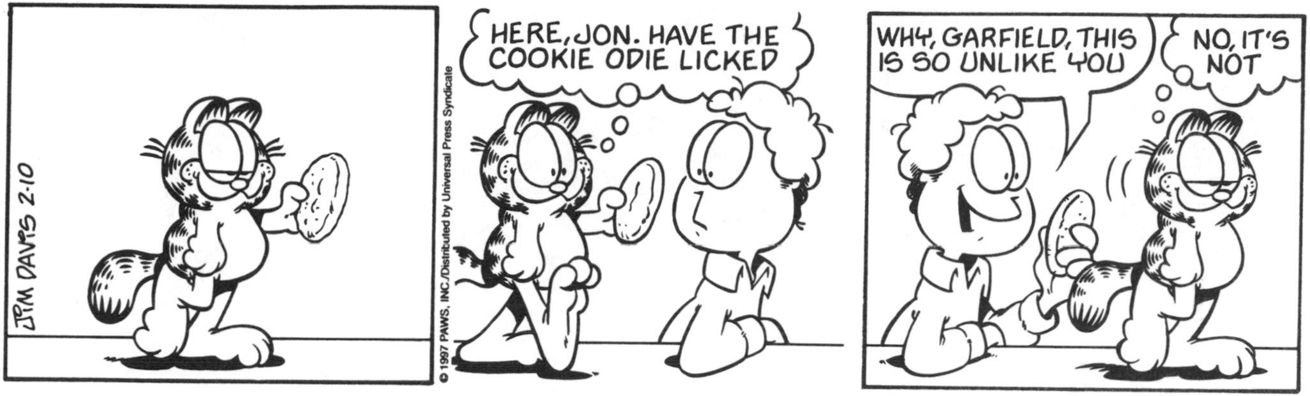
JIM DAVIS 2·10
© 1997 PAWS, INC./Distributed by Universal Press Syndicate
HERE, JON. HAVE THE COOKIE ODIE LICKED
WHY, GARFIELD, THIS IS SO UNLIKE YOU
NO, IT'S NOT

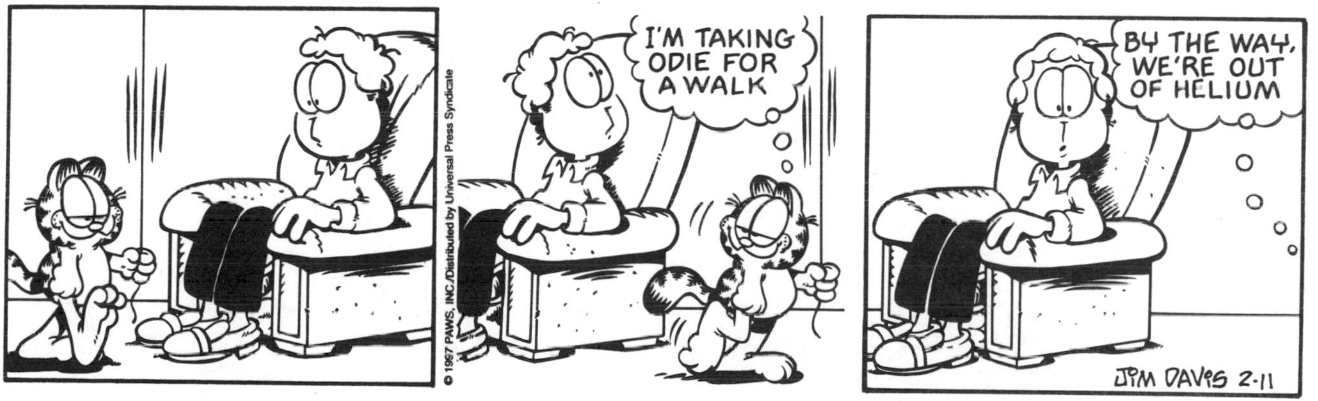
© 1997 PAWS, INC./Distributed by Universal Press Syndicate
I'M TAKING ODIE FOR A WALK
BY THE WAY, WE'RE OUT OF HELIUM
JIM DAVIS 2·11

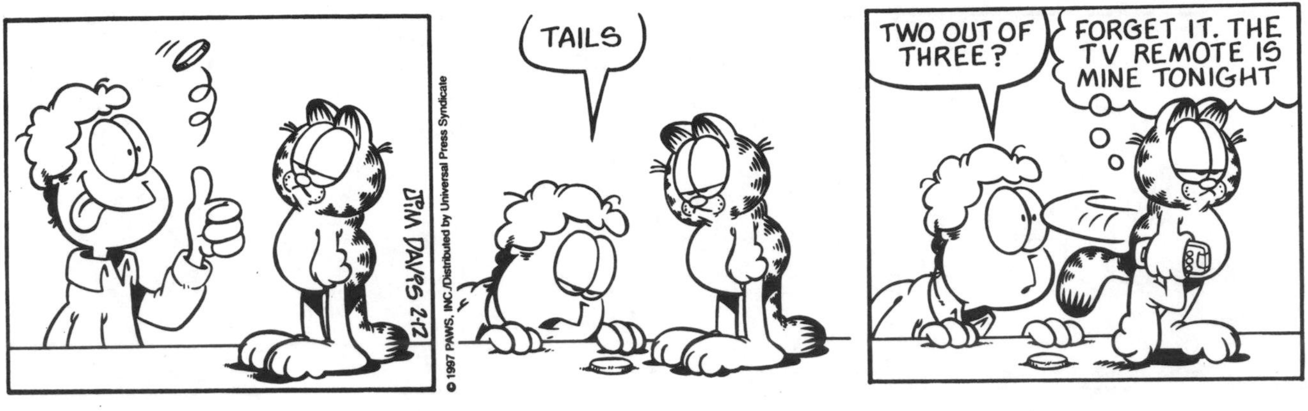
TAILS
TWO OUT OF THREE?
FORGET IT. THE TV REMOTE IS MINE TONIGHT
JIM DAVIS 2-12

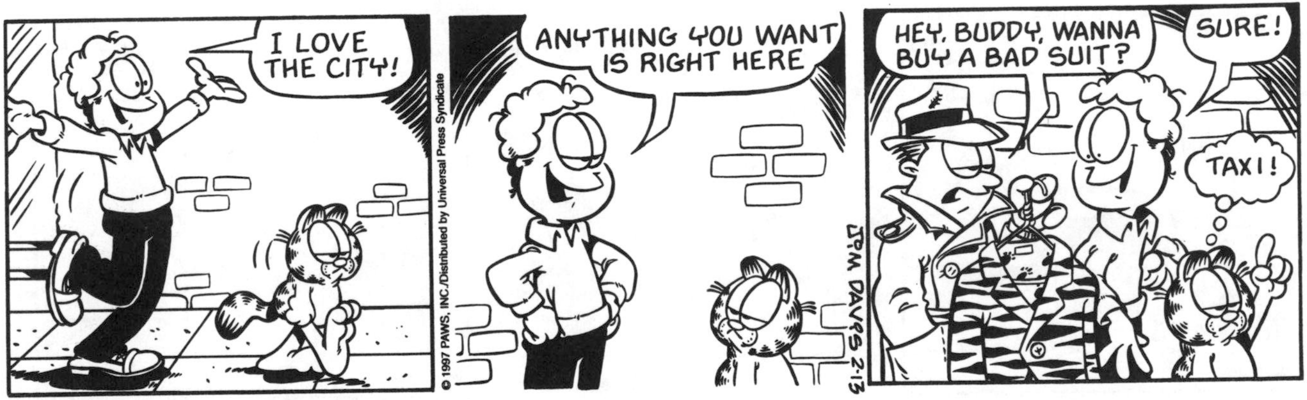
I LOVE THE CITY!
ANYTHING YOU WANT IS RIGHT HERE
HEY, BUDDY, WANNA BUY A BAD SUIT?
SURE!
TAXI!
JIM DAVIS 2-13

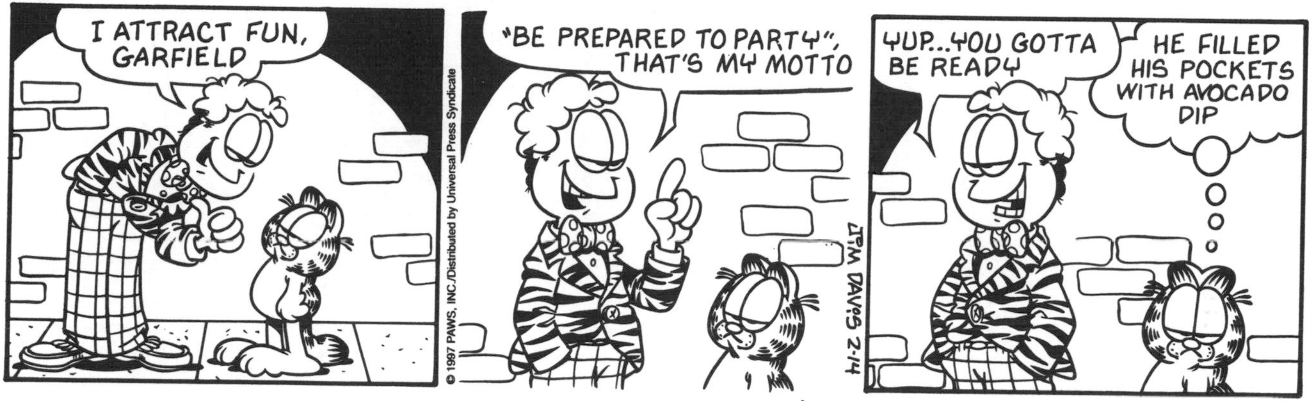
I ATTRACT FUN, GARFIELD
"BE PREPARED TO PARTY", THAT'S MY MOTTO
YUP...YOU GOTTA BE READY
HE FILLED HIS POCKETS WITH AVOCADO DIP
© 1997 PAWS, INC./Distributed by Universal Press Syndicate
JIM DAVIS 2-14

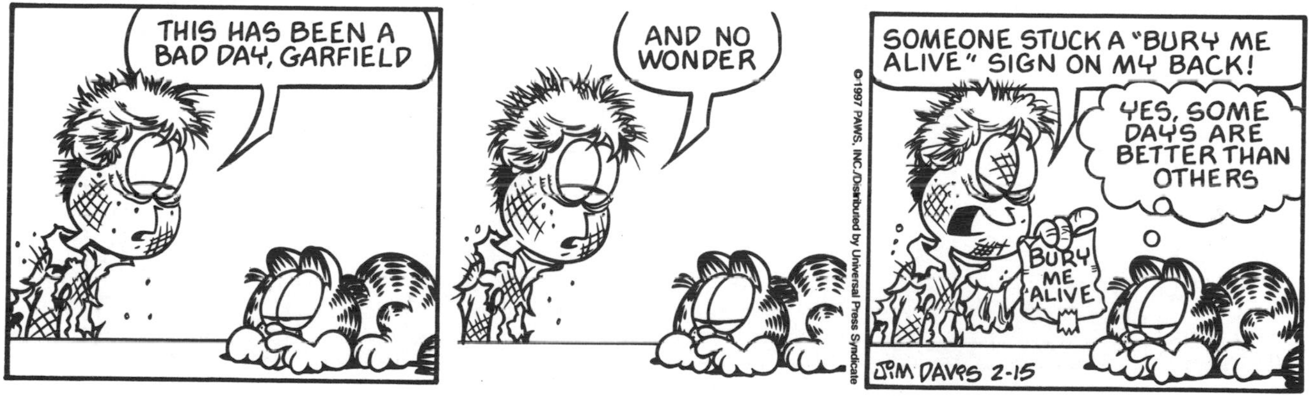
THIS HAS BEEN A BAD DAY, GARFIELD
AND NO WONDER
SOMEONE STUCK A "BURY ME ALIVE" SIGN ON MY BACK!
BURY ME ALIVE
YES, SOME DAYS ARE BETTER THAN OTHERS
© 1997 PAWS, INC./Distributed by Universal Press Syndicate
JIM DAVIS 2-15

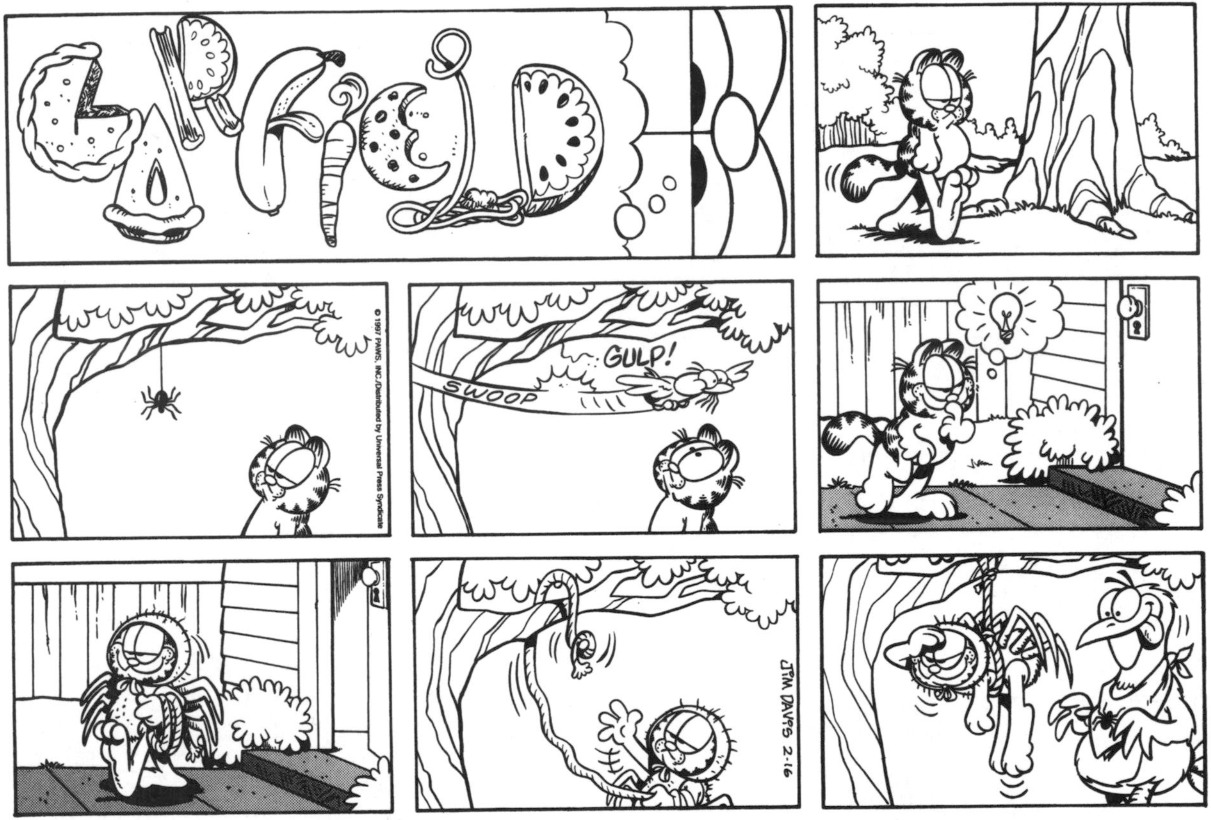

© 1997 PAWS, INC./Distributed by Universal Press Syndicate
SWOOP
GULP!
JIM DAVIS 2-16

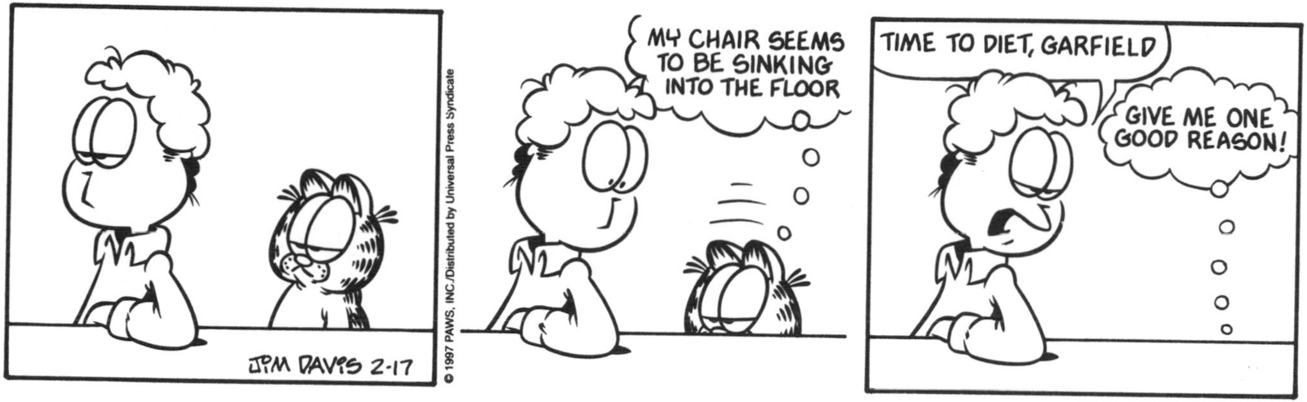
JIM DAVIS 2-17
© 1997 PAWS, INC./Distributed by Universal Press Syndicate
MY CHAIR SEEMS TO BE SINKING INTO THE FLOOR
TIME TO DIET, GARFIELD
GIVE ME ONE GOOD REASON!

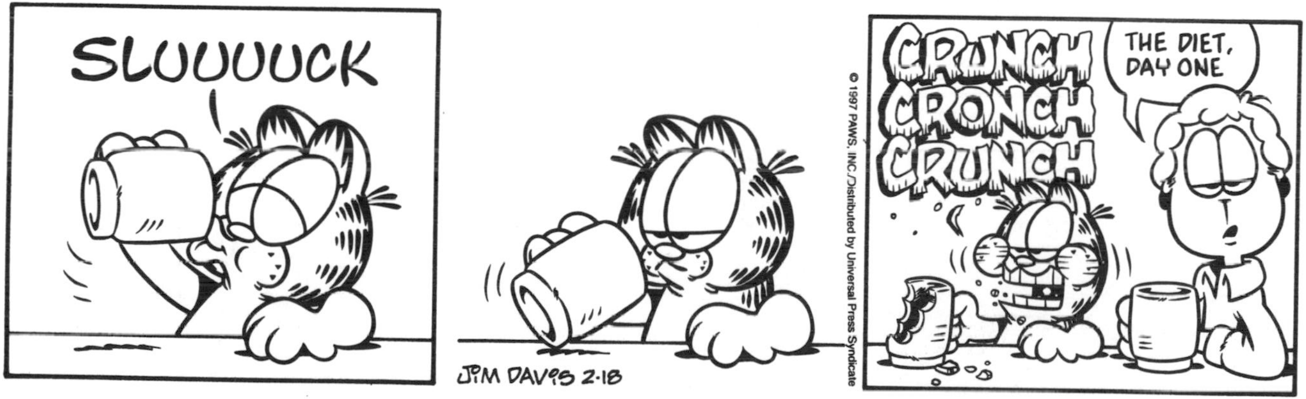
SLUUUUCK
JIM DAVIS 2-18
© 1997 PAWS, INC./Distributed by Universal Press Syndicate
CRUNCH
CRONCH
CRUNCH
THE DIET, DAY ONE

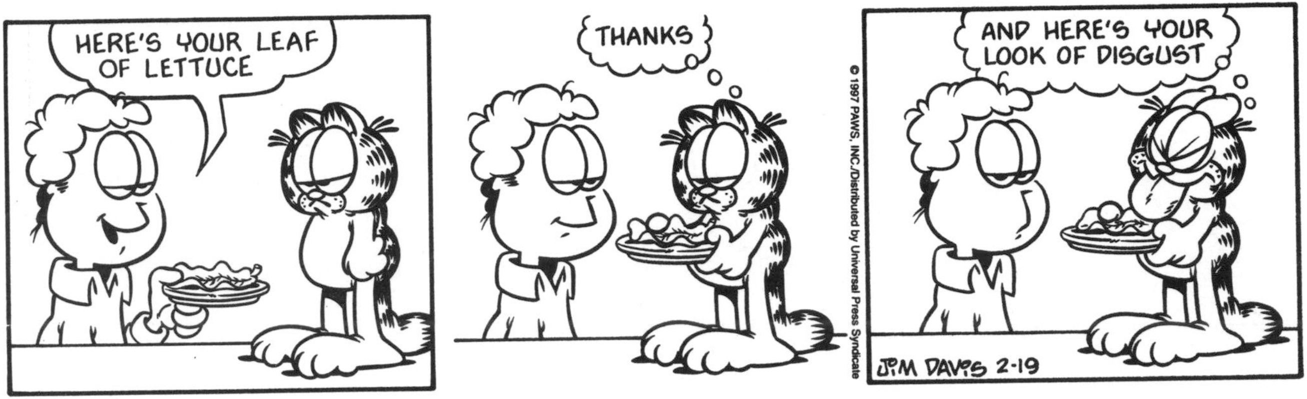
HERE'S YOUR LEAF OF LETTUCE
THANKS
AND HERE'S YOUR LOOK OF DISGUST
JIM DAVIS 2-19
© 1997 PAWS, INC./Distributed by Universal Press Syndicate

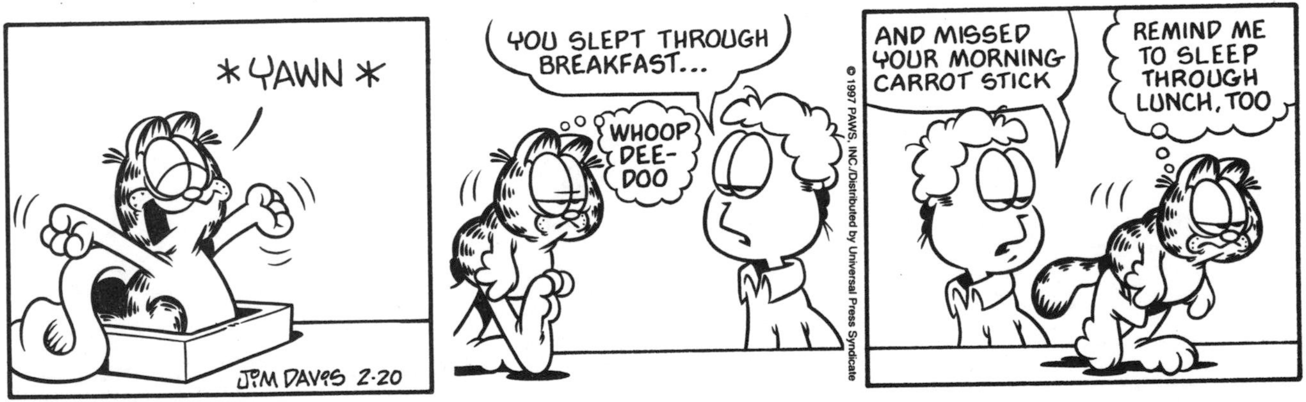
YAWN
JIM DAVIS 2-20
YOU SLEPT THROUGH BREAKFAST...
WHOOP DEE-DOO
AND MISSED YOUR MORNING CARROT STICK
REMIND ME TO SLEEP THROUGH LUNCH, TOO
© 1997 PAWS, INC./Distributed by Universal Press Syndicate

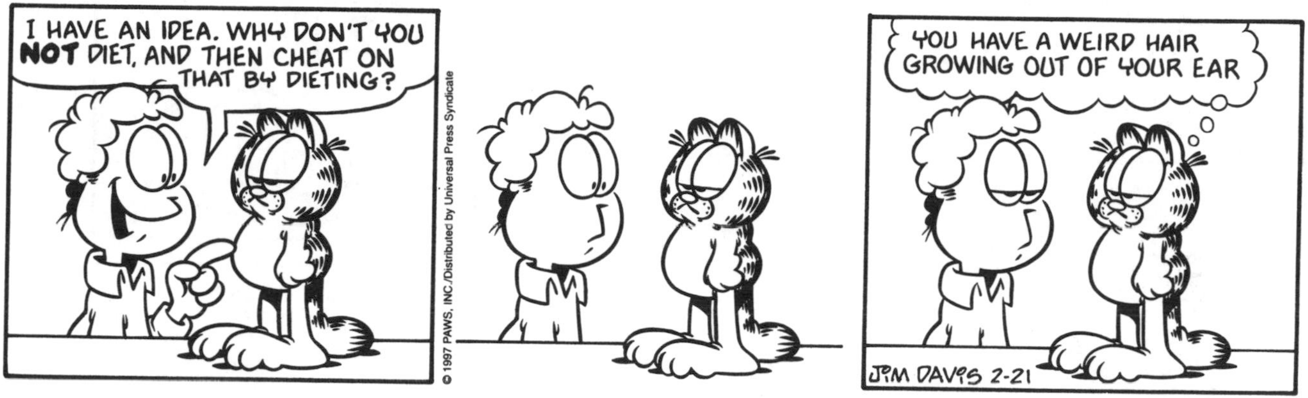
I HAVE AN IDEA. WHY DON'T YOU NOT DIET, AND THEN CHEAT ON THAT BY DIETING?
YOU HAVE A WEIRD HAIR GROWING OUT OF YOUR EAR
JIM DAVIS 2-21
© 1997 PAWS, INC./Distributed by Universal Press Syndicate

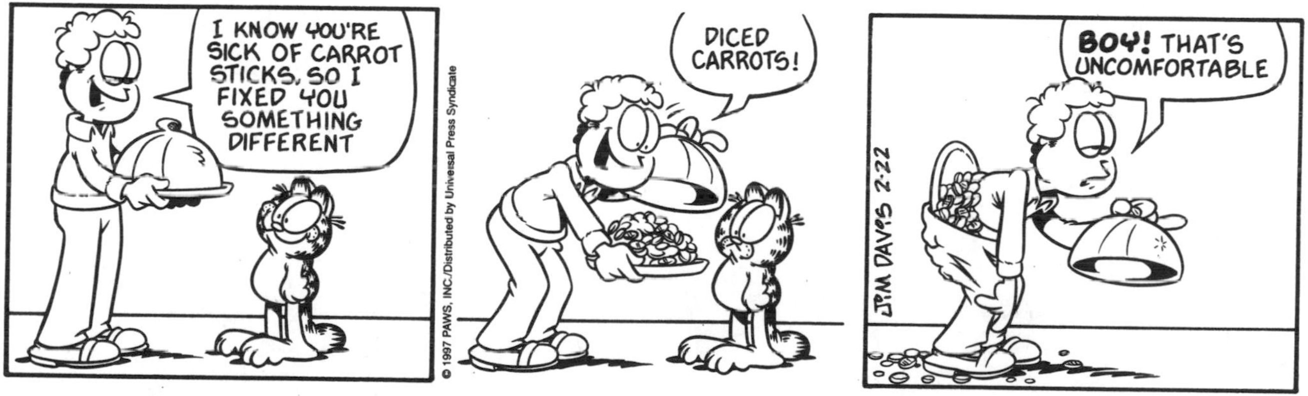
I KNOW YOU'RE SICK OF CARROT STICKS, SO I FIXED YOU SOMETHING DIFFERENT
DICED CARROTS!
BOY! THAT'S UNCOMFORTABLE
JIM DAVIS 2-22
© 1997 PAWS, INC./Distributed by Universal Press Syndicate

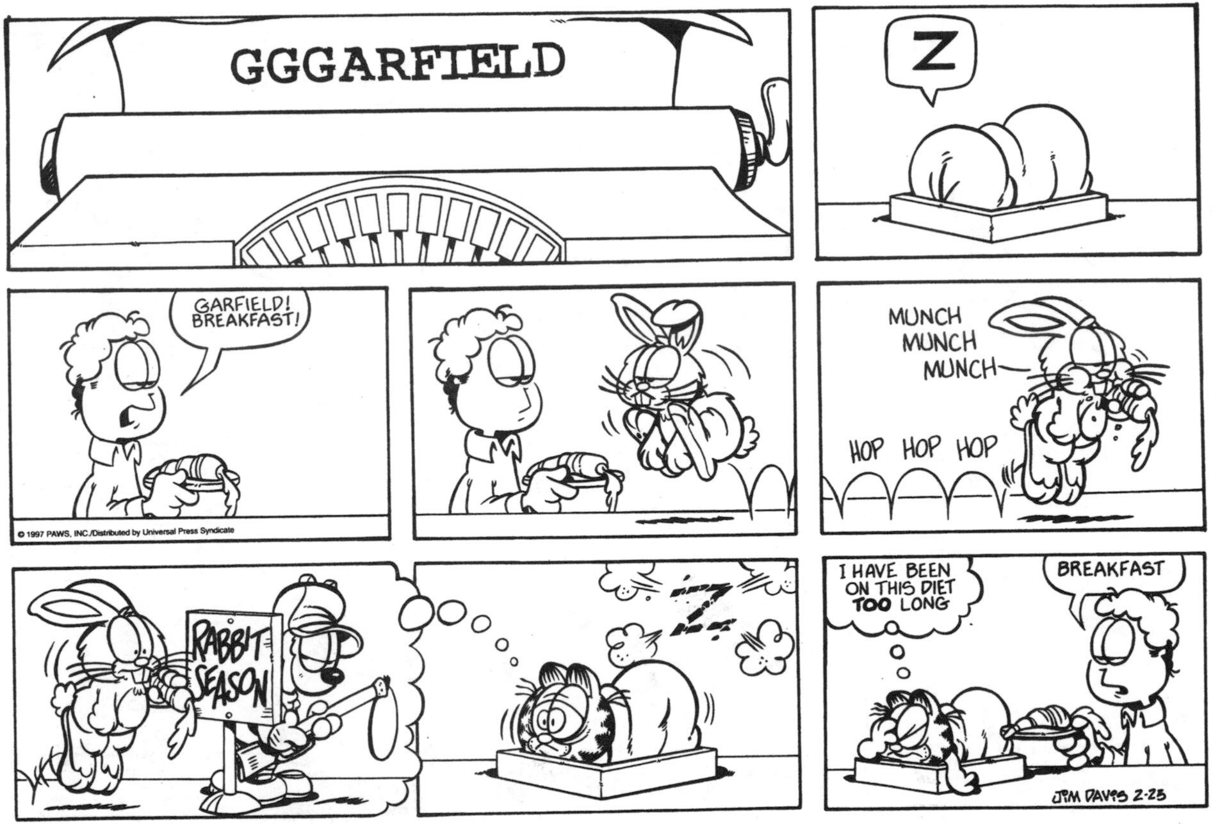
GGGARFIELD
Z
GARFIELD! BREAKFAST!
MUNCH MUNCH MUNCH
HOP HOP HOP
RABBIT SEASON
I HAVE BEEN ON THIS DIET TOO LONG
BREAKFAST
JIM DAVIS 2-23

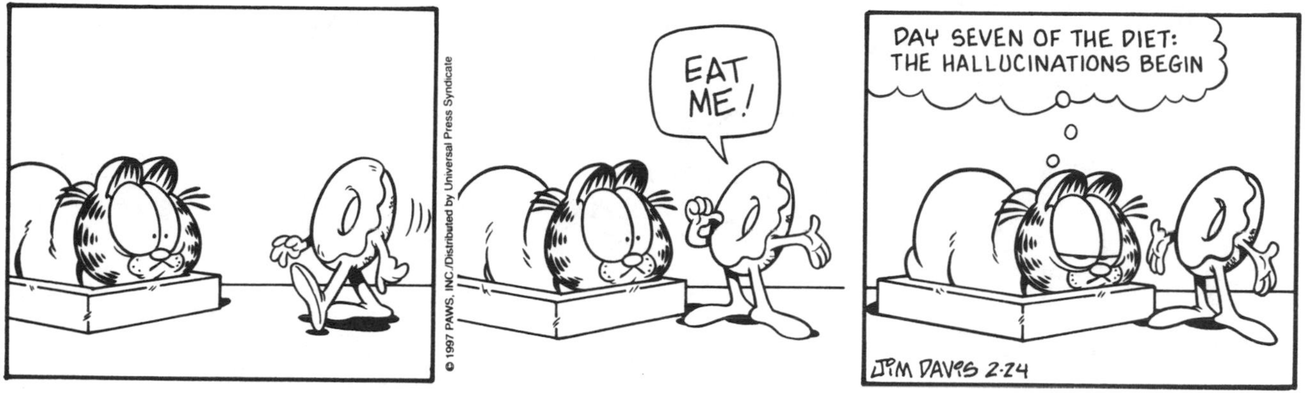
© 1997 PAWS, INC./Distributed by Universal Press Syndicate
EAT ME!
DAY SEVEN OF THE DIET: THE HALLUCINATIONS BEGIN
JIM DAVIS 2-24

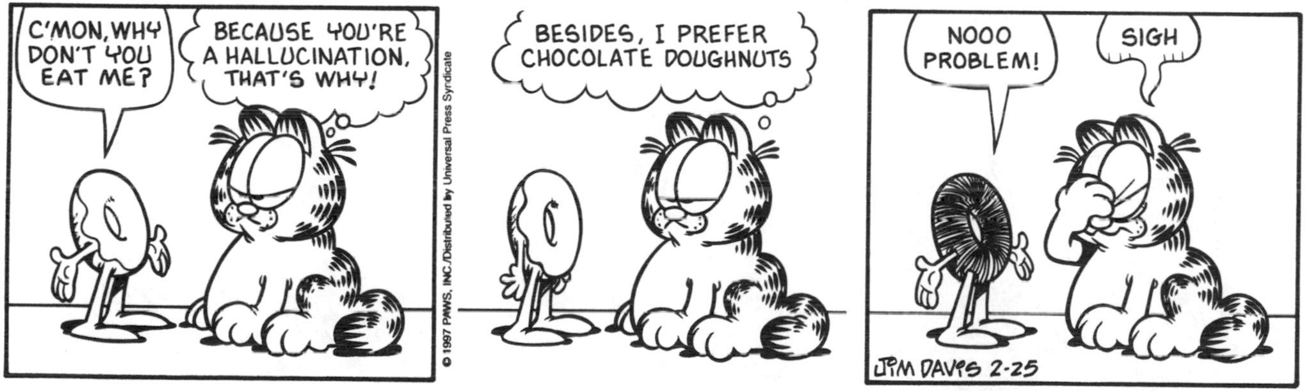
C'MON, WHY DON'T YOU EAT ME?
BECAUSE YOU'RE A HALLUCINATION, THAT'S WHY!
© 1997 PAWS, INC./Distributed by Universal Press Syndicate
BESIDES, I PREFER CHOCOLATE DOUGHNUTS
NOOO PROBLEM!
SIGH
JIM DAVIS 2-25

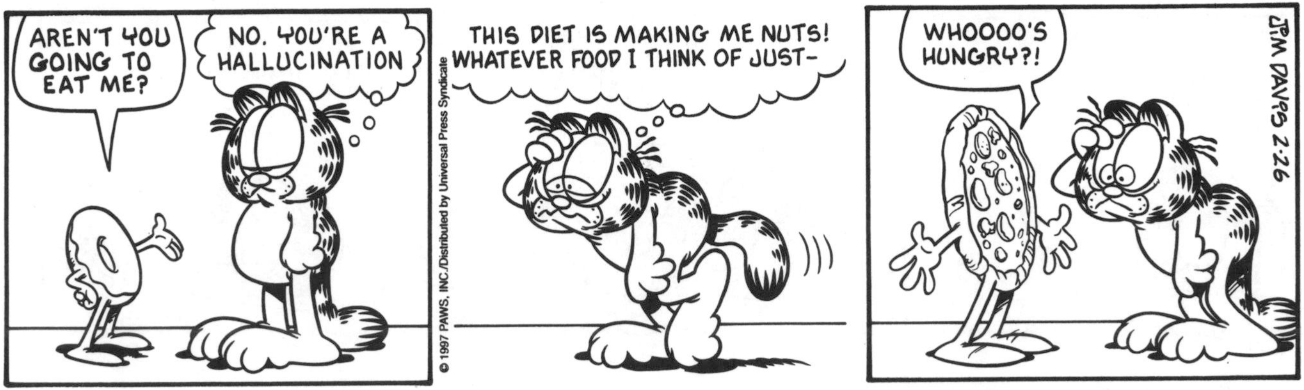
AREN'T YOU GOING TO EAT ME?
NO. YOU'RE A HALLUCINATION
© 1997 PAWS, INC./Distributed by Universal Press Syndicate
THIS DIET IS MAKING ME NUTS! WHATEVER FOOD I THINK OF JUST-
WHOOOO'S HUNGRY?!
JIM DAVIS 2-26

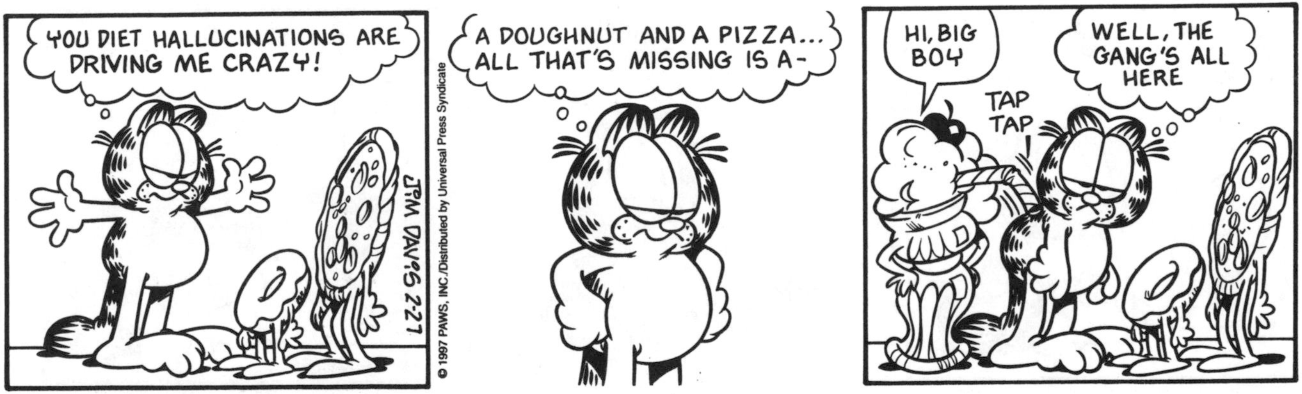
YOU DIET HALLUCINATIONS ARE DRIVING ME CRAZY!
JIM DAVIS 2-27
© 1997 PAWS, INC./Distributed by Universal Press Syndicate
A DOUGHNUT AND A PIZZA... ALL THAT'S MISSING IS A-
HI, BIG BOY
TAP TAP
WELL, THE GANG'S ALL HERE

HOW'S IT GOING, SCALE?
NOT SO GOOD... YOU?
AWFUL. THIS DIET IS KILLING ME
SOUNDS LIKE WE COULD BOTH USE A GOOD LAUGH...
WHY DON'T YOU HOP ON?
JPM DAVIS 2-28
© 1997 PAWS, INC./Distributed by Universal Press Syndicate

I'M PROUD OF YOU, GARFIELD
YOU STUCK TO YOUR DIET, AND ACTUALLY LOST A FEW POUNDS
I KNOW
AND I CAN'T WAIT TO FIND THOSE SUCKERS AGAIN!
JPM DAVIS 3-1
© 1997 PAWS, INC./Distributed by Universal Press Syndicate

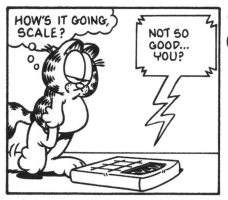

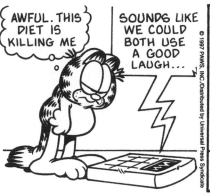

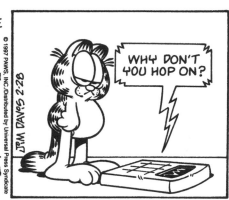

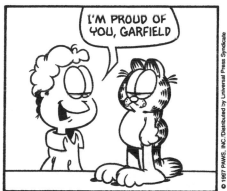

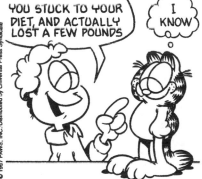

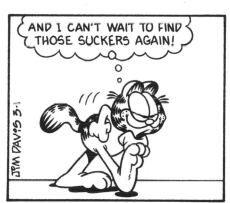

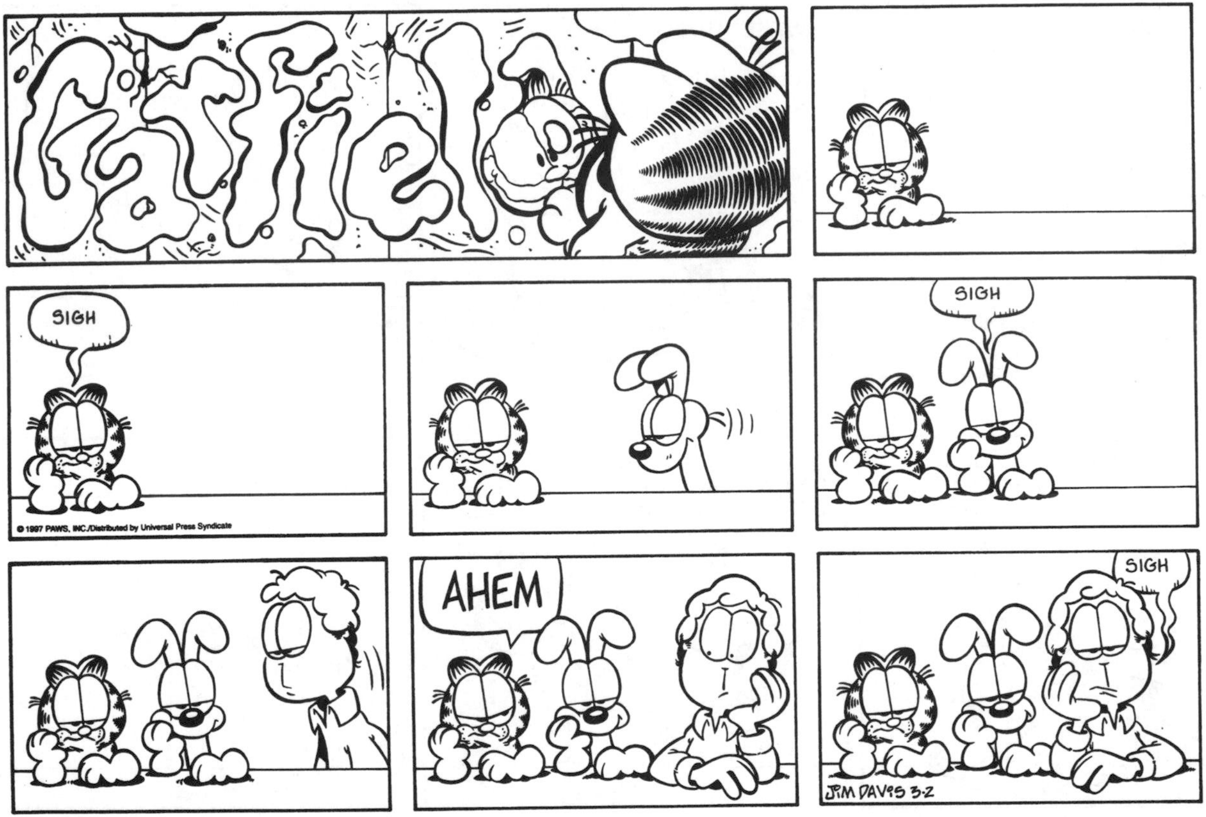

GARFIELD
SIGH
SIGH
AHEM
SIGH
JIM DAVIS 3-2

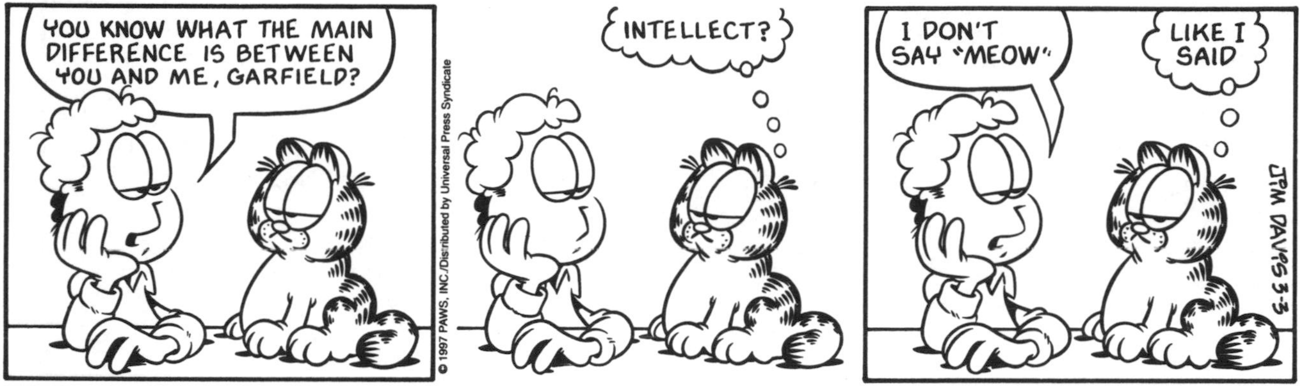
YOU KNOW WHAT THE MAIN DIFFERENCE IS BETWEEN YOU AND ME, GARFIELD?
© 1997 PAWS, INC./Distributed by Universal Press Syndicate
INTELLECT?
I DON'T SAY "MEOW"
LIKE I SAID
JIM DAVIS 3-3

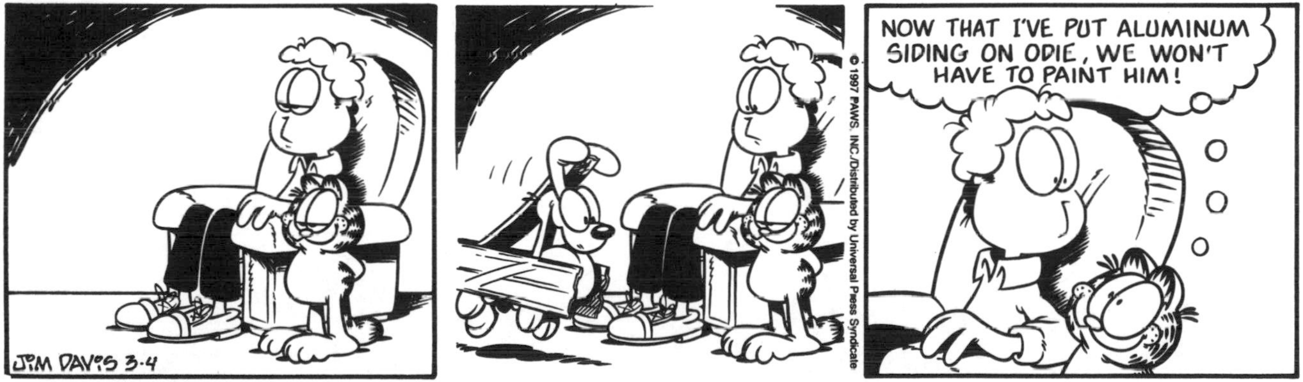
JIM DAVIS 3-4
© 1997 PAWS, INC./Distributed by Universal Press Syndicate
NOW THAT I'VE PUT ALUMINUM SIDING ON ODIE, WE WON'T HAVE TO PAINT HIM!

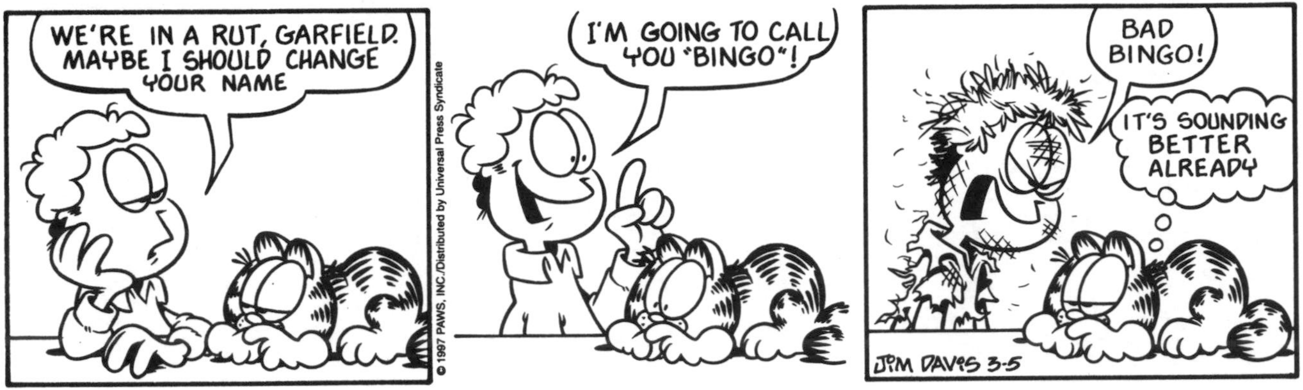
WE'RE IN A RUT, GARFIELD. MAYBE I SHOULD CHANGE YOUR NAME
I'M GOING TO CALL YOU "BINGO"!
BAD BINGO!
IT'S SOUNDING BETTER ALREADY
JIM DAVIS 3-5
© 1997 PAWS, INC./Distributed by Universal Press Syndicate

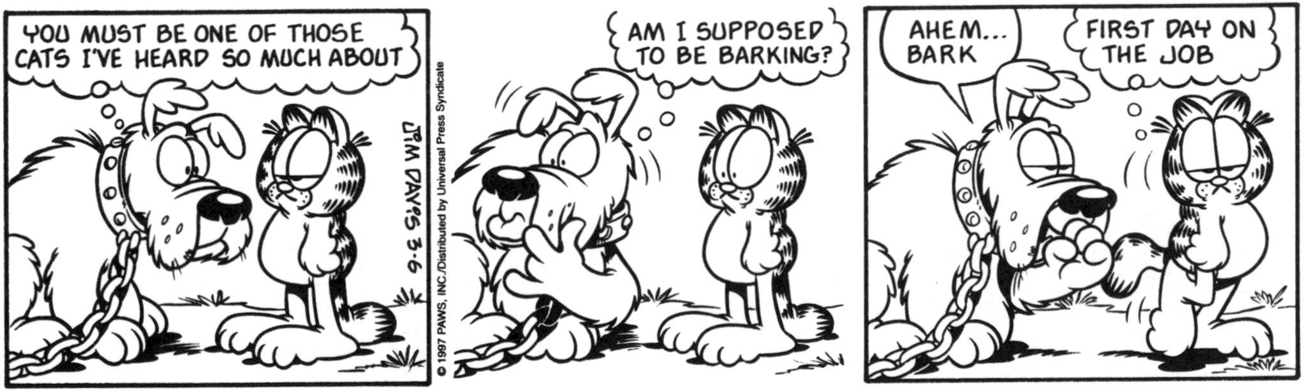
YOU MUST BE ONE OF THOSE CATS I'VE HEARD SO MUCH ABOUT
JIM DAVIS 3-6
AM I SUPPOSED TO BE BARKING?
AHEM... BARK
FIRST DAY ON THE JOB
© 1997 PAWS, INC./Distributed by Universal Press Syndicate

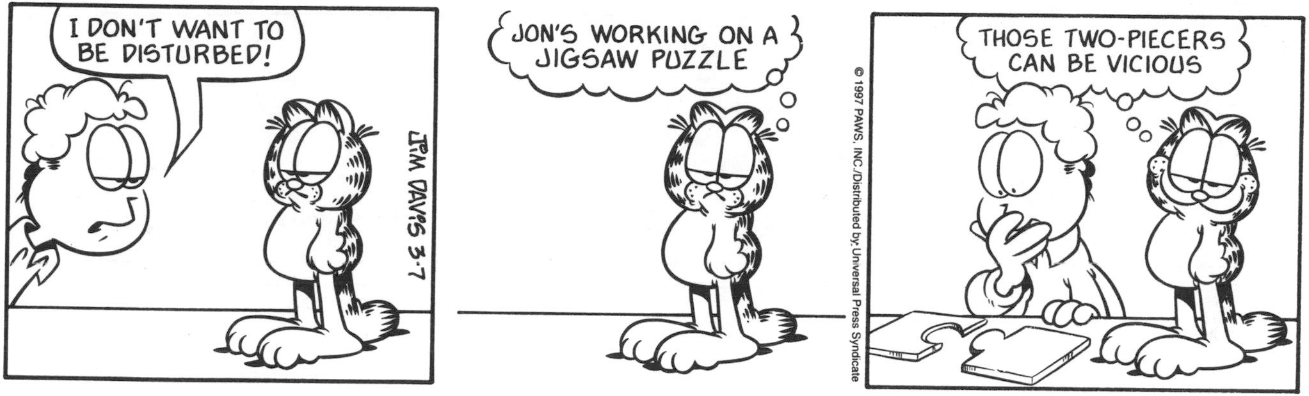
I DON'T WANT TO BE DISTURBED!
JIM DAVIS 3-7
JON'S WORKING ON A JIGSAW PUZZLE
THOSE TWO-PIECERS CAN BE VICIOUS
© 1997 PAWS, INC./Distributed by Universal Press Syndicate

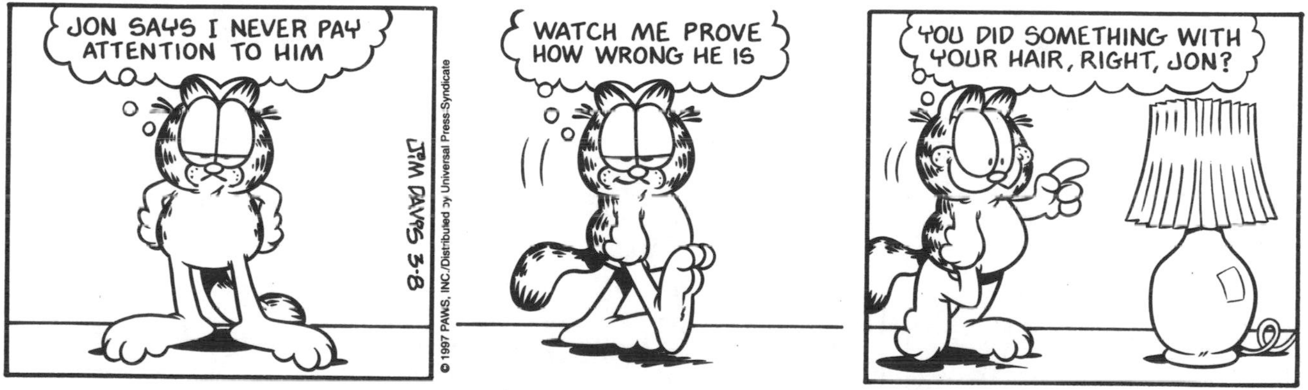
JON SAYS I NEVER PAY ATTENTION TO HIM
JIM DAVIS 3-8
© 1997 PAWS, INC./Distributed by Universal Press Syndicate
WATCH ME PROVE HOW WRONG HE IS
YOU DID SOMETHING WITH YOUR HAIR, RIGHT, JON?

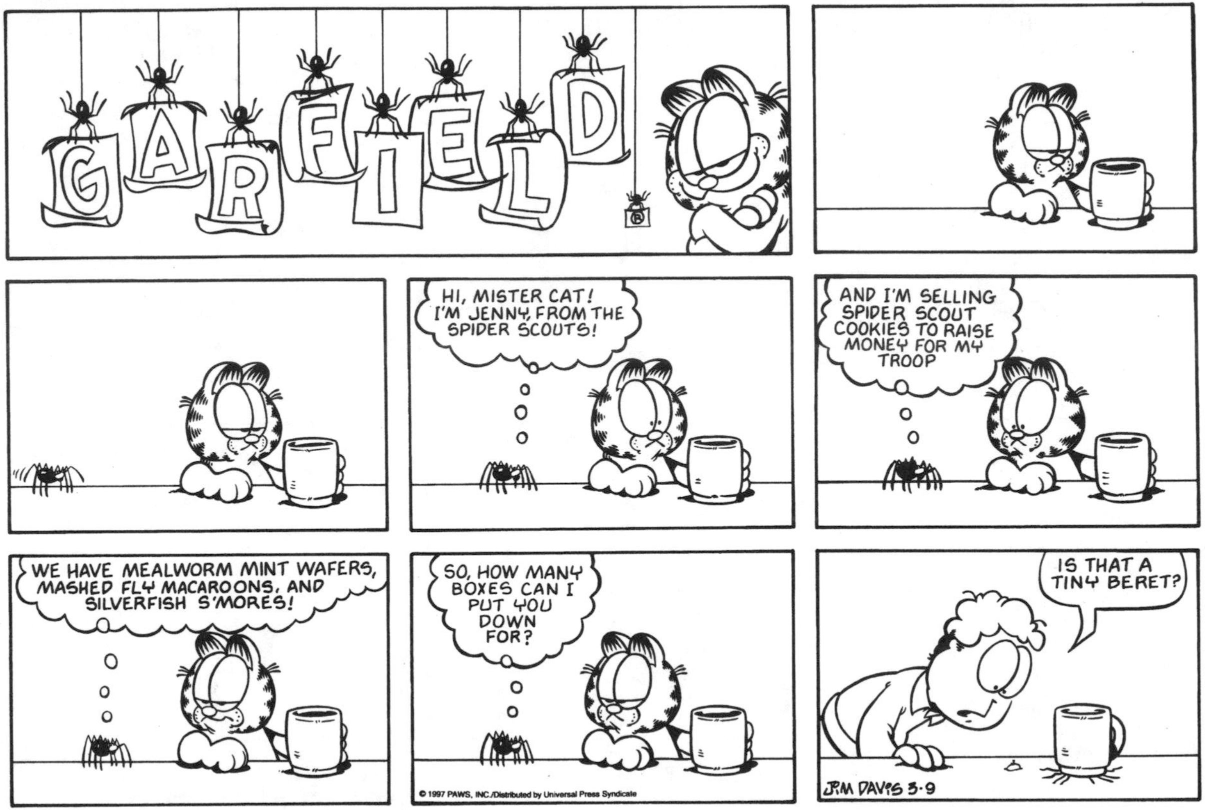
GARFIELD
®
HI, MISTER CAT! I'M JENNY, FROM THE SPIDER SCOUTS!
AND I'M SELLING SPIDER SCOUT COOKIES TO RAISE MONEY FOR MY TROOP
WE HAVE MEALWORM MINT WAFERS, MASHED FLY MACAROONS, AND SILVERFISH S'MORES!
SO, HOW MANY BOXES CAN I PUT YOU DOWN FOR?
© 1997 PAWS, INC./Distributed by Universal Press Syndicate
IS THAT A TINY BERET?
JIM DAVIS 3-9

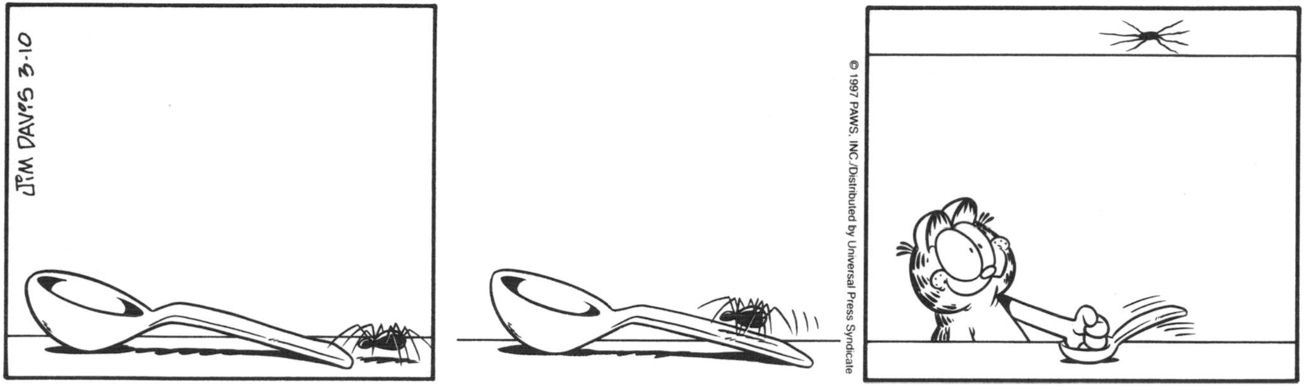
JIM DAVIS 3-10
© 1997 PAWS, INC./Distributed by Universal Press Syndicate

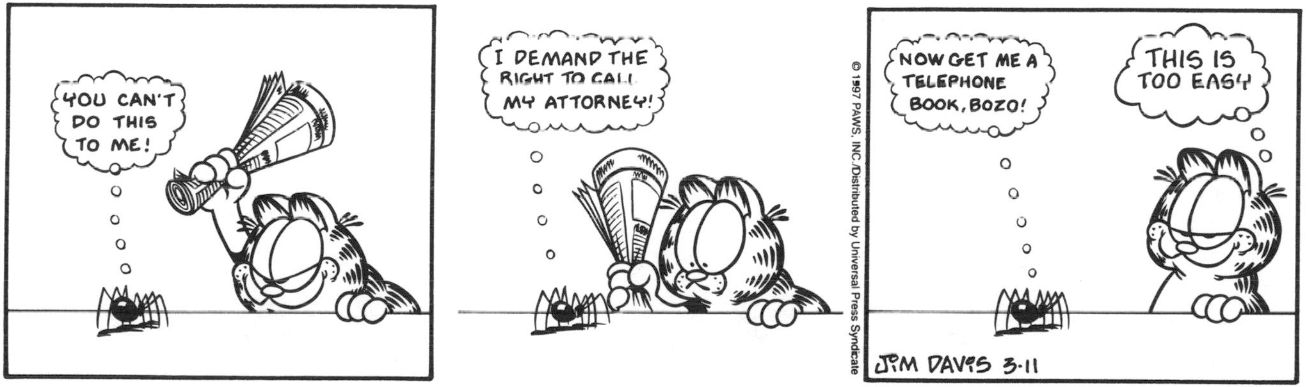
YOU CAN'T DO THIS TO ME!
I DEMAND THE RIGHT TO CALL MY ATTORNEY!
© 1997 PAWS, INC./Distributed by Universal Press Syndicate
NOW GET ME A TELEPHONE BOOK, BOZO!
THIS IS TOO EASY
JIM DAVIS 3-11

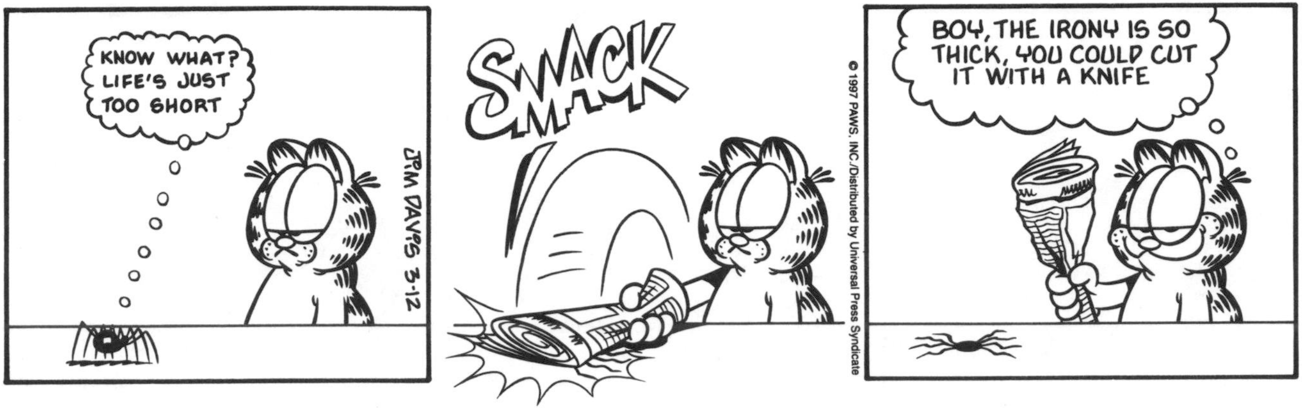
KNOW WHAT? LIFE'S JUST TOO SHORT
JIM DAVIS 3-12
SMACK
BOY, THE IRONY IS SO THICK, YOU COULD CUT IT WITH A KNIFE
© 1997 PAWS, INC./Distributed by Universal Press Syndicate

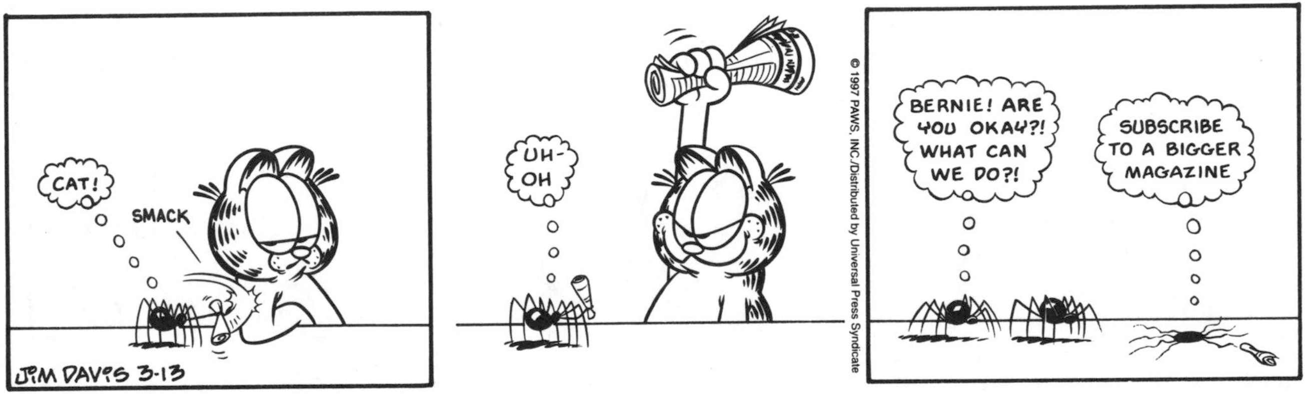
CAT!
SMACK
JIM DAVIS 3-13
UH-OH
© 1997 PAWS, INC./Distributed by Universal Press Syndicate
BERNIE! ARE YOU OKAY?! WHAT CAN WE DO?!
SUBSCRIBE TO A BIGGER MAGAZINE

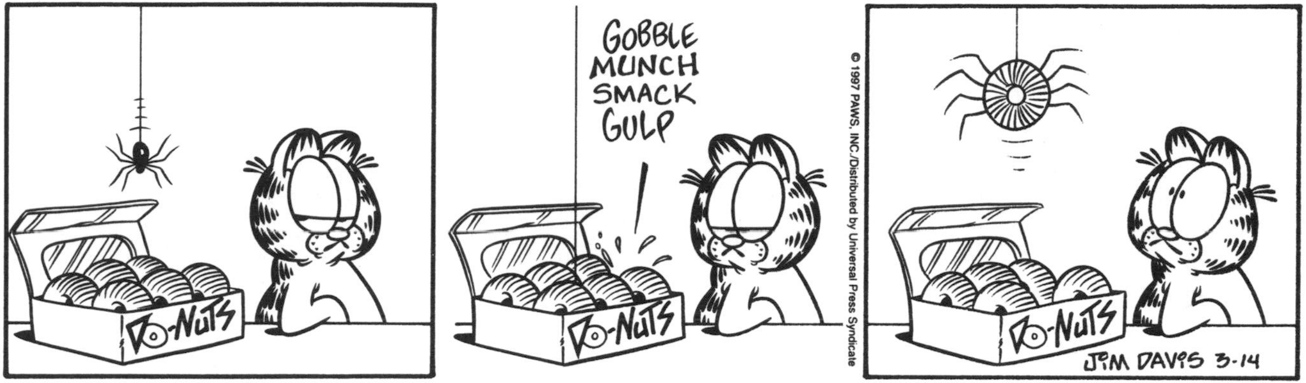
GOBBLE
MUNCH
SMACK
GULP
DO-NUTS
JIM DAVIS 3-14

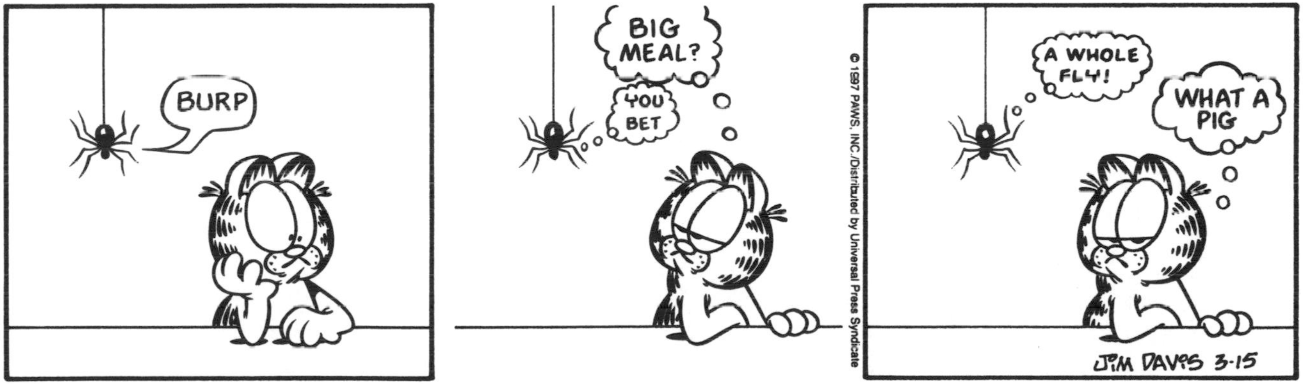
BURP
BIG MEAL?
YOU BET
A WHOLE FLY!
WHAT A PIG
JIM DAVIS 3-15

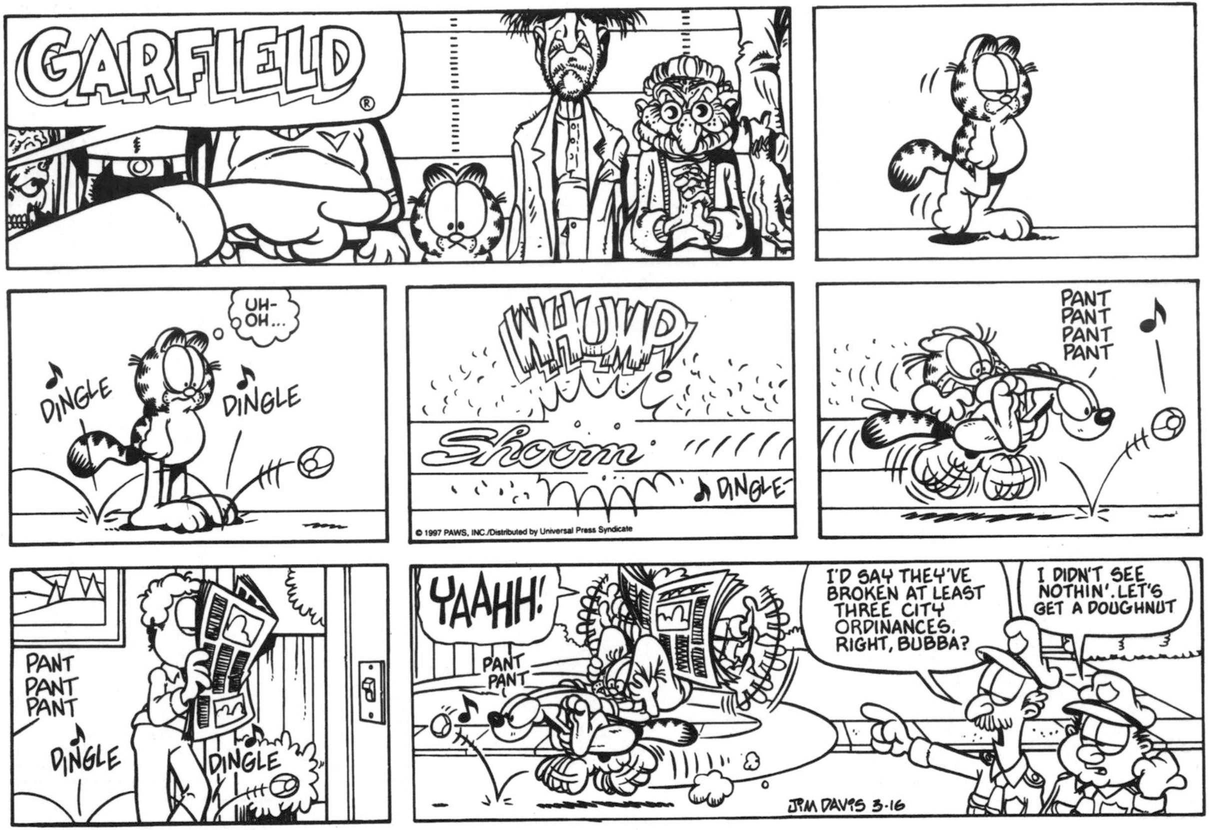
GARFIELD®
UH-OH...
DINGLE
DINGLE
WHUMP!
Shoom
DINGLE
© 1997 PAWS, INC./Distributed by Universal Press Syndicate
PANT PANT PANT PANT
PANT PANT PANT
DINGLE
DINGLE
YAAHH!
PANT PANT
I'D SAY THEY'VE BROKEN AT LEAST THREE CITY ORDINANCES. RIGHT, BUBBA?
I DIDN'T SEE NOTHIN'. LET'S GET A DOUGHNUT
JIM DAVIS 3-16

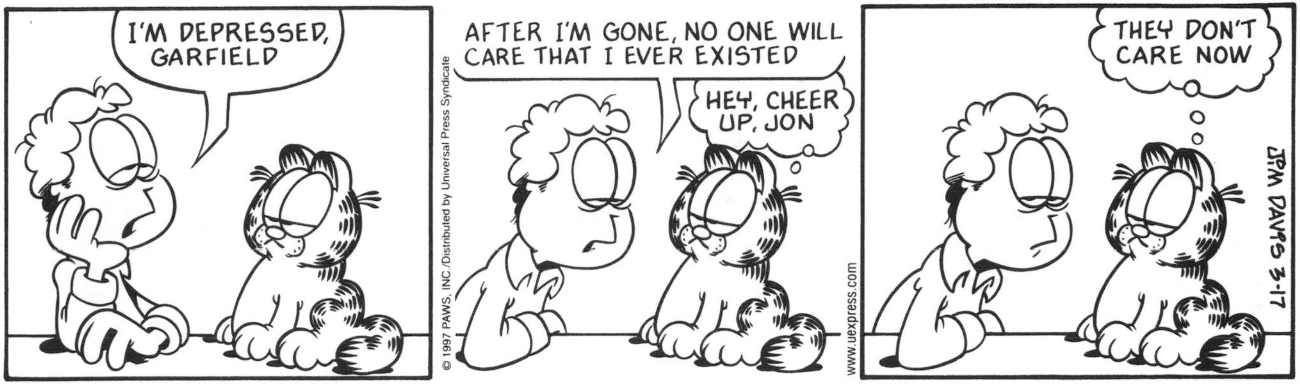
I'M DEPRESSED, GARFIELD
AFTER I'M GONE, NO ONE WILL CARE THAT I EVER EXISTED
HEY, CHEER UP, JON
THEY DON'T CARE NOW
© 1997 PAWS, INC./Distributed by Universal Press Syndicate
www.uexpress.com
JIM DAVIS 3-17

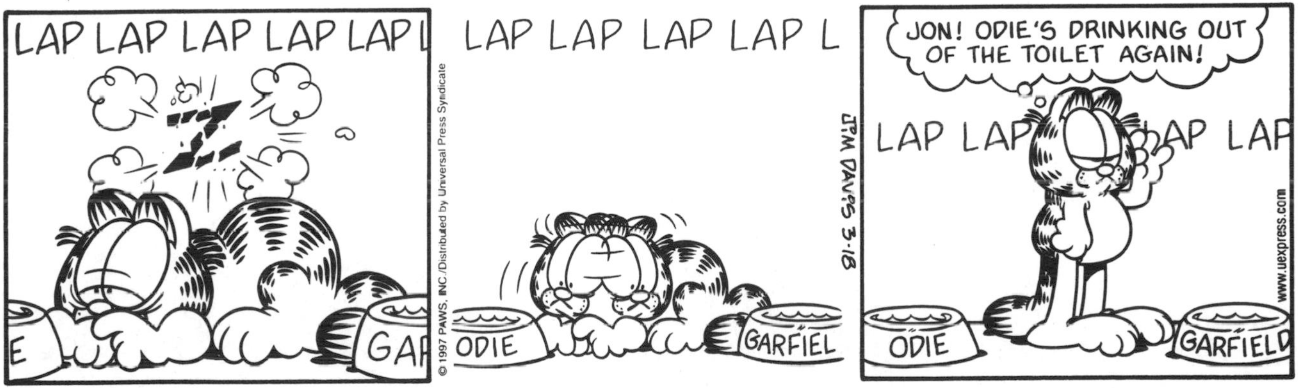
LAP LAP LAP LAP LAP L
Z
E
GA
LAP LAP LAP LAP L
ODIE
GARFIEL
JON! ODIE'S DRINKING OUT OF THE TOILET AGAIN!
LAP LAP LAP LAP
ODIE
GARFIELD
© 1997 PAWS, INC./Distributed by Universal Press Syndicate
www.uexpress.com
JIM DAVIS 3-18

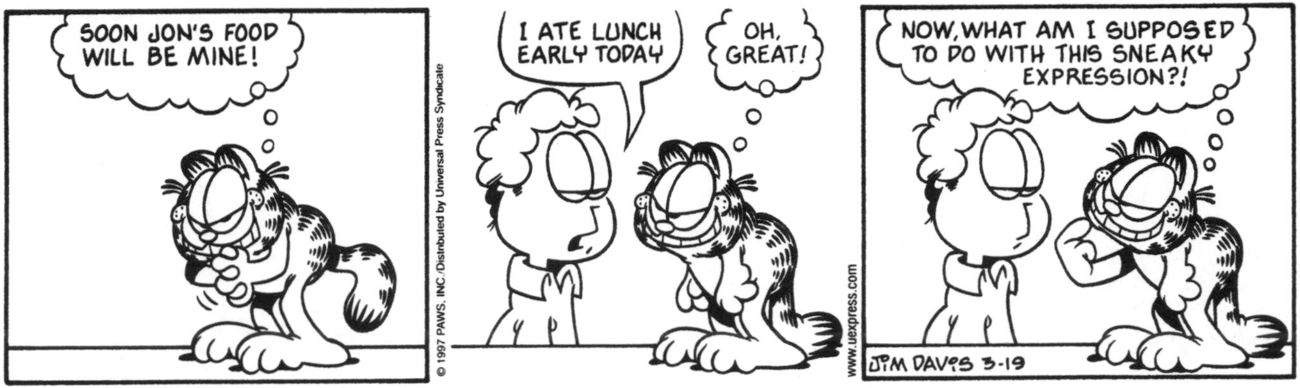
SOON JON'S FOOD WILL BE MINE!
I ATE LUNCH EARLY TODAY
OH, GREAT!
NOW, WHAT AM I SUPPOSED TO DO WITH THIS SNEAKY EXPRESSION?!
JIM DAVIS 3-19
© 1997 PAWS, INC./Distributed by Universal Press Syndicate
www.uexpress.com

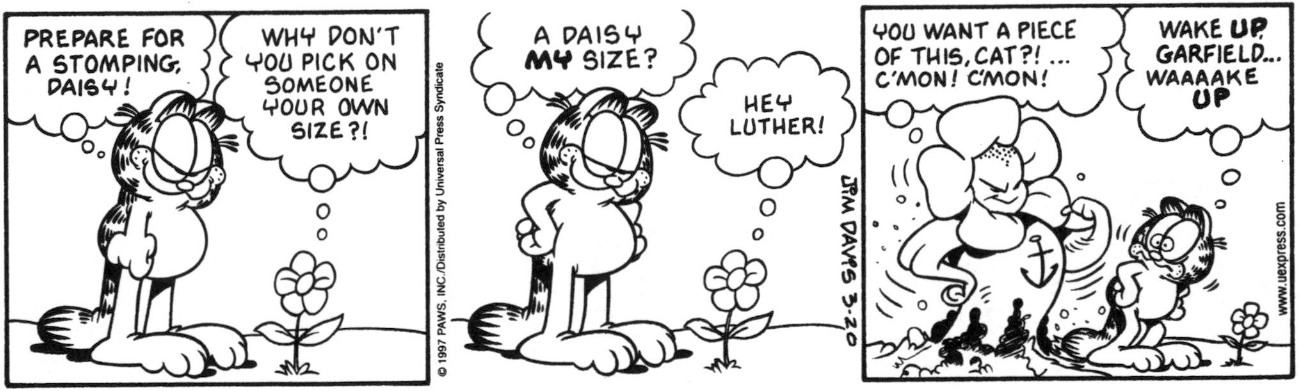
PREPARE FOR A STOMPING, DAISY!
WHY DON'T YOU PICK ON SOMEONE YOUR OWN SIZE?!
A DAISY **MY** SIZE?
HEY LUTHER!
YOU WANT A PIECE OF THIS, CAT?! ... C'MON! C'MON!
WAKE **UP**, GARFIELD... WAAAAKE **UP**
JIM DAVIS 3-20
© 1997 PAWS, INC./Distributed by Universal Press Syndicate
www.uexpress.com

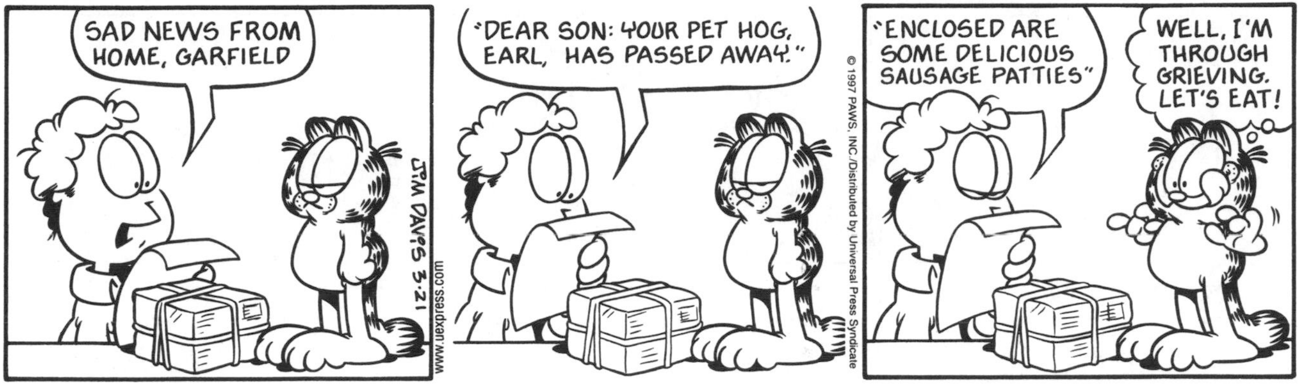
SAD NEWS FROM HOME, GARFIELD
JIM DAVIS 3-21
www.uexpress.com
"DEAR SON: YOUR PET HOG, EARL, HAS PASSED AWAY."
© 1997 PAWS, INC./Distributed by Universal Press Syndicate
"ENCLOSED ARE SOME DELICIOUS SAUSAGE PATTIES"
WELL, I'M THROUGH GRIEVING. LET'S EAT!

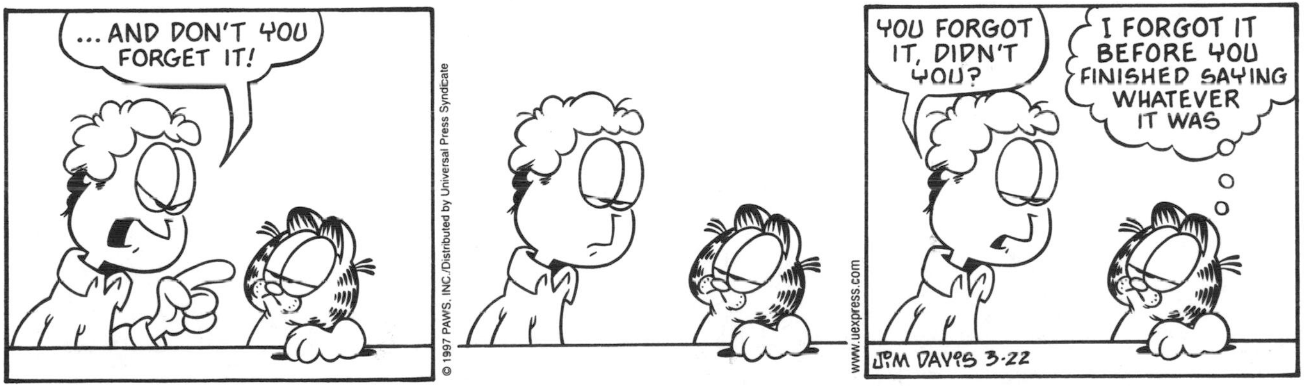
...AND DON'T YOU FORGET IT!
© 1997 PAWS, INC./Distributed by Universal Press Syndicate
www.uexpress.com
YOU FORGOT IT, DIDN'T YOU?
I FORGOT IT BEFORE YOU FINISHED SAYING WHATEVER IT WAS
JIM DAVIS 3-22

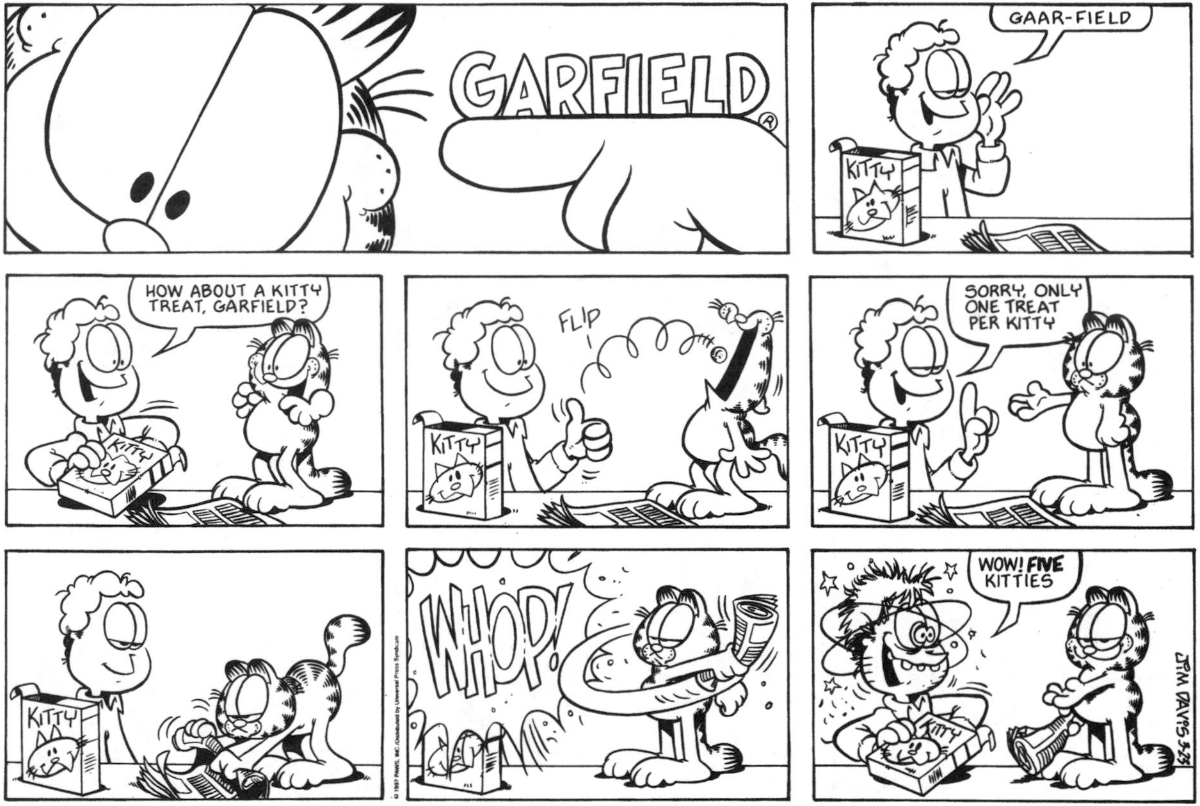
GARFIELD®
GAAR-FIELD
HOW ABOUT A KITTY TREAT, GARFIELD?
FLIP
SORRY, ONLY ONE TREAT PER KITTY
WHOP!
WOW! **FIVE** KITTIES
JIM DAVIS 3-23
© 1997 PAWS, INC./Distributed by Universal Press Syndicate

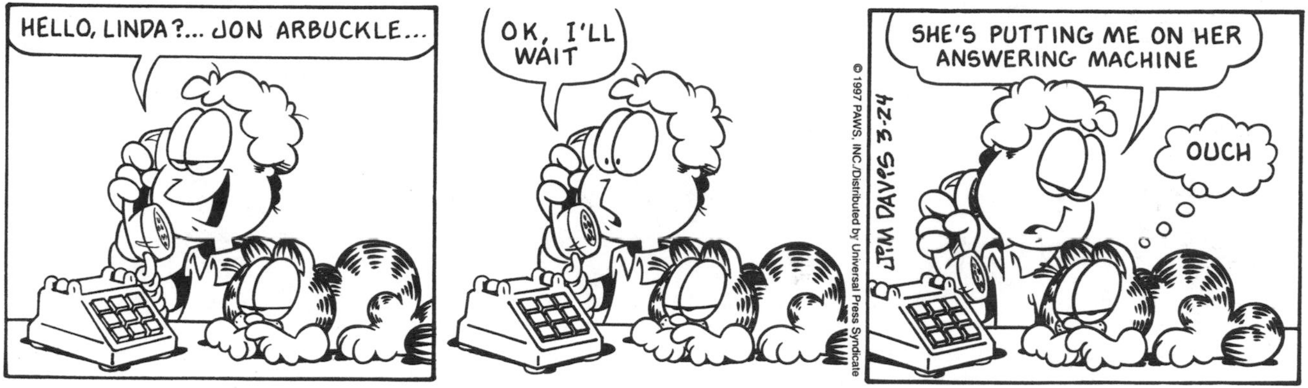
HELLO, LINDA?... JON ARBUCKLE...
OK, I'LL WAIT
JIM DAVIS 3-24
© 1997 PAWS, INC./Distributed by Universal Press Syndicate
SHE'S PUTTING ME ON HER ANSWERING MACHINE
OUCH

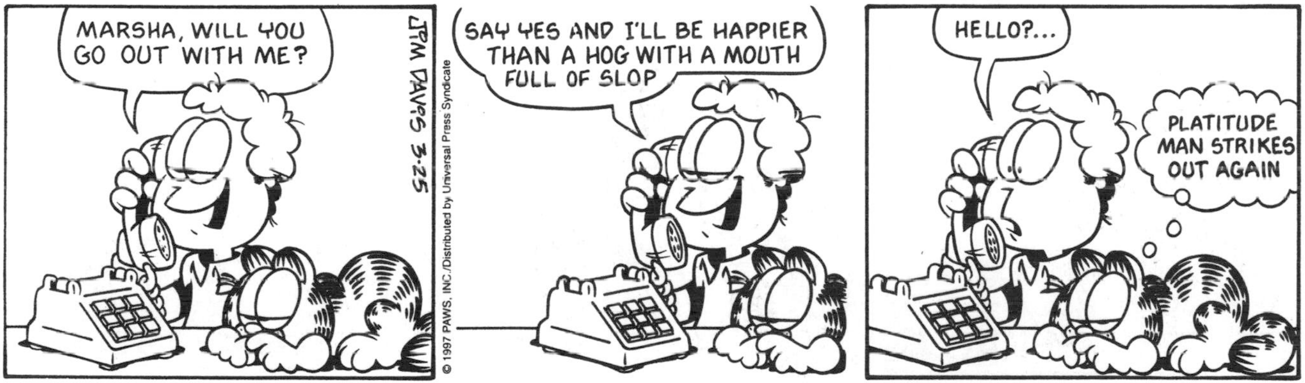
MARSHA, WILL YOU GO OUT WITH ME?
JIM DAVIS 3-25
© 1997 PAWS, INC./Distributed by Universal Press Syndicate
SAY YES AND I'LL BE HAPPIER THAN A HOG WITH A MOUTH FULL OF SLOP
HELLO?...
PLATITUDE MAN STRIKES OUT AGAIN

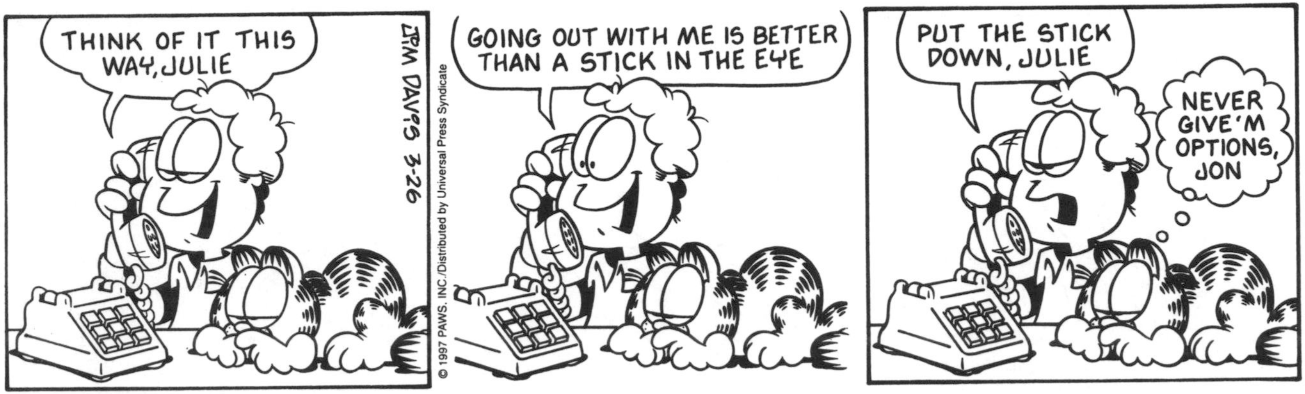
THINK OF IT THIS WAY, JULIE
JIM DAVIS 3-26
GOING OUT WITH ME IS BETTER THAN A STICK IN THE EYE
PUT THE STICK DOWN, JULIE
NEVER GIVE'M OPTIONS, JON

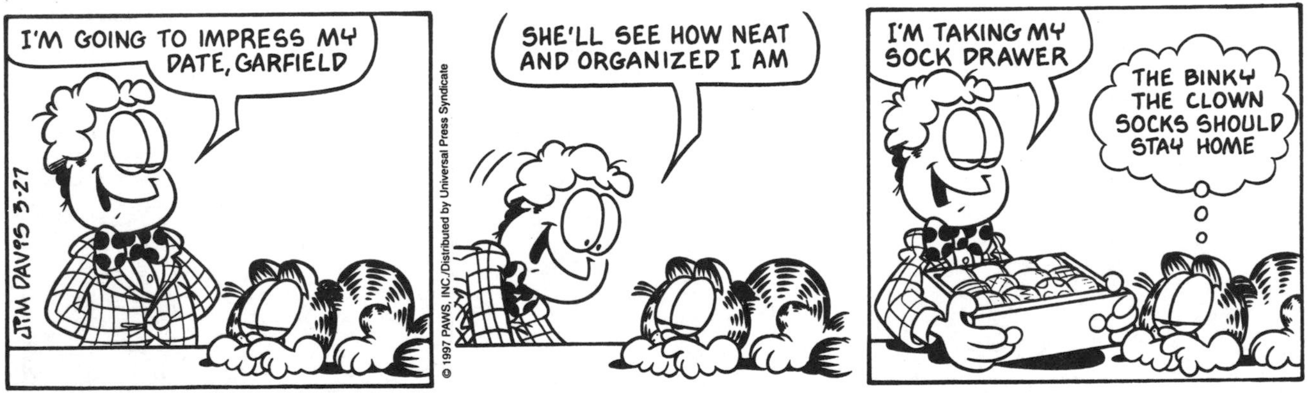
I'M GOING TO IMPRESS MY DATE, GARFIELD
JIM DAVIS 3-27
SHE'LL SEE HOW NEAT AND ORGANIZED I AM
I'M TAKING MY SOCK DRAWER
THE BINKY THE CLOWN SOCKS SHOULD STAY HOME

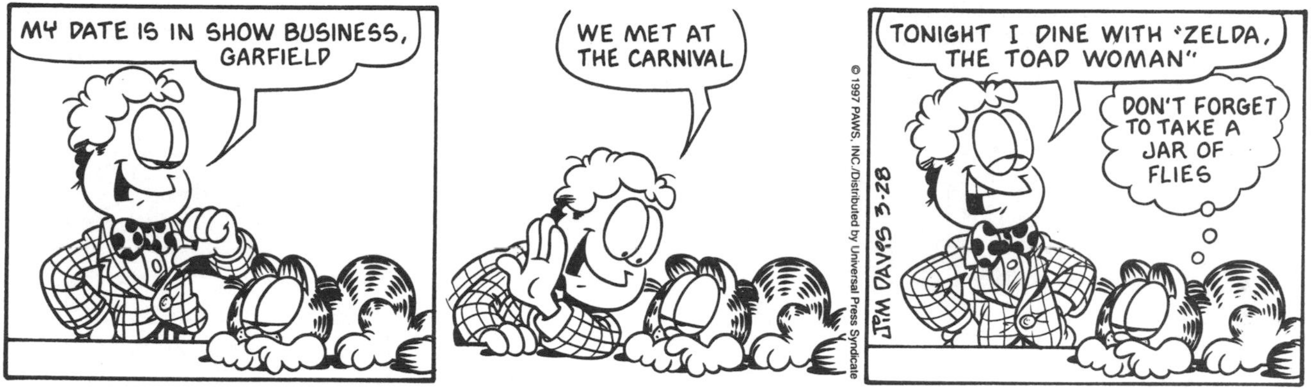
MY DATE IS IN SHOW BUSINESS, GARFIELD
WE MET AT THE CARNIVAL
TONIGHT I DINE WITH "ZELDA, THE TOAD WOMAN"
DON'T FORGET TO TAKE A JAR OF FLIES
JIM DAVIS 3-28
© 1997 PAWS, INC./Distributed by Universal Press Syndicate

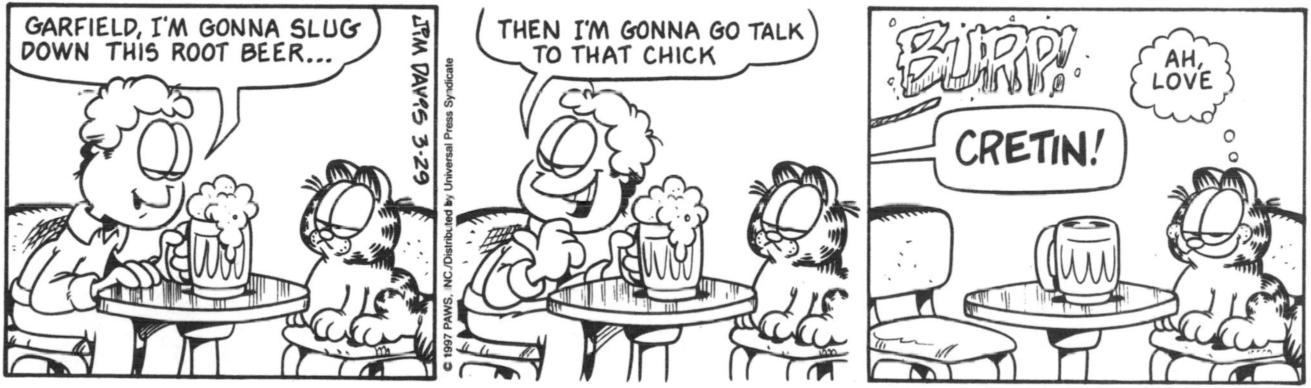
GARFIELD, I'M GONNA SLUG DOWN THIS ROOT BEER...
JIM DAVIS 3-29
© 1997 PAWS, INC./Distributed by Universal Press Syndicate
THEN I'M GONNA GO TALK TO THAT CHICK
BURP!
CRETIN!
AH, LOVE

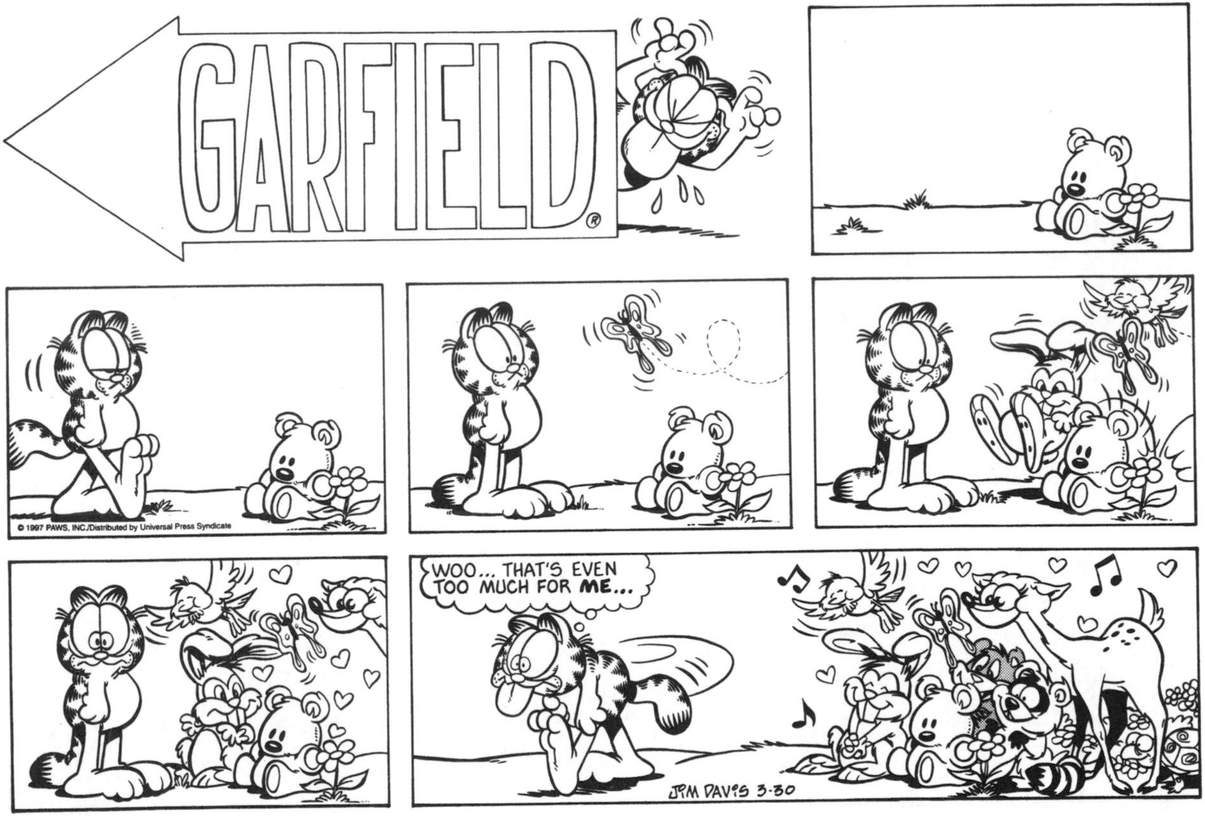
GARFIELD®
© 1997 PAWS, INC./Distributed by Universal Press Syndicate
WOO... THAT'S EVEN TOO MUCH FOR **ME**...
JIM DAVIS 3-30

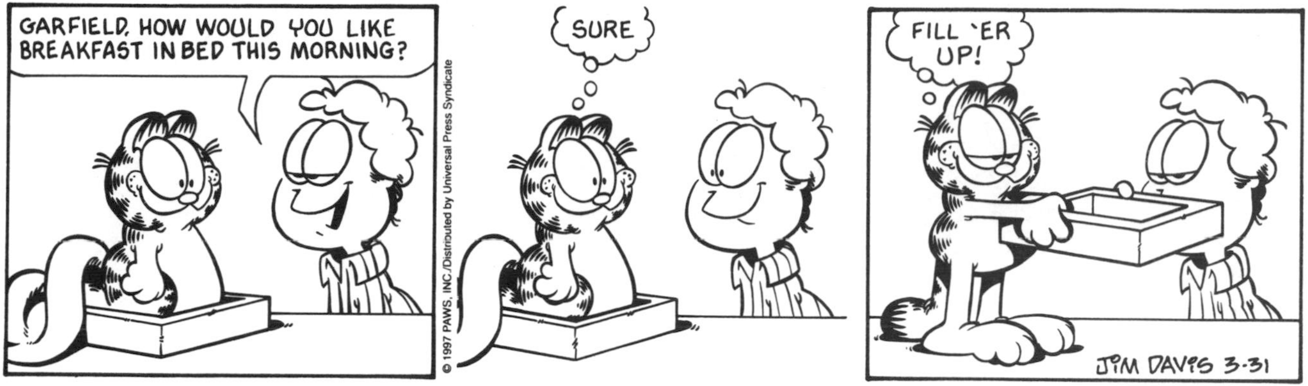
GARFIELD, HOW WOULD YOU LIKE BREAKFAST IN BED THIS MORNING?
SURE
FILL 'ER UP!
© 1997 PAWS, INC./Distributed by Universal Press Syndicate
JIM DAVIS 3-31

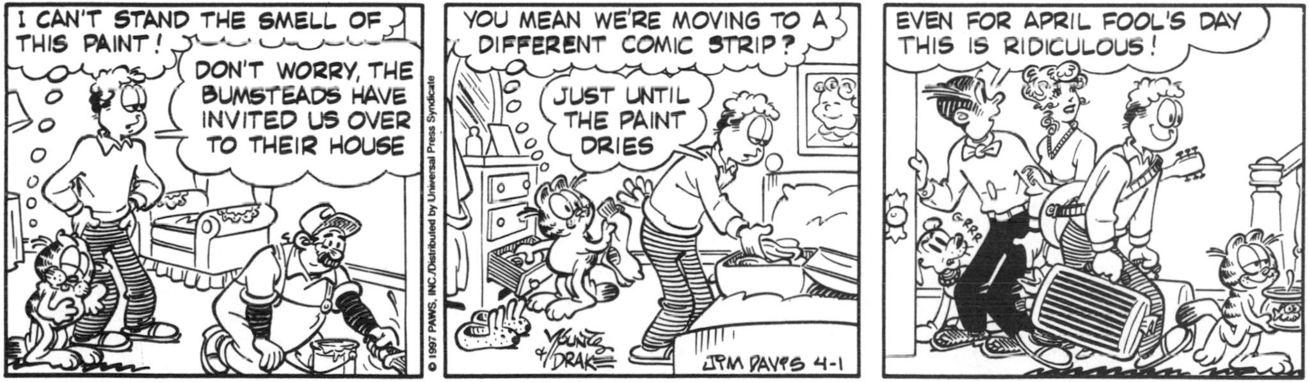
I CAN'T STAND THE SMELL OF THIS PAINT!
DON'T WORRY, THE BUMSTEADS HAVE INVITED US OVER TO THEIR HOUSE
YOU MEAN WE'RE MOVING TO A DIFFERENT COMIC STRIP?
JUST UNTIL THE PAINT DRIES
EVEN FOR APRIL FOOL'S DAY THIS IS RIDICULOUS!
GRRR
YOUNG & DRAKE
© 1997 PAWS, INC./Distributed by Universal Press Syndicate
JIM DAVIS 4-1

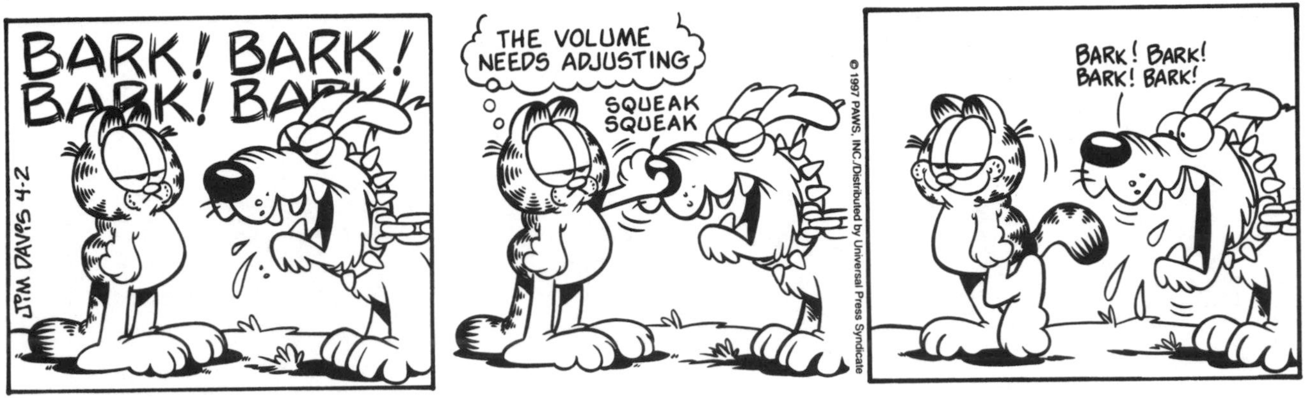
BARK! BARK! BARK! BARK!
JIM DAVIS 4-2
THE VOLUME NEEDS ADJUSTING
SQUEAK SQUEAK
© 1997 PAWS, INC./Distributed by Universal Press Syndicate
BARK! BARK! BARK! BARK!

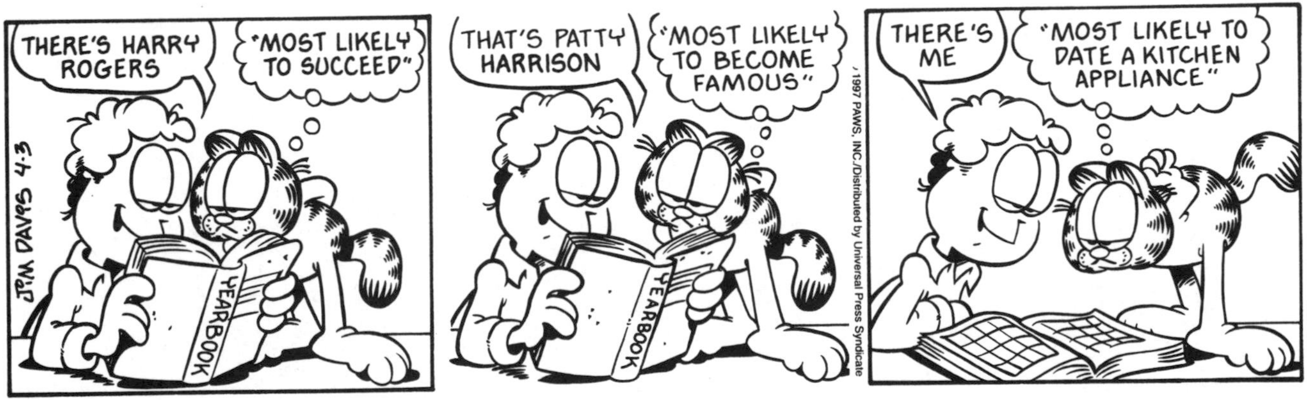
THERE'S HARRY ROGERS
"MOST LIKELY TO SUCCEED"
JIM DAVIS 4-3
YEARBOOK
THAT'S PATTY HARRISON
"MOST LIKELY TO BECOME FAMOUS"
YEARBOOK
© 1997 PAWS, INC./Distributed by Universal Press Syndicate
THERE'S ME
"MOST LIKELY TO DATE A KITCHEN APPLIANCE"

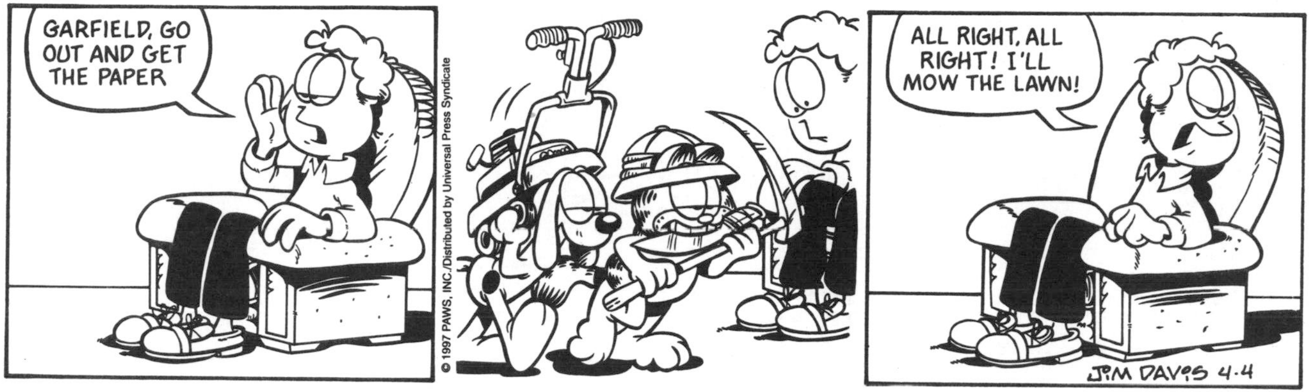
GARFIELD, GO OUT AND GET THE PAPER
© 1997 PAWS, INC./Distributed by Universal Press Syndicate
ALL RIGHT, ALL RIGHT! I'LL MOW THE LAWN!
JIM DAVIS 4-4

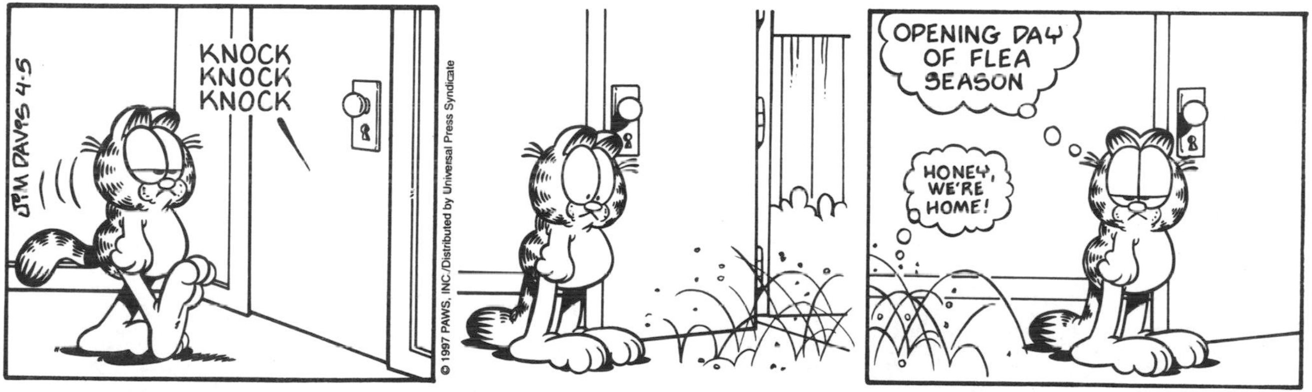
JIM DAVIS 4-5
KNOCK KNOCK KNOCK
© 1997 PAWS, INC./Distributed by Universal Press Syndicate
OPENING DAY OF FLEA SEASON
HONEY, WE'RE HOME!

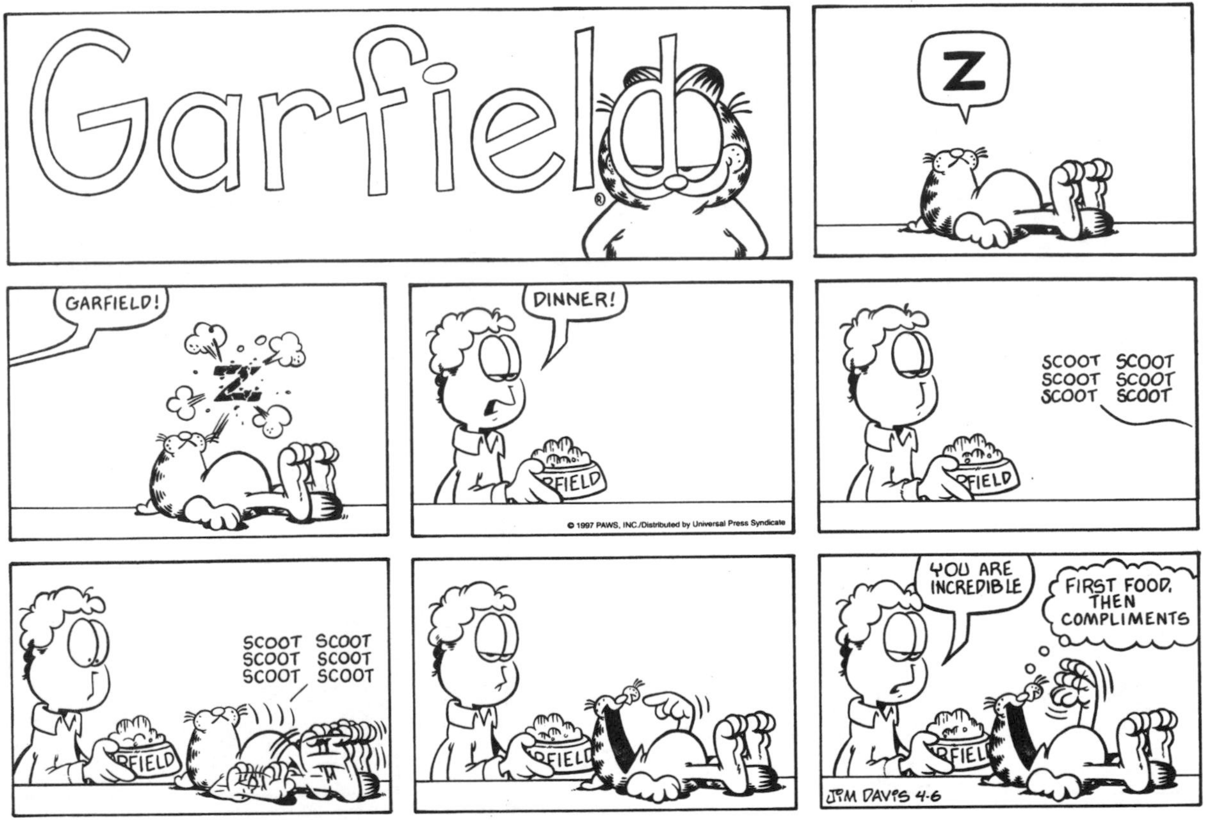
Garfield®
Z
GARFIELD!
Z
DINNER!
GARFIELD
© 1997 PAWS, INC./Distributed by Universal Press Syndicate
SCOOT SCOOT
SCOOT SCOOT
SCOOT SCOOT
RFIELD
SCOOT SCOOT
SCOOT SCOOT
SCOOT SCOOT
RFIELD
RFIELD
YOU ARE INCREDIBLE
FIRST FOOD, THEN COMPLIMENTS
RFIELD
JIM DAVIS 4-6

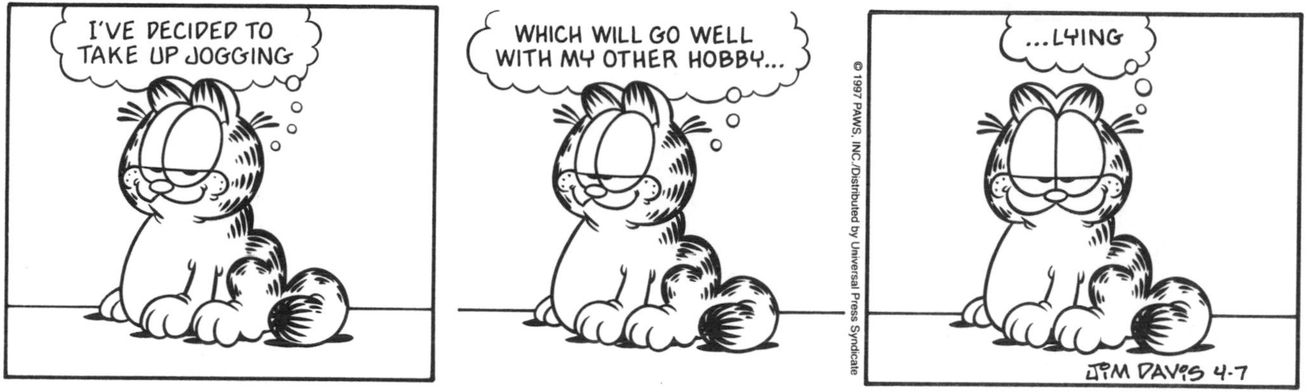
I'VE DECIDED TO TAKE UP JOGGING
WHICH WILL GO WELL WITH MY OTHER HOBBY...
...LYING
© 1997 PAWS, INC./Distributed by Universal Press Syndicate
JIM DAVIS 4-7

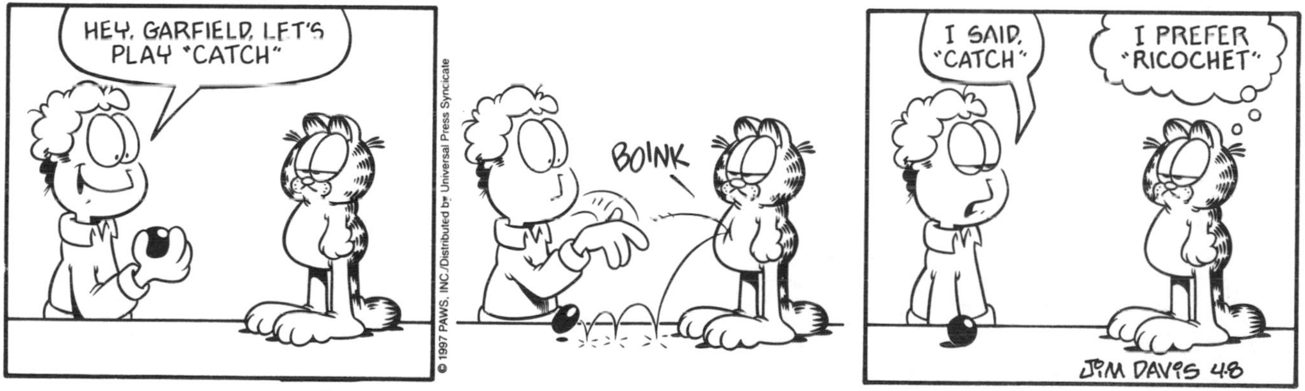
HEY, GARFIELD, LET'S PLAY "CATCH"
© 1997 PAWS, INC./Distributed by Universal Press Syndicate
BOINK
I SAID, "CATCH"
I PREFER "RICOCHET"
JIM DAVIS 4-8

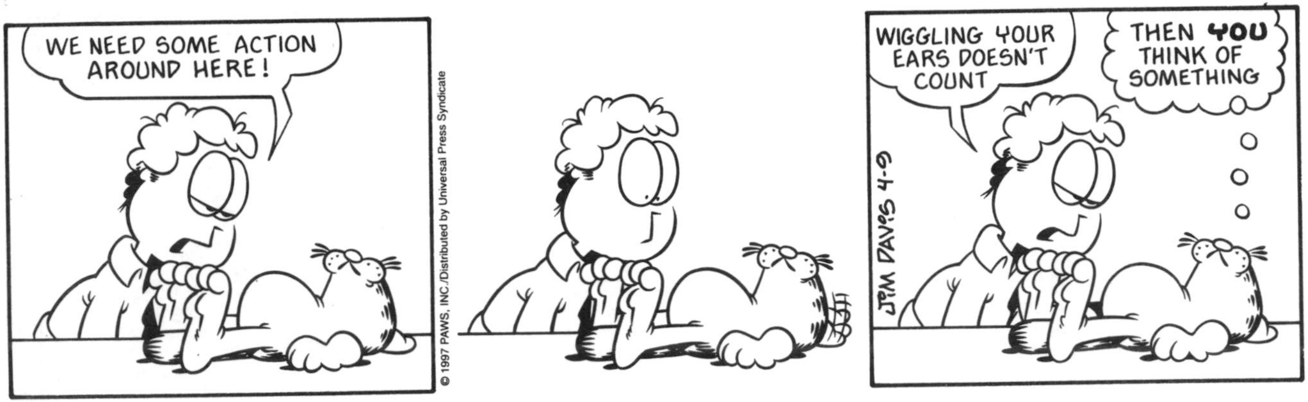
WE NEED SOME ACTION AROUND HERE!
© 1997 PAWS, INC./Distributed by Universal Press Syndicate
WIGGLING YOUR EARS DOESN'T COUNT
THEN **YOU** THINK OF SOMETHING
JPM DAVIS 4-9

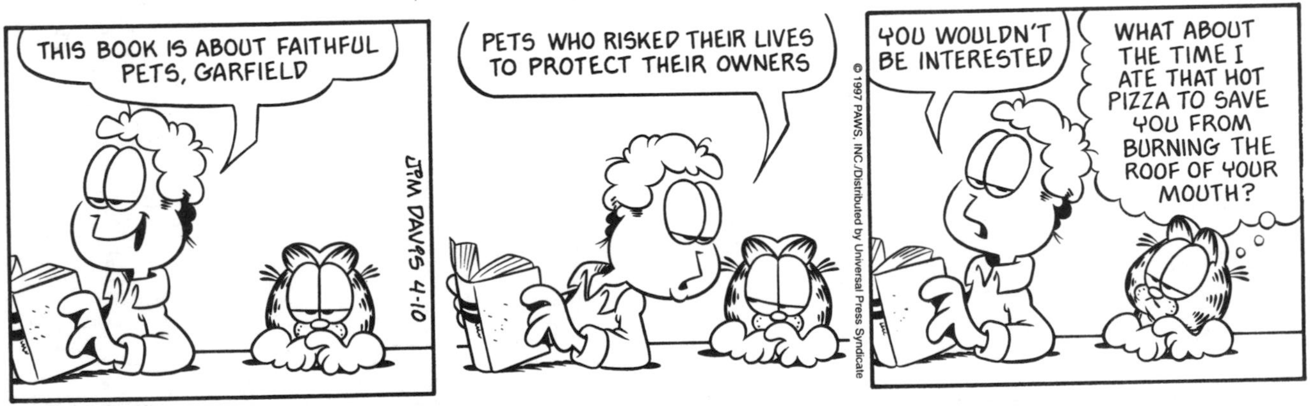
THIS BOOK IS ABOUT FAITHFUL PETS, GARFIELD
JPM DAVIS 4-10
PETS WHO RISKED THEIR LIVES TO PROTECT THEIR OWNERS
© 1997 PAWS, INC./Distributed by Universal Press Syndicate
YOU WOULDN'T BE INTERESTED
WHAT ABOUT THE TIME I ATE THAT HOT PIZZA TO SAVE YOU FROM BURNING THE ROOF OF YOUR MOUTH?

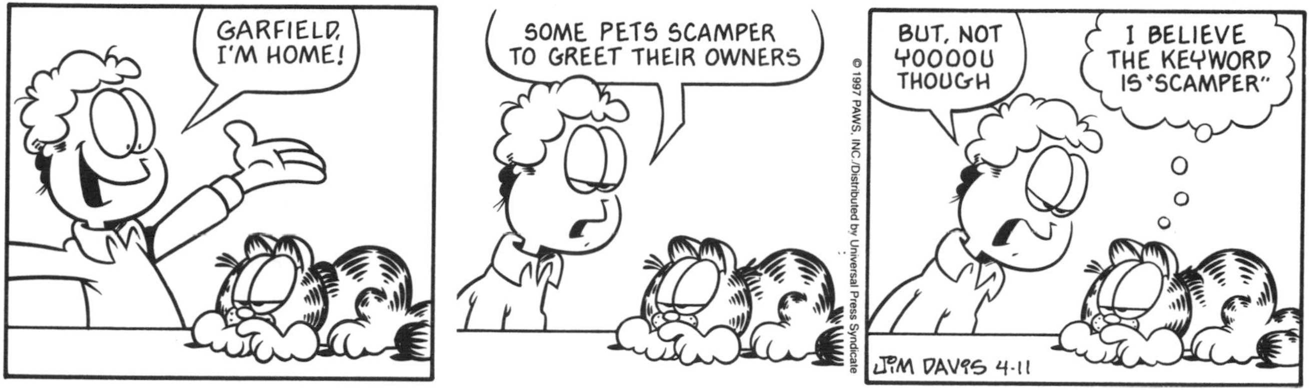
GARFIELD, I'M HOME!
SOME PETS SCAMPER TO GREET THEIR OWNERS
BUT, NOT YOOOOU THOUGH
I BELIEVE THE KEYWORD IS "SCAMPER"
© 1997 PAWS, INC./Distributed by Universal Press Syndicate
JIM DAVIS 4-11

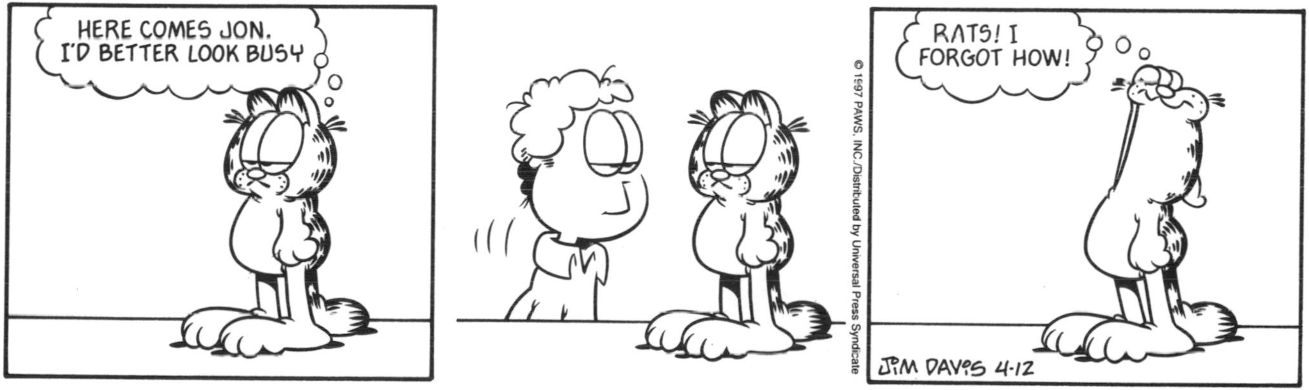
HERE COMES JON. I'D BETTER LOOK BUSY
RATS! I FORGOT HOW!
© 1997 PAWS, INC./Distributed by Universal Press Syndicate
JIM DAVIS 4-12

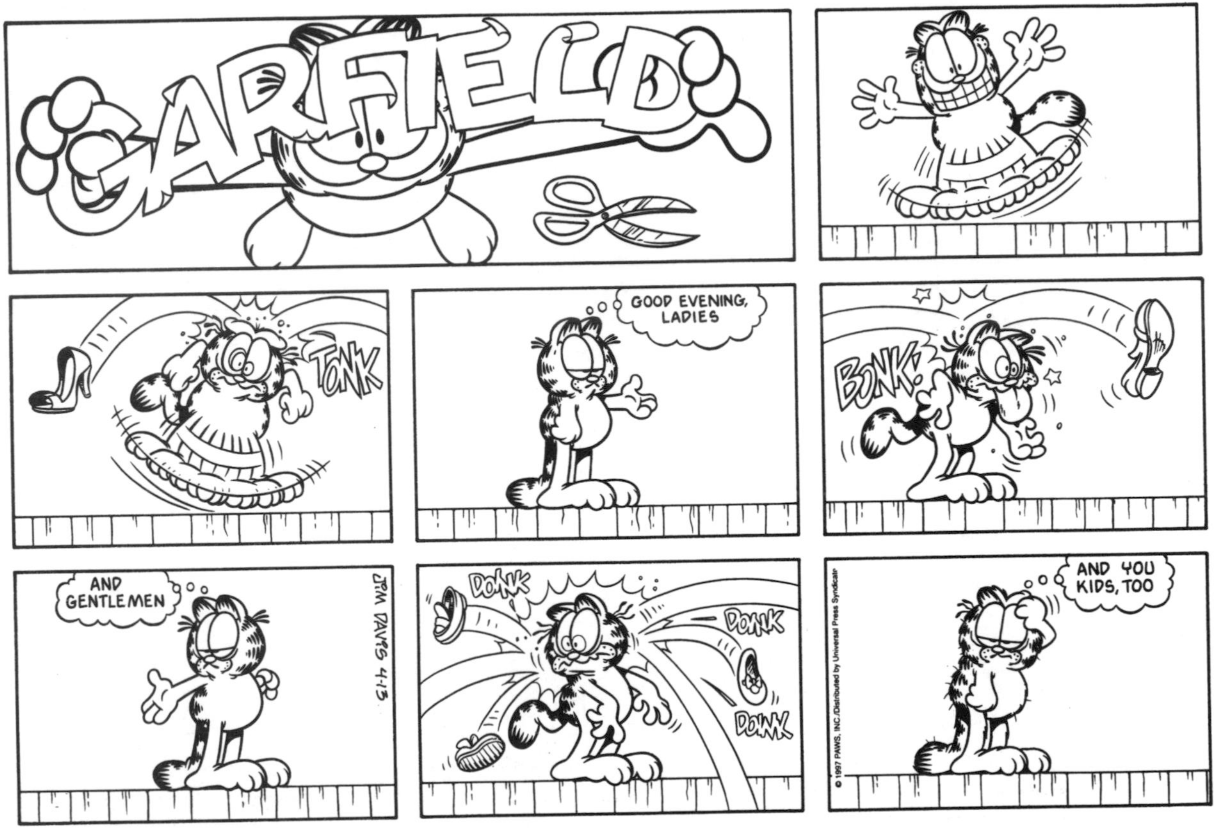
GARFIELD
TONK
GOOD EVENING, LADIES
BONK!
AND GENTLEMEN
JIM DAVIS 4-13
DONK
DONK
DONK
AND YOU KIDS, TOO
© 1997 PAWS, INC./Distributed by Universal Press Syndicate

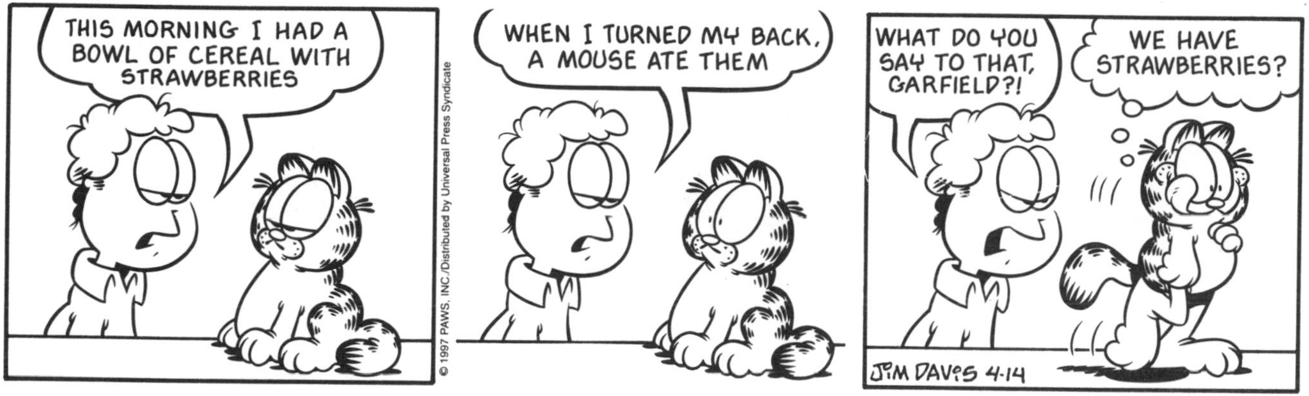
THIS MORNING I HAD A BOWL OF CEREAL WITH STRAWBERRIES
© 1997 PAWS, INC./Distributed by Universal Press Syndicate
WHEN I TURNED MY BACK, A MOUSE ATE THEM
WHAT DO YOU SAY TO THAT, GARFIELD?!
WE HAVE STRAWBERRIES?
JIM DAVIS 4-14

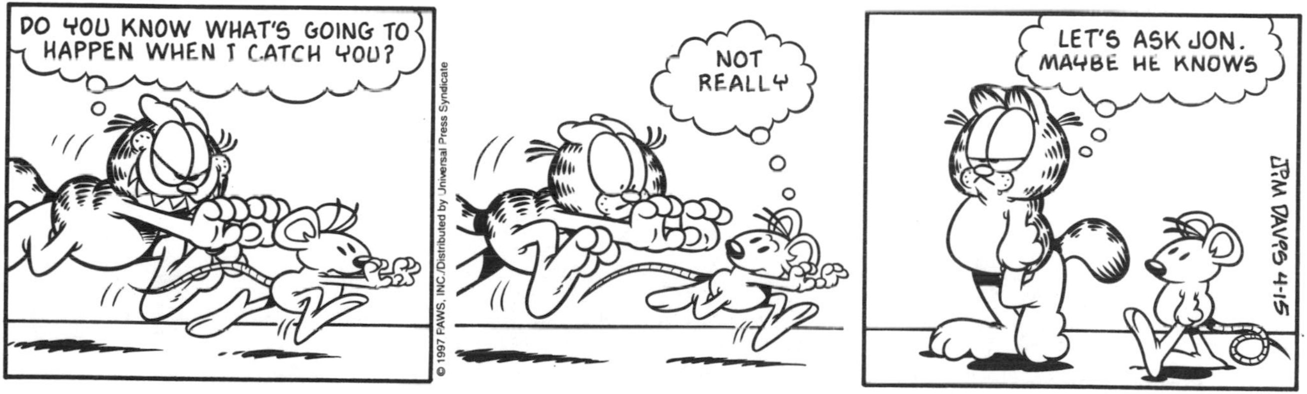
DO YOU KNOW WHAT'S GOING TO HAPPEN WHEN I CATCH YOU?
© 1997 PAWS, INC./Distributed by Universal Press Syndicate
NOT REALLY
LET'S ASK JON. MAYBE HE KNOWS
JIM DAVIS 4-15

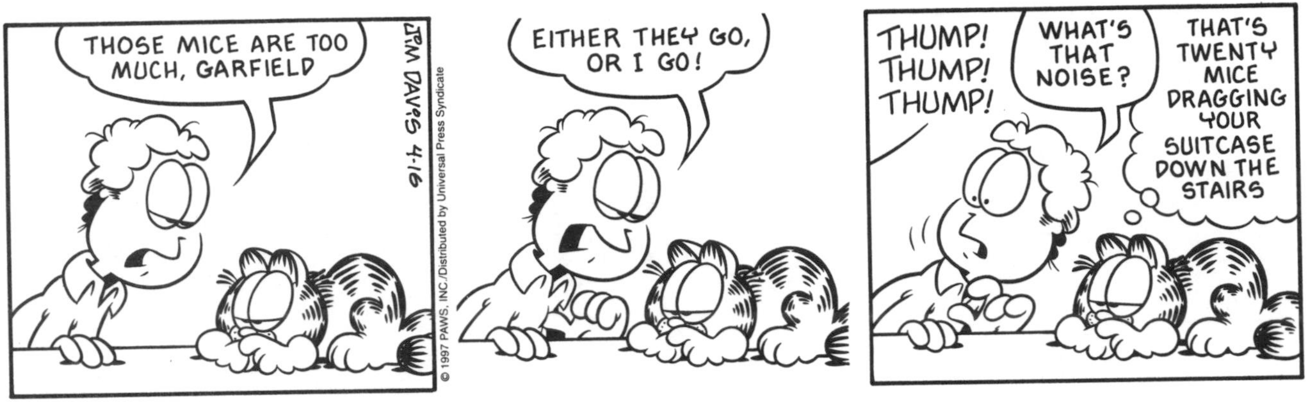
THOSE MICE ARE TOO MUCH, GARFIELD
JIM DAVIS 4-16
© 1997 PAWS, INC./Distributed by Universal Press Syndicate
EITHER THEY GO, OR I GO!
THUMP! THUMP! THUMP!
WHAT'S THAT NOISE?
THAT'S TWENTY MICE DRAGGING YOUR SUITCASE DOWN THE STAIRS

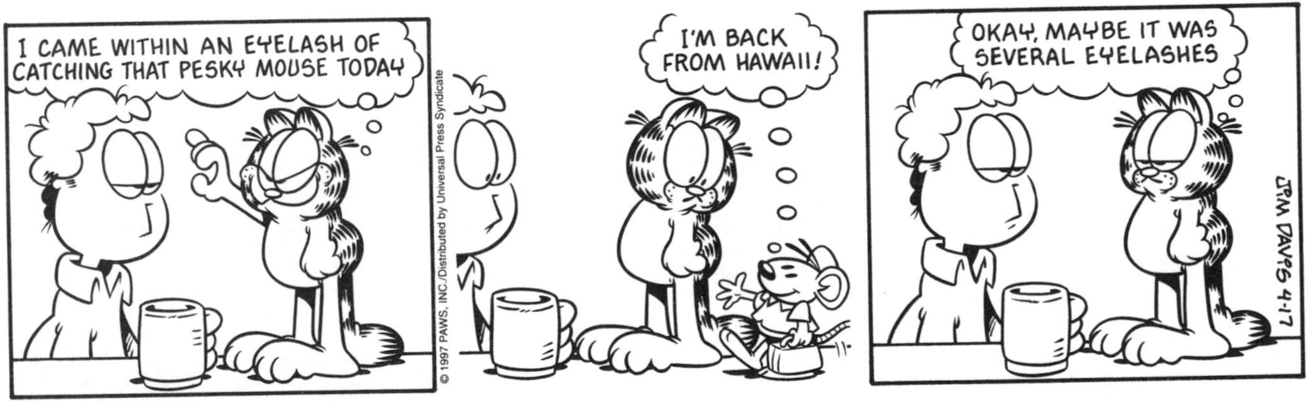
I CAME WITHIN AN EYELASH OF CATCHING THAT PESKY MOUSE TODAY
© 1997 PAWS, INC./Distributed by Universal Press Syndicate
I'M BACK FROM HAWAII!
OKAY, MAYBE IT WAS SEVERAL EYELASHES
JIM DAVIS 4-17

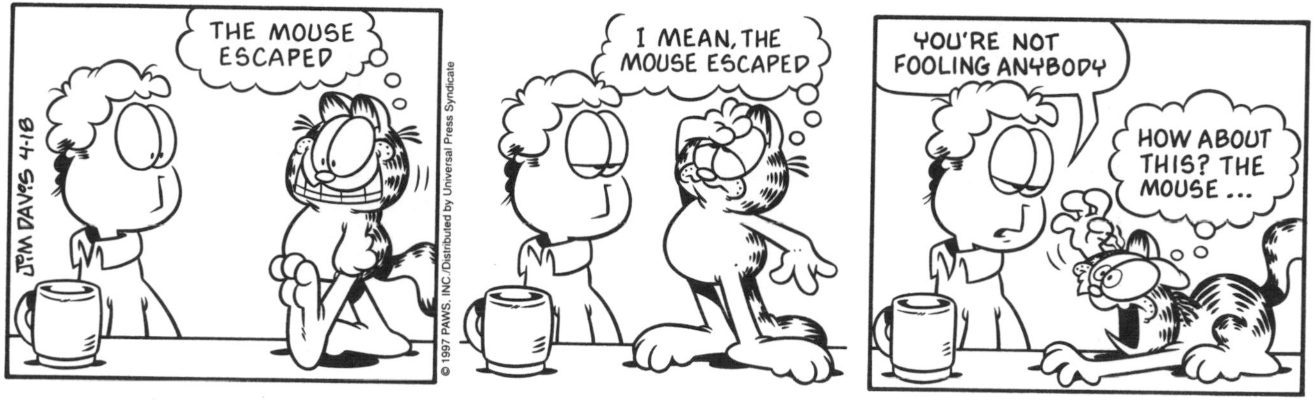
JIM DAVIS 4-18
THE MOUSE ESCAPED
I MEAN, THE MOUSE ESCAPED
YOU'RE NOT FOOLING ANYBODY
HOW ABOUT THIS? THE MOUSE ...
© 1997 PAWS, INC./Distributed by Universal Press Syndicate

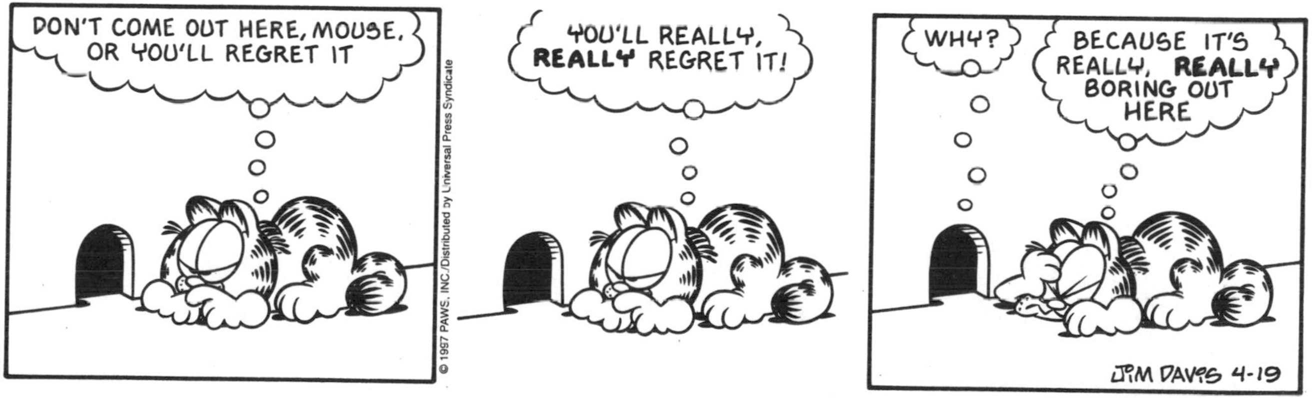
DON'T COME OUT HERE, MOUSE, OR YOU'LL REGRET IT
YOU'LL REALLY, **REALLY** REGRET IT!
WHY?
BECAUSE IT'S REALLY, **REALLY** BORING OUT HERE
JIM DAVIS 4-19
© 1997 PAWS, INC./Distributed by Universal Press Syndicate

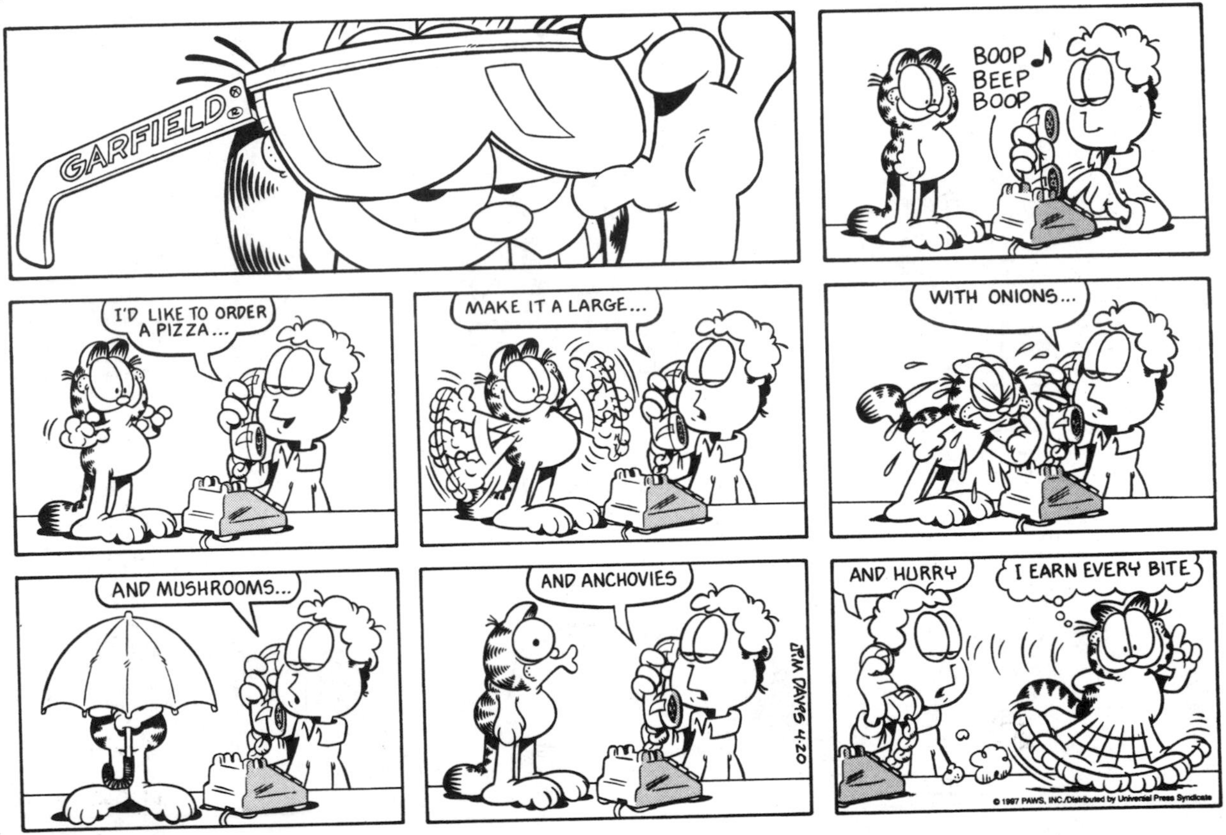
GARFIELD
BOOP BEEP BOOP
I'D LIKE TO ORDER A PIZZA...
MAKE IT A LARGE...
WITH ONIONS...
AND MUSHROOMS...
AND ANCHOVIES
JIM DAVIS 4-20
AND HURRY
I EARN EVERY BITE
© 1987 PAWS, INC./Distributed by Universal Press Syndicate

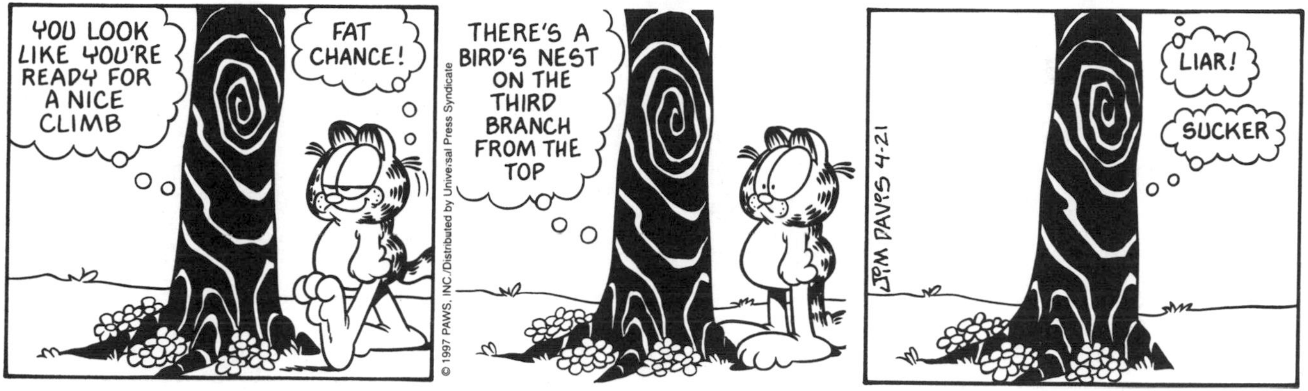
YOU LOOK LIKE YOU'RE READY FOR A NICE CLIMB
FAT CHANCE!
THERE'S A BIRD'S NEST ON THE THIRD BRANCH FROM THE TOP
LIAR!
SUCKER
JIM DAVIS 4-21
© 1997 PAWS, INC./Distributed by Universal Press Syndicate

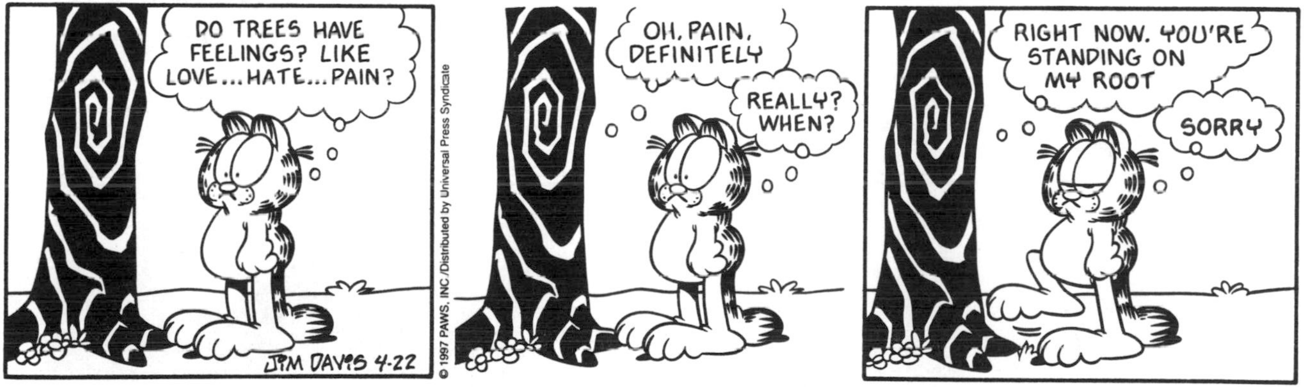
DO TREES HAVE FEELINGS? LIKE LOVE... HATE... PAIN?
OH, PAIN, DEFINITELY
REALLY? WHEN?
RIGHT NOW. YOU'RE STANDING ON MY ROOT
SORRY
JIM DAVIS 4-22
© 1997 PAWS, INC./Distributed by Universal Press Syndicate

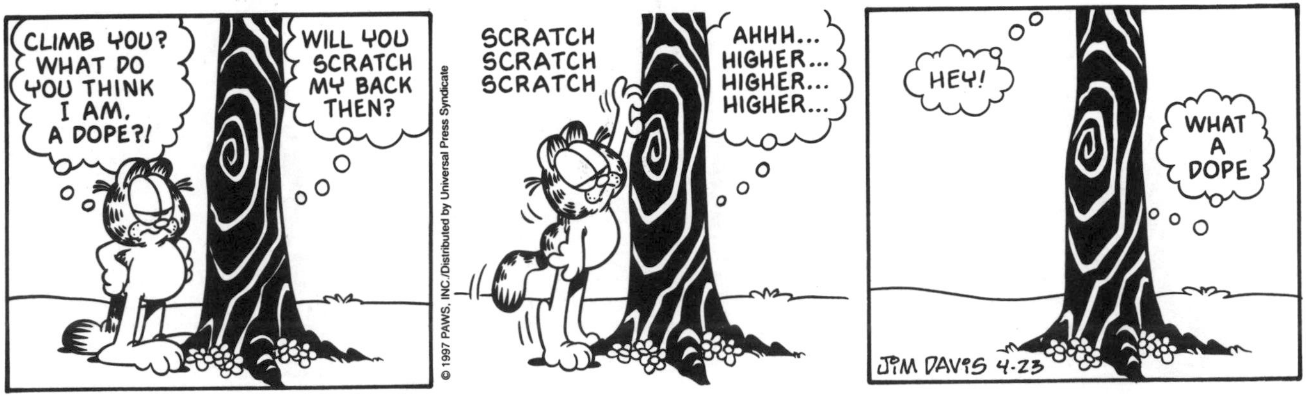
CLIMB YOU? WHAT DO YOU THINK I AM, A DOPE?!
WILL YOU SCRATCH MY BACK THEN?
SCRATCH SCRATCH SCRATCH
AHHH... HIGHER... HIGHER... HIGHER...
HEY!
WHAT A DOPE
JIM DAVIS 4-23

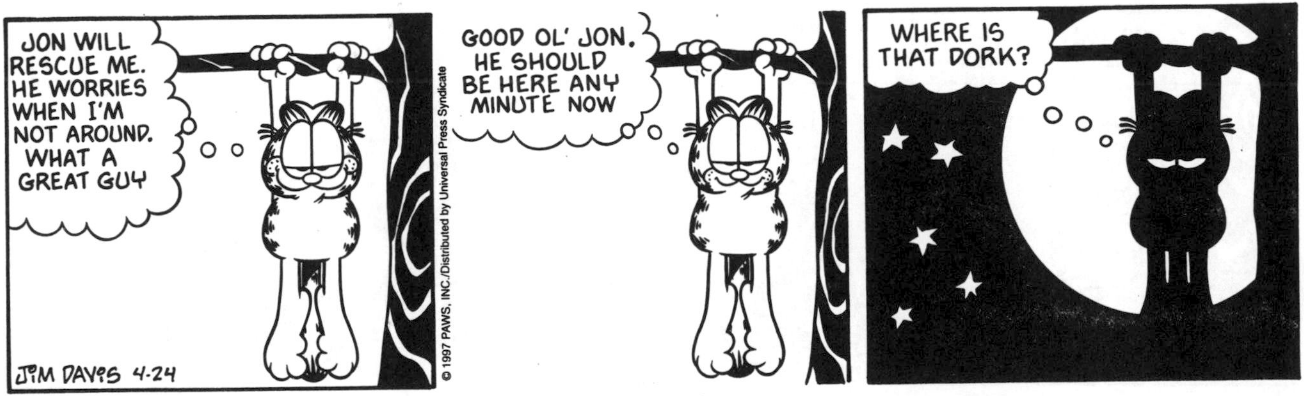
JON WILL RESCUE ME. HE WORRIES WHEN I'M NOT AROUND. WHAT A GREAT GUY
GOOD OL' JON. HE SHOULD BE HERE ANY MINUTE NOW
WHERE IS THAT DORK?
JIM DAVIS 4-24

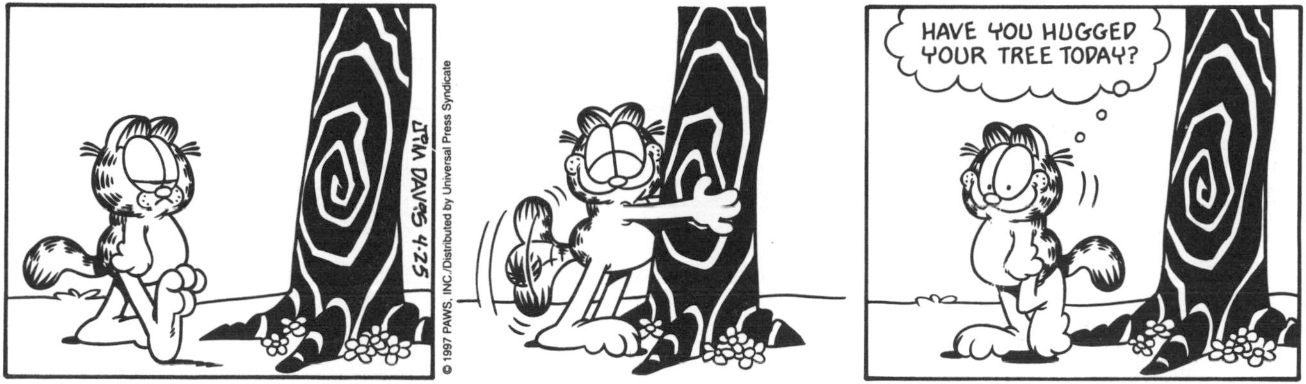
JIM DAVIS 4-25
© 1997 PAWS, INC./Distributed by Universal Press Syndicate
HAVE YOU HUGGED YOUR TREE TODAY?

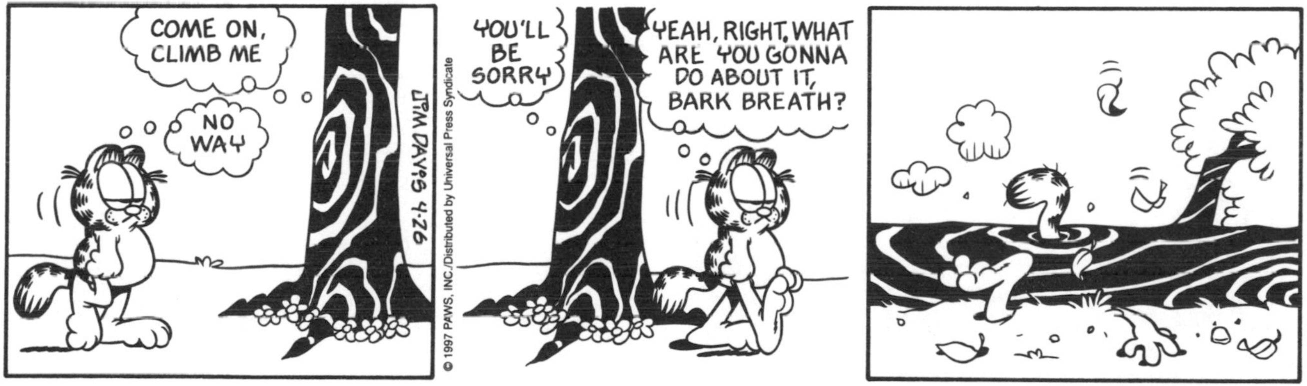
COME ON, CLIMB ME
NO WAY
JIM DAVIS 4-26
© 1997 PAWS, INC./Distributed by Universal Press Syndicate
YOU'LL BE SORRY
YEAH, RIGHT. WHAT ARE YOU GONNA DO ABOUT IT, BARK BREATH?

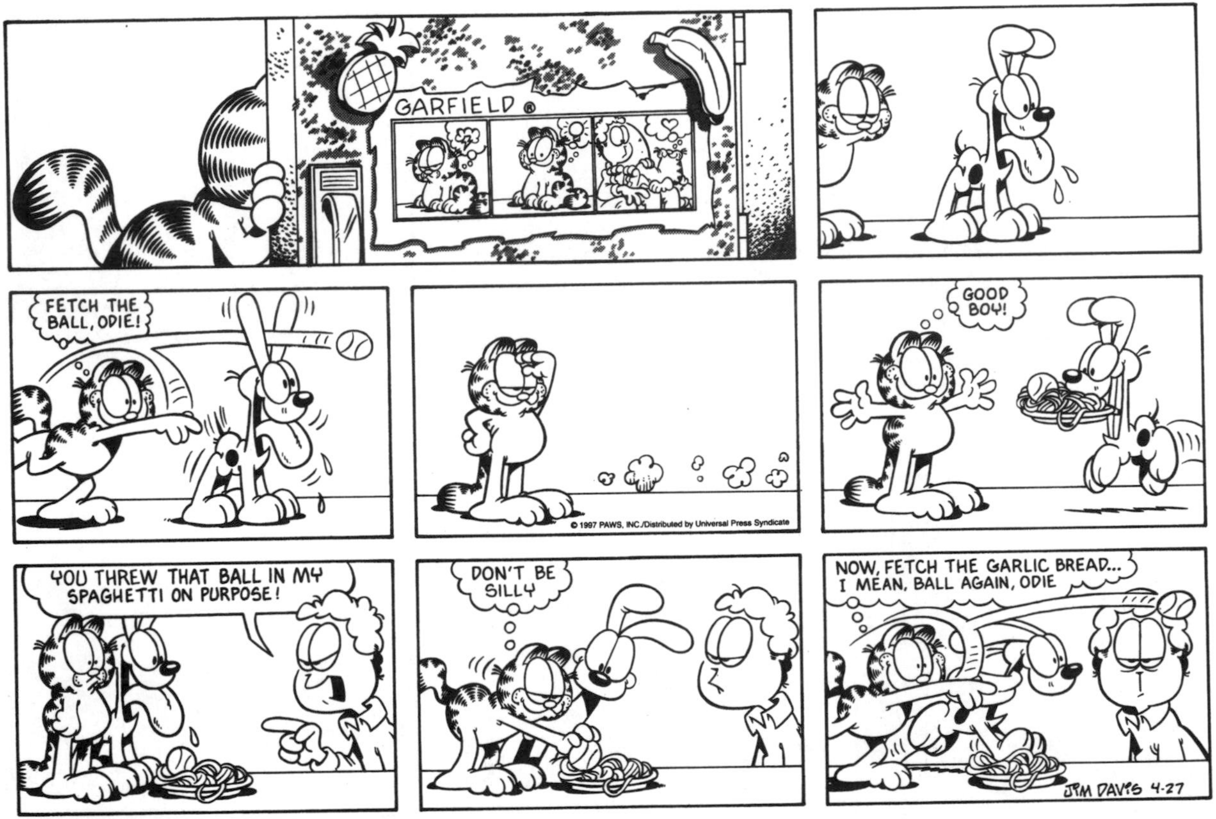
GARFIELD ®
FETCH THE BALL, ODIE!
© 1997 PAWS, INC./Distributed by Universal Press Syndicate
GOOD BOY!
YOU THREW THAT BALL IN MY SPAGHETTI ON PURPOSE!
DON'T BE SILLY
NOW, FETCH THE GARLIC BREAD... I MEAN, BALL AGAIN, ODIE
JIM DAVIS 4-27

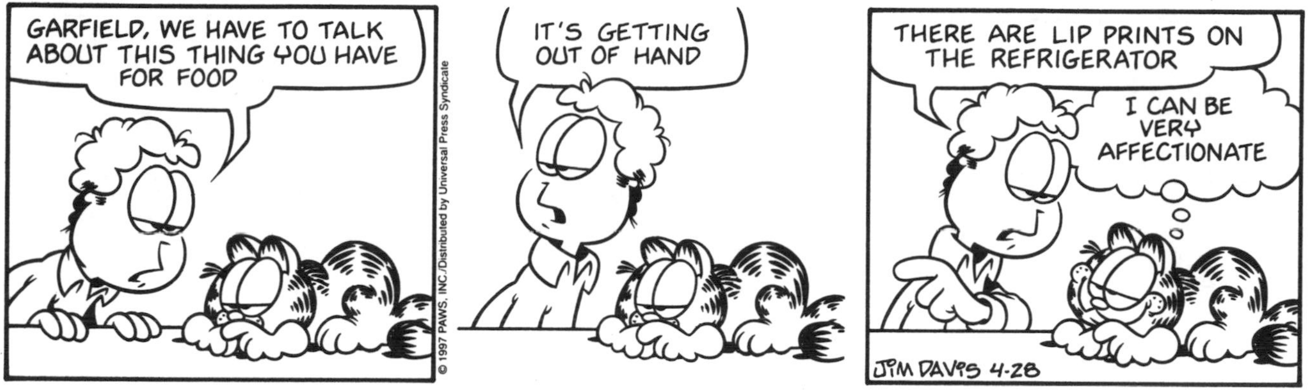
GARFIELD, WE HAVE TO TALK ABOUT THIS THING YOU HAVE FOR FOOD
© 1997 PAWS, INC./Distributed by Universal Press Syndicate
IT'S GETTING OUT OF HAND
THERE ARE LIP PRINTS ON THE REFRIGERATOR
I CAN BE VERY AFFECTIONATE
JIM DAVIS 4-28

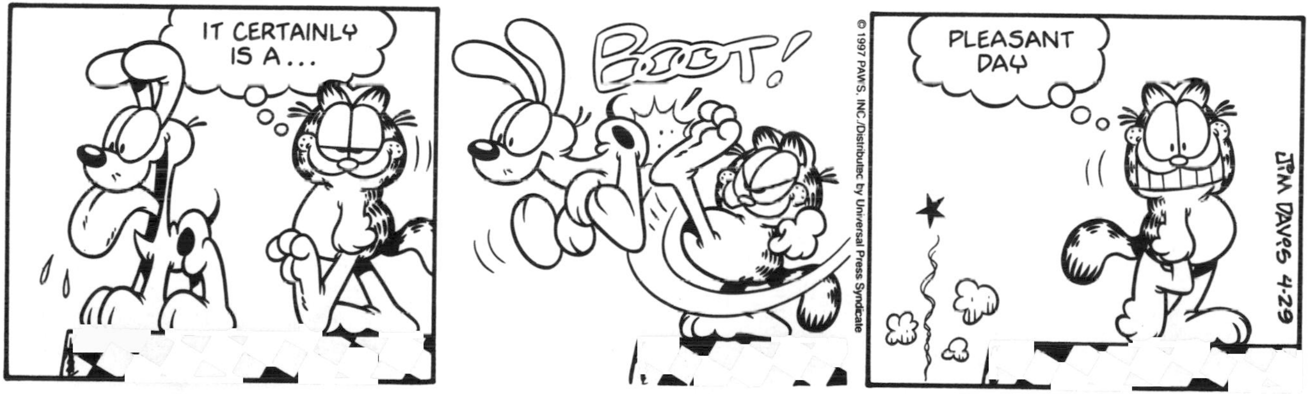
IT CERTAINLY IS A...
BOOT!
© 1997 PAWS, INC./Distributed by Universal Press Syndicate
PLEASANT DAY
JIM DAVIS 4-29

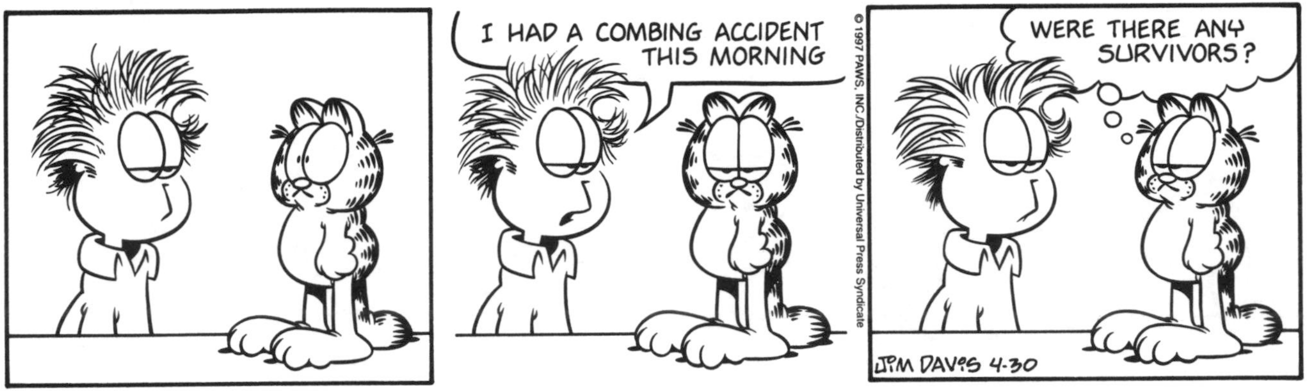

I HAD A COMBING ACCIDENT THIS MORNING
© 1997 PAWS, INC./Distributed by Universal Press Syndicate
WERE THERE ANY SURVIVORS?
JIM DAVIS 4-30

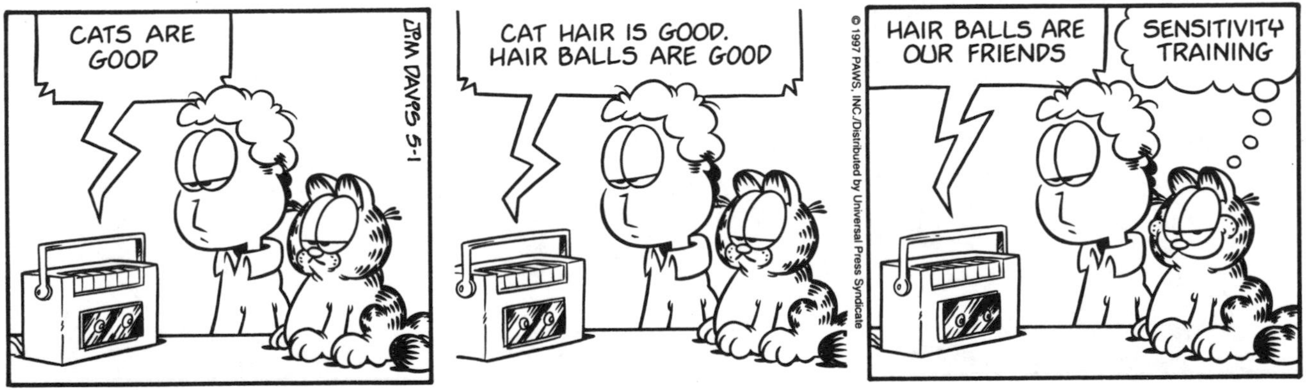

CATS ARE GOOD
JIM DAVIS 5-1
CAT HAIR IS GOOD. HAIR BALLS ARE GOOD
© 1997 PAWS, INC./Distributed by Universal Press Syndicate
HAIR BALLS ARE OUR FRIENDS
SENSITIVITY TRAINING

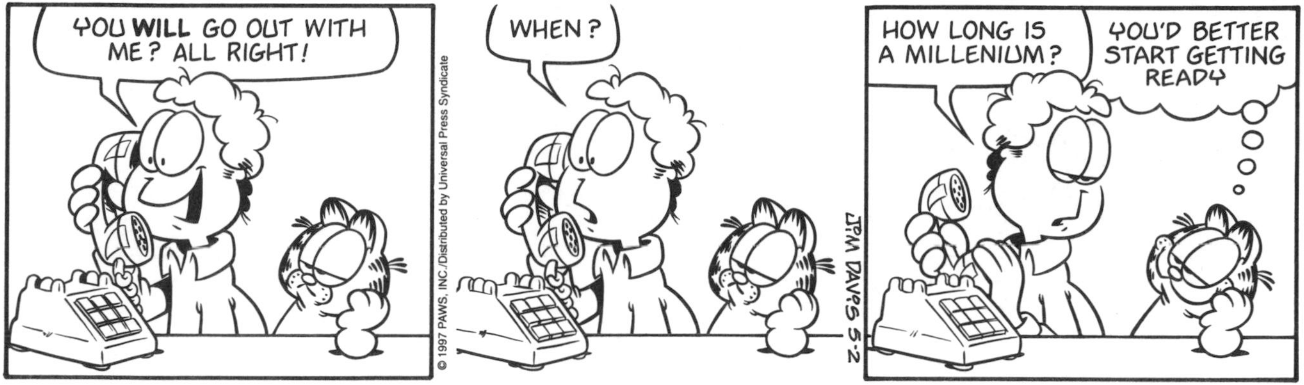
YOU WILL GO OUT WITH ME? ALL RIGHT!
WHEN?
HOW LONG IS A MILLENIUM?
YOU'D BETTER START GETTING READY
JIM DAVIS 5-2

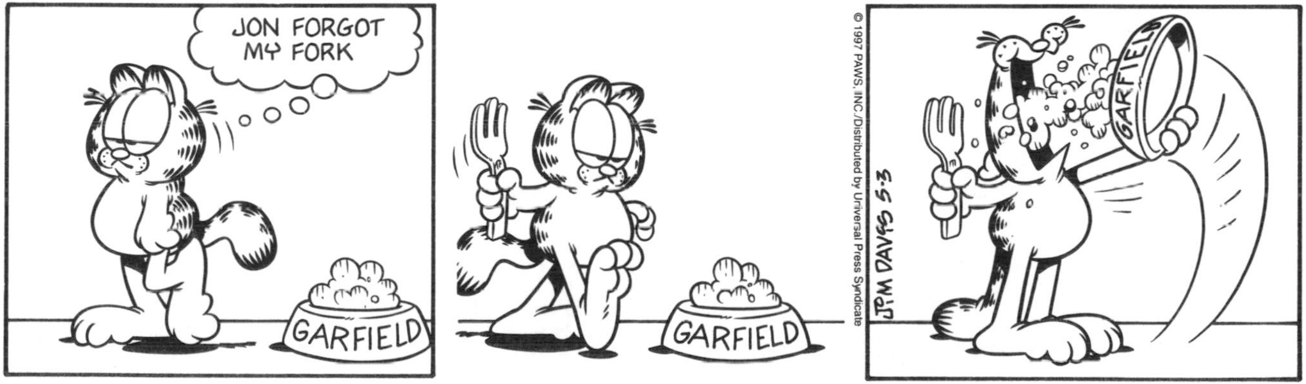
JON FORGOT MY FORK
GARFIELD
GARFIELD
GARFIELD
JIM DAVIS 5-3

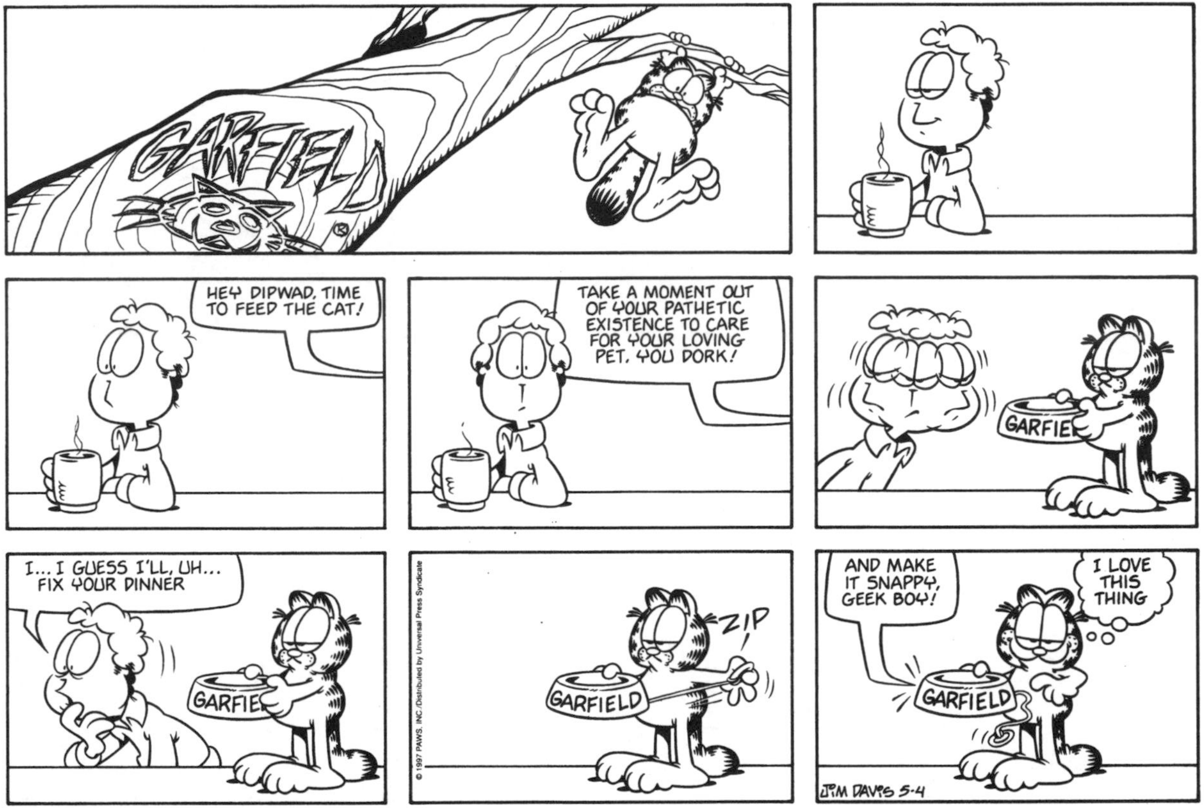
GARFIELD
HEY DIPWAD, TIME TO FEED THE CAT!
TAKE A MOMENT OUT OF YOUR PATHETIC EXISTENCE TO CARE FOR YOUR LOVING PET, YOU DORK!
GARFIE
I... I GUESS I'LL, UH... FIX YOUR DINNER
GARFIE
© 1997 PAWS, INC./Distributed by Universal Press Syndicate
GARFIELD
ZIP
AND MAKE IT SNAPPY, GEEK BOY!
I LOVE THIS THING
GARFIELD
JIM DAVIS 5-4

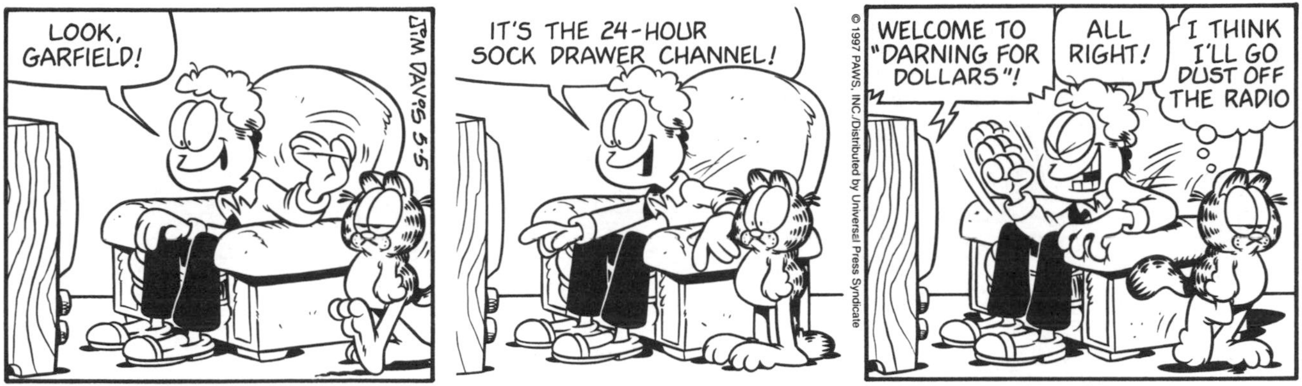
LOOK, GARFIELD!
JIM DAVIS 5-5
IT'S THE 24-HOUR SOCK DRAWER CHANNEL!
© 1997 PAWS, INC./Distributed by Universal Press Syndicate
WELCOME TO "DARNING FOR DOLLARS"!
ALL RIGHT!
I THINK I'LL GO DUST OFF THE RADIO

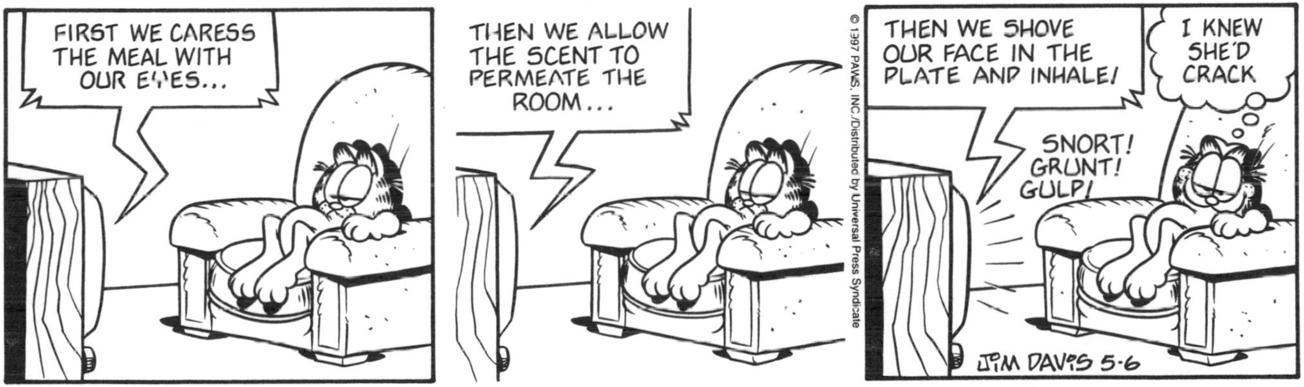
FIRST WE CARESS THE MEAL WITH OUR EYES...
THEN WE ALLOW THE SCENT TO PERMEATE THE ROOM...
© 1997 PAWS, INC./Distributed by Universal Press Syndicate
THEN WE SHOVE OUR FACE IN THE PLATE AND INHALE!
SNORT! GRUNT! GULP!
I KNEW SHE'D CRACK
JIM DAVIS 5-6

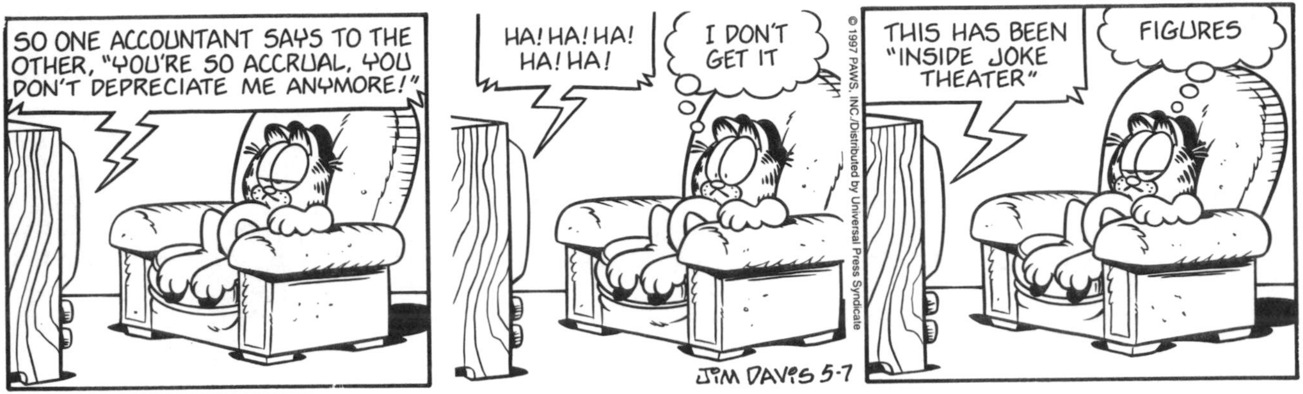
SO ONE ACCOUNTANT SAYS TO THE OTHER, "YOU'RE SO ACCRUAL, YOU DON'T DEPRECIATE ME ANYMORE!"
HA! HA! HA! HA! HA!
I DON'T GET IT
THIS HAS BEEN "INSIDE JOKE THEATER"
FIGURES
JIM DAVIS 5-7
© 1997 PAWS, INC./Distributed by Universal Press Syndicate

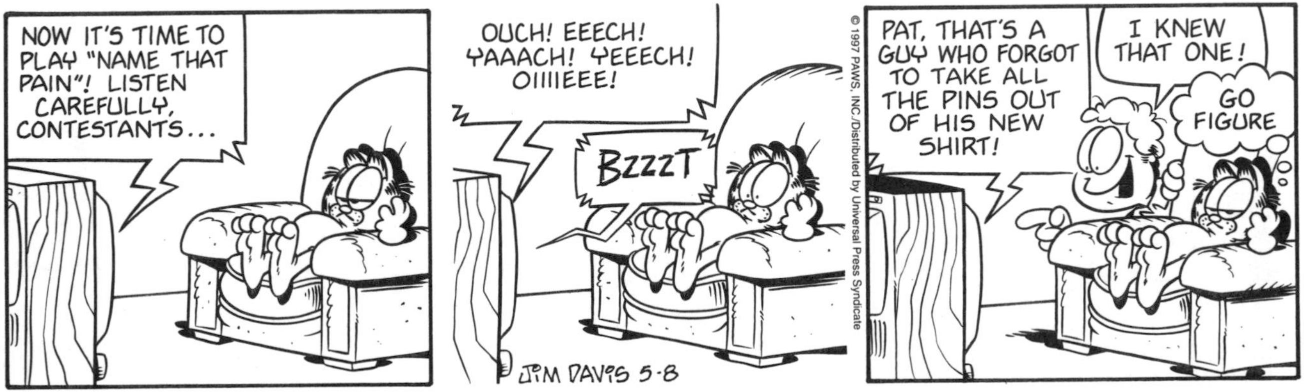
NOW IT'S TIME TO PLAY "NAME THAT PAIN"! LISTEN CAREFULLY, CONTESTANTS...
OUCH! EEECH! YAAACH! YEEECH! OIIIIEEE!
BZZZT
PAT, THAT'S A GUY WHO FORGOT TO TAKE ALL THE PINS OUT OF HIS NEW SHIRT!
I KNEW THAT ONE!
GO FIGURE
JIM DAVIS 5-8
© 1997 PAWS, INC./Distributed by Universal Press Syndicate

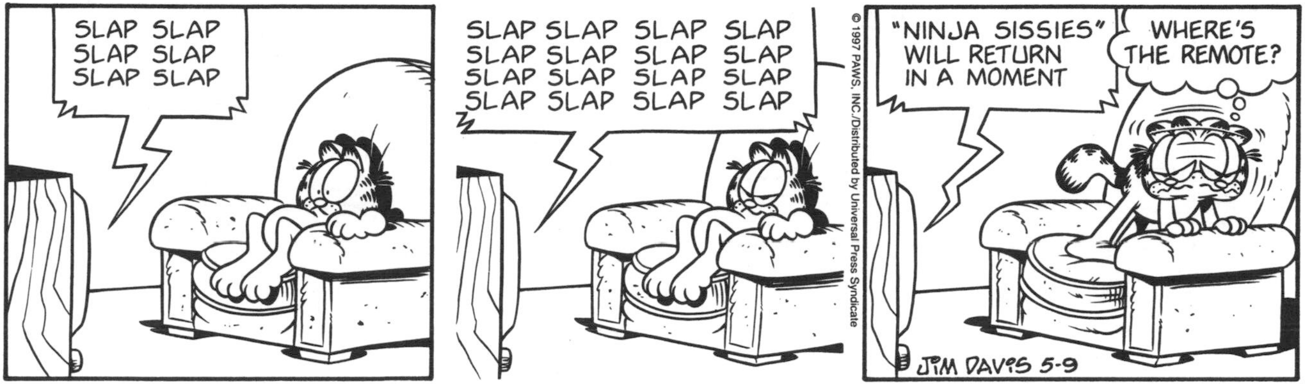
SLAP SLAP SLAP SLAP SLAP SLAP
SLAP SLAP SLAP SLAP SLAP SLAP SLAP SLAP SLAP SLAP SLAP SLAP SLAP SLAP SLAP SLAP
© 1997 PAWS, INC./Distributed by Universal Press Syndicate
"NINJA SISSIES" WILL RETURN IN A MOMENT
WHERE'S THE REMOTE?
JIM DAVIS 5-9

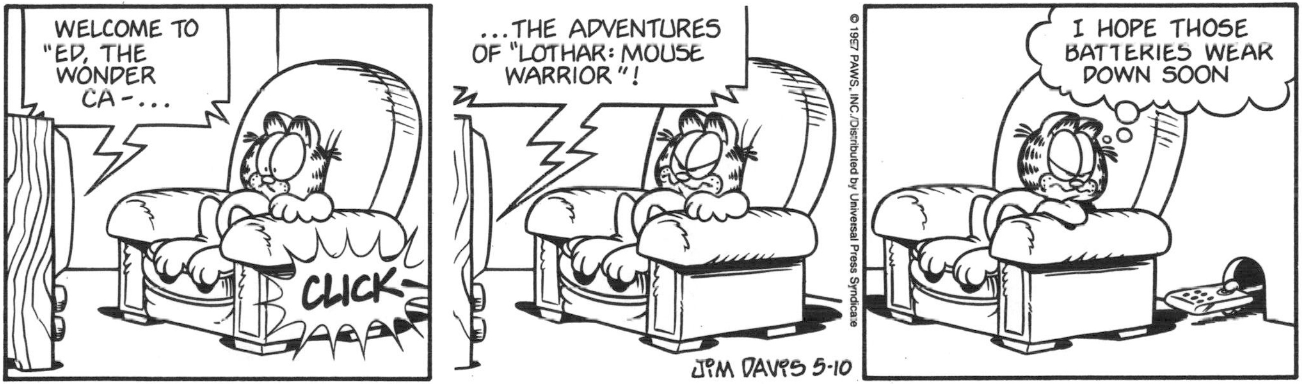
WELCOME TO "ED, THE WONDER CA-...
CLICK
...THE ADVENTURES OF "LOTHAR: MOUSE WARRIOR"!
JIM DAVIS 5-10
© 1997 PAWS, INC./Distributed by Universal Press Syndicate
I HOPE THOSE BATTERIES WEAR DOWN SOON

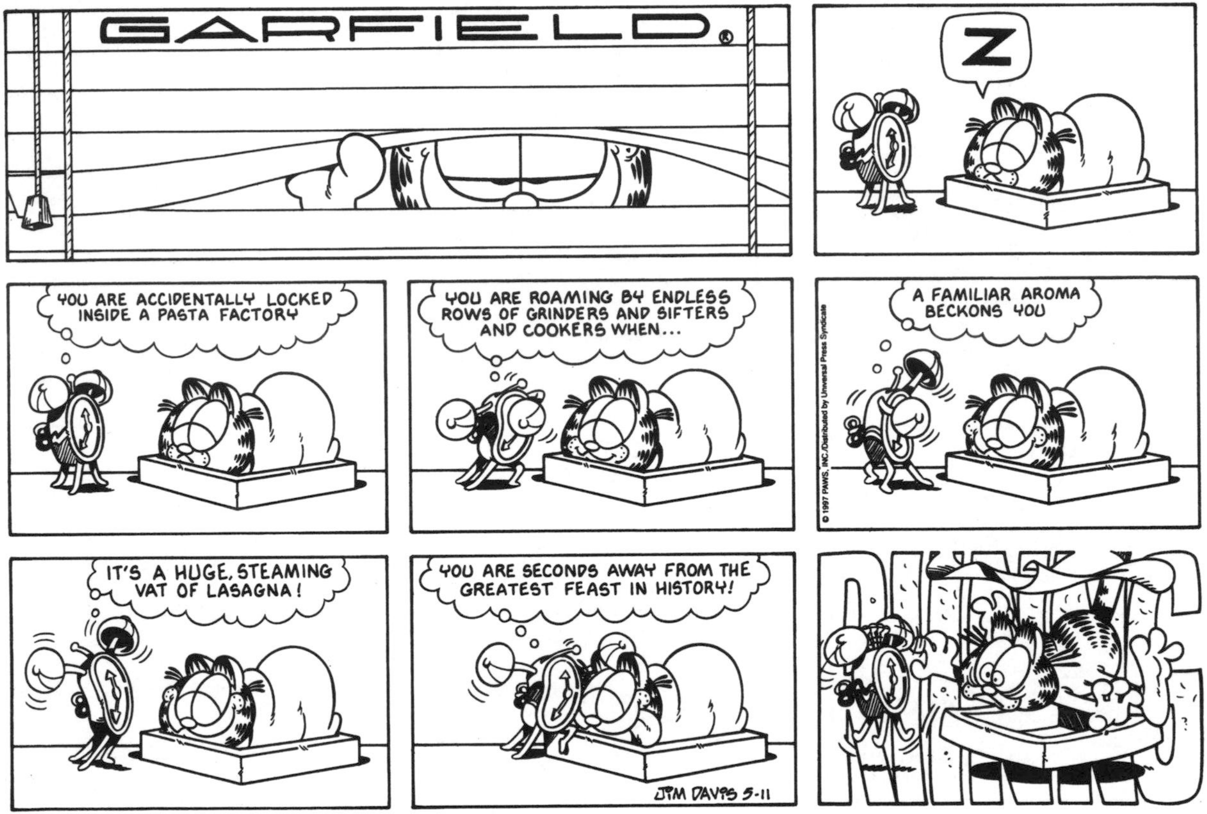
GARFIELD®
Z
YOU ARE ACCIDENTALLY LOCKED INSIDE A PASTA FACTORY
YOU ARE ROAMING BY ENDLESS ROWS OF GRINDERS AND SIFTERS AND COOKERS WHEN...
A FAMILIAR AROMA BECKONS YOU
© 1997 PAWS, INC./Distributed by Universal Press Syndicate
IT'S A HUGE, STEAMING VAT OF LASAGNA!
YOU ARE SECONDS AWAY FROM THE GREATEST FEAST IN HISTORY!
JIM DAVIS 5-11

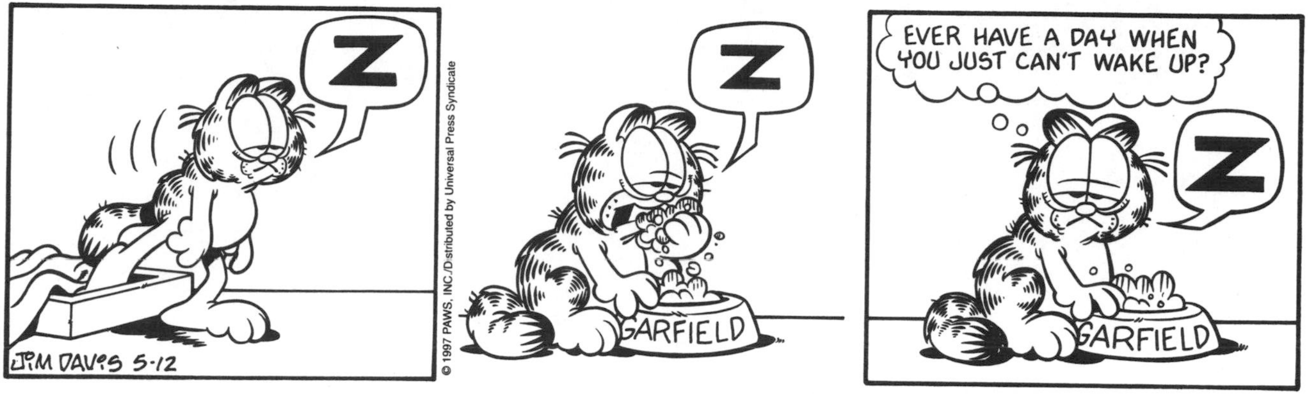
Z
Z
GARFIELD
EVER HAVE A DAY WHEN YOU JUST CAN'T WAKE UP?
Z
GARFIELD
JIM DAVIS 5-12
© 1997 PAWS, INC./Distributed by Universal Press Syndicate

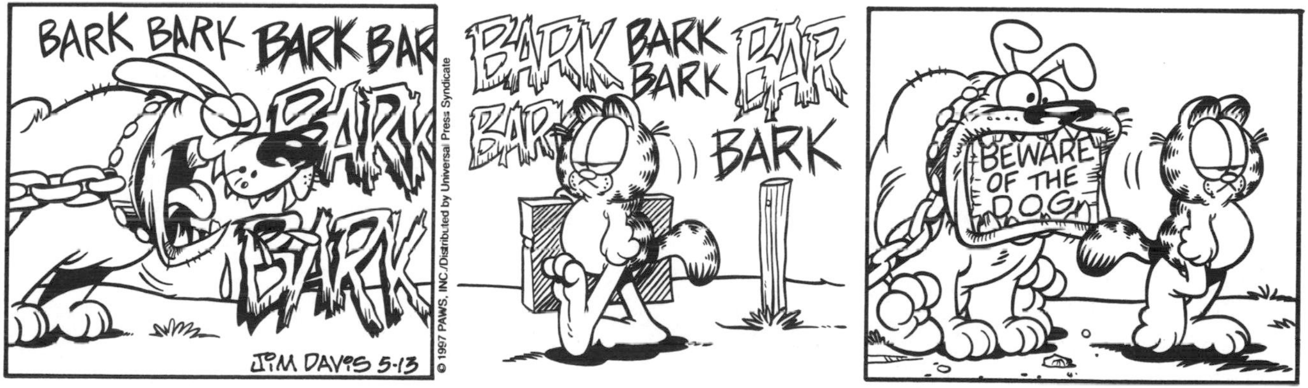
BARK BARK BARK BAR
BARK
BARK
BARK BARK BARK BAR
BAR
BARK
BEWARE OF THE DOG
JIM DAVIS 5-13
© 1997 PAWS, INC./Distributed by Universal Press Syndicate

SIGNS YOU'RE GOING TO A BAD VETERINARIAN...

- moonlights as a taxidermist
- keeps excusing himself to set the traps
- can't work a "pooper scooper"
- only licensed to treat insects
- tries to floss a piranha
- was once fired for trying to put Lassie to sleep
- wears a coonskin cap
- performs surgery with a steak knife
- tries to give mouth-to-mouth to your badger

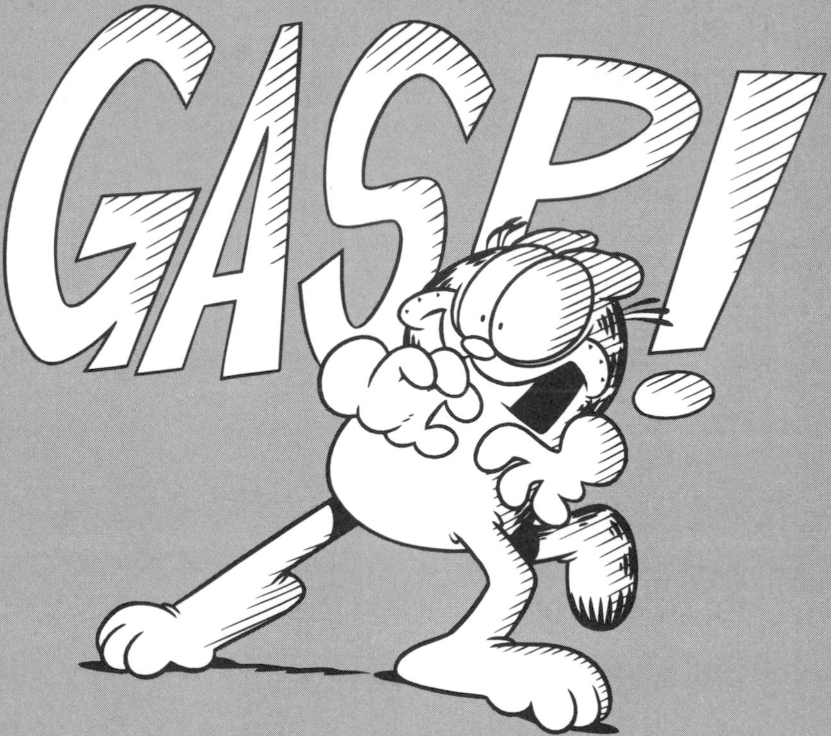
GASP!

STRIPS, SPECIALS, OR BESTSELLING BOOKS . . .
GARFIELD'S ON EVERYONE'S MENU
Don't miss even one episode in the Tubby Tabby's hilarious series!

__GARFIELD AT LARGE (#1)   32013/$6.95
__GARFIELD GAINS WEIGHT (#2)   32008/$6.95
__GARFIELD BIGGER THAN LIFE (#3)   32007/$6.95
__GARFIELD WEIGHS IN (#4)   32010/$6.95
__GARFIELD TAKES THE CAKE (#5)   32009/$6.95
__GARFIELD EATS HIS HEART OUT (#6)   32018/$6.95
__GARFIELD SITS AROUND THE HOUSE (#7)   32011/$6.95
__GARFIELD TIPS THE SCALES (#8)   33580/$6.95
__GARFIELD LOSES HIS FEET (#9)   31805/$6.95
__GARFIELD MAKES IT BIG (#10)   31928/$6.95
__GARFIELD ROLLS ON (#11)   32634/$6.95
__GARFIELD OUT TO LUNCH (#12)   33118/$6.95
__GARFIELD FOOD FOR THOUGHT (#13)   34129/$6.95
__GARFIELD SWALLOWS HIS PRIDE (#14)   34725/$6.95
__GARFIELD WORLDWIDE (#15)   35158/$6.95
__GARFIELD ROUNDS OUT (#16)   35388/$6.95
__GARFIELD CHEWS THE FAT (#17)   35956/$6.95
__GARFIELD GOES TO WAIST (#18)   36430/$6.95
__GARFIELD HANGS OUT (#19)   36835/$6.95
__GARFIELD TAKES UP SPACE (#20)   37029/$6.95

__GARFIELD SAYS A MOUTHFUL (#21)   37368/$6.95
__GARFIELD BY THE POUND (#22)   37579/$6.95
__GARFIELD KEEPS HIS CHINS UP (#23)   37959/$6.95
__GARFIELD TAKES HIS LICKS (#24)   38170/$6.95
__GARFIELD HITS THE BIG TIME (#25)   38332/$6.95
__GARFIELD PULLS HIS WEIGHT (#26)   38666/$6.95
__GARFIELD DISHES IT OUT (#27)   39287/$6.95
__GARFIELD LIFE IN THE FAT LANE (#28)   39776/$6.95
__GARFIELD TONS OF FUN (#29)   40386/$6.95
__GARFIELD BIGGER AND BETTER (#30)   40770/$6.95
__GARFIELD HAMS IT UP (#31)   41241/$6.95
__GARFIELD THINKS BIG (#32)   41671/$6.95

GARFIELD AT HIS SUNDAY BEST!
__GARFIELD TREASURY   32106/$11.95
__THE SECOND GARFIELD TREASURY   33276/$10.95
__THE THIRD GARFIELD TREASURY   32635/$11.00
__THE FOURTH GARFIELD TREASURY   34726/$10.95
__THE FIFTH GARFIELD TREASURY   36268/$12.00
__THE SIXTH GARFIELD TREASURY   37367/$10.95
__THE SEVENTH GARFIELD TREASURY   38427/$10.95
__THE EIGHTH GARFIELD TREASURY   39778/$12.00
__THE NINTH GARFIELD TREASURY   41670/$12.50

Please send me the BALLANTINE BOOKS I have checked above. I am enclosing $_____. (Please add $2.00 for the first book and $.50 for each additional book for postage and handling and include the appropriate state sales tax.) Send check or money order (no cash or C.O.D.'s) to Ballantine Mail Sales Dept. TA, 400 Hahn Road, Westminster, MD 21157.

To order by phone, call 1-800-733-3000 and use your major credit card.

Prices and numbers are subject to change without notice. Valid in the U.S. only. All orders are subject to availability.

Name_____

Address_____

City_____ State_____ Zip_____

Allow at least 4 weeks for delivery   5/97

Like to get a **COOL CATalog** stuffed with great **GARFIELD** products? Then just write down the information below, stuff it in an envelope and mail it back to us...or you can fill in the card on our website - HTTP://www.GARFIELD.com. We'll get one out to you in two shakes of a cat's tail!

Name:
Address:
City:
State:
Zip:
Phone:
Date of Birth:
Sex:

Please mail your information to:

Garfield Stuff Customer Service Center
100 Fusion Way
Country Club Hills, Illinois 60478-3113

© PAWS